UNEXPECTED REVOLUTIONARIES

A VOLUME IN THE SERIES

Cornell Studies in Money

Edited by Eric Helleiner and Jonathan Kirshner

A list of titles in this series is available at cornellpress.cornell.edu.

UNEXPECTED REVOLUTIONARIES

How Central Banks Made and Unmade
Economic Orthodoxy

Manuela Moschella

CORNELL UNIVERSITY PRESS   ITHACA AND LONDON

Copyright © 2024 by Cornell University

First published 2024 by Cornell University Press

Librarians: A CIP catalog record for this book is available from the Library of Congress.

ISBN 978-1-5017-7485-0 (hardcover)
ISBN 978-1-5017-7486-7 (pdf)
ISBN 978-1-5017-7487-4 (epub)

To my boys

Contents

Preface

Some say the best way to describe the job of a central bank is to say that a central bank's job is to worry. Looking at the recent historical period, there have been plenty of reasons for central banks—as well as other economic policymakers—to be worried. Indeed, since the Great Recession of 2008, the economic context whipsawed from low and stable inflation to persistent deflation and secular stagnation and, later, to post-pandemic scenarios of rampant inflation and 1970s-style stagflation. In confronting these economic gyrations, central banks have been put in the front seat of economic decision making and crisis management. Their traditional power in steering domestic economies by affecting output and employment has also become greater and much more visible. In this process, central banks have become significantly different institutions from the ones that have underpinned the pillar of the neoliberal macroeconomic regime that has spread around the world since the 1980s.

I have been intrigued observing how much central banks have changed in such a short—although momentous—timespan. Since around the 1980s, the unchallenged monetary orthodoxy had revolved around the narrow pursuit of low inflation through the use of interest rate policy. However, since 2008, balance sheet policies came to dominate monetary policymaking while the boundaries of monetary policy stretched to include issues that were once anathema to central bankers, including financial stability, social inequality, and even climate change. The transformation of monetary policy has also brought about a profound change in the relationship with domestic governments. The large-scale purchase of government bonds under the various quantitative easing programs has indeed challenged the central banks' mantra against any form of fiscal dominance and their same cherished independence.

As a political economy scholar, I found this transformation extremely puzzling in light of the traditional view that our scholarship had of central banks, namely the view according to which central banks are the conservative guardians of the dominant neoliberal macroeconomic regime. These same guardians had just turned out to be the most active heralds of change.

I thus started looking into explanations that could help make sense of this puzzle, and I was largely dissatisfied with what I found. Most analyses were based on a peculiar understanding of central banks as technocratic actors whose behavior is explained by the expert ideas developed within a politically insulated epistemic community. This understanding, however, clouds the complexity of the nature of central banks, which are technocratic actors but still operate within a political context. Recovering this political dimension is a key goal that this book seeks to achieve. In particular, the purpose of the book is to shed light on the fact that even if central banks are formally independent and made up of monetary experts, as public institutions they need political support to implement monetary policy and survive under changed external conditions. Reputation is the key tool that central banks use to secure and maintain such political support. The institutional evolution of central banking cannot be fully understood without taking into account central banks' need for political support through reputation building and protection. Indeed, reputation protection led central banks to move away from well-established monetary practices only when political support for such deviations was in place (i.e., when governments supported central banks' unconventional policies) or when support was waning (i.e., on the back on increasing public contestation), thereby requiring new policies to win back that support.

In short, this book is my attempt to make sense of what happened since the 2008 crisis and rethink the role of central banks from technocratic to political actors. Ultimately, the complex relationship between technocracy and politics is the reason I got interested in central banks in the first place.

As with most academic books, this one took far too long to write. More importantly, though, this book also took a village to be finished! So many colleagues and friends have inspired me with their work and devoted their time to providing generous advice and precious suggestions. I am not sure I will be able to do justice to all of them here, but at least I will try. My special thanks go to Kate McNamara who helped me clarify my thinking with her lucid comments and whose works have and continue to be a wonderful example of scholarly craft. For their invaluable and detailed comments on the entire manuscript, I am deeply grateful to Randy Germain, Elliot Posner, Lucia Quaglia, and two anonymous reviewers at Cornell University Press. Their close reading and suggestions helped me improve my thinking so much. I am also particularly grateful to Eric Helleiner for his sharp insights and interest in and enthusiasm for this book, even at a time when it was more an idea than a real project.

Over the past few years, I was very lucky to share ideas with many generous colleagues that offered advice on specific aspects of the book at different stages of its development. For the helpful suggestions and conversations, I want to thank Cornel Ban, Jacquie Best, Mark Blyth, Henry Farrell, Federico Ferrara, Orfeo Fioretos, Daniela Gabor, Julia Gray, Scott James, Juliet Johnson, Erik Jones, Saori Katada, Ronen Mandelkern, Donato Masciandaro, Matthias Matthjis, Samuel McPhilemy, Abe Newman, Stefano Pagliari, Luca Pinto, Aidan Regan,

Davide Romelli, Waltraud Schelkle, Cheryl Schonardt-Bailey, Matthias Thiemann, Eleni Tsingou, and Kevin Young.

During the preparation of the book, I had the opportunity to present parts of this manuscript at several conferences and workshops. While it is not possible for me to mention everyone who helped shape my thinking with helpful questions and comments on various presentations, I am particularly grateful to the colleagues who invited me and discussed my papers in detail. In this spirit, I am particularly indebted to Benjamin Braun, Björn Bremer, Sebastian Diessner, Leah Downey, Clément Fontan, Nicolò Fraccaroli, Oddny Helgadóttir, Charlotte Rommerskirchen, Jens van 't Klooster, and Mattias Vermeiren.

I am also grateful to the PhD students at the Scuola Normale and the European University Institute Political Economy Working Group who read parts of the manuscript and came back with some of the most difficult criticisms to deal with. A special mention goes to my former student and inspiring scholar Palma Polyak, who provided invaluable research assistance during the writing stages of this book.

The book was written at quite a challenging time—during the COVID-19 pandemic and the repeated lockdowns. I confess that it was not always an easy task to focus on writing as our way of living was basically called into question. Sharing my home office with "my boys" also elevated the task of writing to levels that remain unrivaled for me. Ultimately, however, this book could not have been written without their special inspiration and unwavering encouragement.

Abbreviations

ABCP	asset-backed commercial paper
AIG	American International Group
BIS	Bank for International Settlements
BoE	Bank of England
BoJ	Bank of Japan
CSPP	Corporate Sector Purchase Programme
ECB	European Central Bank
EFSF	European Financial Stability Facility
EMU	European Monetary Union
ESM	European Stability Mechanism
EU	European Union
Fed	Federal Reserve System of the United States
FOMC	Federal Open Market Committee
GDP	gross domestic product
HICP	harmonized index of consumer prices
IMF	International Monetary Fund
IT	inflation targeting
LSAPs	large-scale asset purchase programs
LTROs	longer-term refinancing operations
MBS	mortgage-backed securities
NCBs	national central banks
OMT	Outright Monetary Transactions
PEPP	Pandemic Emergency Purchase Program
PSPP	Public Sector Purchase Program
QE	quantitative easing
repos	repurchase agreements
SMP	Securities Market Program
TALF	Term Asset-Backed Securities Loan Facility
TARP	Troubled Asset Relief Program
UK	United Kingdom
US	United States
WWII	World War II

UNEXPECTED REVOLUTIONARIES

THE EVOLUTION OF CENTRAL BANKS

It is important to recognize the role of an independent central bank is different in inflationary and deflationary environments. In the face of inflation, which is often associated with excessive monetization of government debt, the virtue of an independent central bank is its ability to say "no" to the government. With protracted deflation, however, excessive money creation is unlikely to be the problem, and a more cooperative stance on the part of the central bank may be called for.

—Bernanke 2003

Central bank independence is one of the most widely accepted principles of successful economic governance. Forged in the aftermath of the Great Inflation of the 1970s, the notion that central bankers should be free from political interference to keep inflation low and stable has become an almost universally accepted principle of macroeconomic doctrine. Nowhere is this consensus more evident than in the delegation of monetary responsibilities to unelected technocrats that has taken place since the 1980s. As a wealth of studies indicate, countries around the world have progressively opted for a clearly defined type of monetary governance—namely, an independent agency specializing in achieving the overarching objective of price stability through the tool of interest rate policy.[1] This new institutional setup was so successful in taming inflation through the 1990s that it won central banks the title of kings of economic stability and placed them at the core of the neoliberal macroeconomic regime that was embraced around the world.[2] By the early 2000s, central bank independence and the pursuit of low inflation through interest rate technology had become unchallenged economic orthodoxy.

Soon afterwards, however, orthodoxy was suddenly shaken. The deflationary forces unleashed by the 2008 global financial crisis and the 2020 COVID-19 crisis have indeed led central banks away from the "tidy and cozy" central banking world that had reigned since the 1980s.[3] The transformation started as central banks ventured into unconventional policies that had been considered a "theoretical curiosity" at best.[4] Policies such as lending to banks (and even to non-banks) in huge volume and large-scale asset purchases (so-called quantitative

1

easing) have indeed caused central banks to stray from the orthodox terrain of interest rate policy and price stabilization to give pride of place to balance sheet policy and financial stability. In what seems an anathema to any casual central banking observer, postcrises central banks have even stretched the orthodox view that monetary policy can influence only the level of inflation by claiming overt responsibility for employment objectives and even issues such as inclusive growth and climate change. Central banks' new policies have also tested the principle of independence as monetary authorities have often taken controversial decisions regarding which firms to support and which assets to buy. By including government debt into their asset purchases, central banks have further tested their cherished independence by reducing the traditional arm's-length distance from fiscal policy.

The return of inflation in the aftermath of the COVID-19 pandemic and Russia's invasion of Ukraine, which has been associated with a significant amount of upward pressure on commodity prices, marks a new turning point for the evolution of central banks. With inflation back in focus, for instance, central banks can be expected to switch back to the precrisis monetary playbook. The unwinding of unconventional policies and the synchronized tightening of monetary policy that has taken place in high-income countries since 2022 seems to corroborate this expectation.[5] While the return to "business as usual" is a plausible scenario, a serious and informed discussion about the future direction of monetary policy and the macroeconomic regime it underpins must start with an analysis of the recent past and the initial conditions that central banks have been confronted with as economic conditions whipsawed from persistent deflation to post-pandemic inflation.

This book thus looks at the recent past to explain the institutional evolution of central banks and to offer insights into its future directions. In particular, the book examines central banks' journey from the heydays of monetary orthodoxy that started in the 1980s to the 2008 global financial crisis and the 2020 COVID-19 crisis. In doing so, the book explains why central banks responded to changed economic conditions by breaking with monetary orthodoxy and what consequences this evolutionary path entails for the role of central banks in domestic societies.

In answering these questions, the book challenges the widespread narrative that depicts central banks as technocratic actors. According to this narrative, central banks' behavior can basically be explained in light of either their independence from political constraints or the expert ideas developed and embraced within central banks themselves. For instance, standard accounts of central banks' responses to the 2008 and 2020 crises have generally revolved around two different lines of arguments—both of which stress the technocratic nature of central banks. One argument posits that central banks have adapted to changed economic circumstances because their independence provided them with the capacity to act when fiscal policymakers were unwilling or politically unable to act. This independence provided the space for central banks to rise as "the only game in town."[6] The other common argument posits that central banks' transformation was instead the outcome of a process of learning and ideational change within the epistemic community of central bankers. That is to say, central banks responded to the crises of 2008 and 2020 in a way that challenged monetary orthodoxy because they had learned lessons from the 1930s, the period when monetary policy failed to counteract the Great Depression.[7] In other words, central banks broke with orthodoxy because they reassessed the tenets of the preexisting monetary consensus following the "battle for ideas" and the learning process that took place among central bank economists.[8]

In contrast to this conventional narrative, the book argues that the key to explaining deviation from orthodoxy lies not in technocracy but rather squarely in politics. In a nutshell, breaking with orthodoxy required a supportive political environment. Paraphrasing Peter Gourevitch's seminal argument, monetary policy, whether traditional or innovative, always needs politics.[9]

It may sound odd to argue that central banks respond to the political environment in which they operate. Indeed, monetary institutions are usually regarded as the quintessential example of non-majoritarian policymakers, which, by legal design, are independent and need not seek political approval to exert their powers. However, this representation of central banks is at least partial. Even if they are legally independent and made up of technocrats who share a distinct set of economic ideas, central banks are still public institutions, and as such, they are dependent on government and public support as well as on positive market actors' reaction to justify their activities, achieve their mandate, and survive over time. Just as politicians have to construct and maintain agreement in domestic societies to adopt specific policies and stay in power, so do central banks. However, the modalities through which central banks build support for their policies and their role in domestic societies across their multiple audiences are different from the modalities that elected policymakers follow. Herein, this book maintains that technocratic institutions such as central banks foster political support through the projection of a distinct organizational image, which I refer to as reputation.[10] In particular, having a reputation for being inflation-averse and politically neutral was the trademark of successful central banks since the 1980s and the crucial channel through which to sustain broad support for central banks' policy and independence.[11]

Relying on reputation implies a built-in tension, however. As economic conditions change, central banks might be required to take actions to achieve their mandate that do not always align with the prescriptions stemming from past reputation.[12] This is what happened to central banks as the economic environment switched to a deflationary environment: to restore price stability, central banks were called to act "irresponsibly."[13] That is, the new context required central banks to foster inflation and broaden their policy tools with policies that carried more visible distributive implications than the interest rate policy. These actions, however, clashed with the conservative and apolitical reputation that central banks had been building d since the 1980s. When external circumstances challenge past reputation, central banks, like other institutions, find themselves in an uncomfortable position: they have to balance the need to preserve their past reputation with the need to deviate from past reputation and adapt to changed conditions. How central banks balance these two competing objectives—this book maintains—is a function of the political context and how supportive it is. Indeed, central banks deviated from orthodoxy under specific conditions, in particular when governments directly or indirectly supported the use of unconventional monetary policies. The politicization of central banks, as evidenced by the increased public salience and contestation of monetary policy and institutions, was also a key condition that pushed central banks away from orthodoxy. Central banks' progressive emphasis on employment, growth, and climate objectives can indeed be read as a strategic way to mitigate the public backlash and shore up public support.

This book illustrates the reputational argument by examining monetary policy in high-income countries in one of the most tumultuous economic periods on historical record. In particular, the book focuses on the transformation in monetary orthodoxy in response to the deflationary period that started in 2008 and continued with the 2020 crisis caused by the pandemic. In doing so, the book focuses on the two central banks that set the monetary policy for the largest economies in the group of high-income countries: namely, the US Federal Reserve (the Fed) and the European Central Bank (ECB). As the United States and the eurozone account for a combined 65.9 percent of global gross domestic product, these two institutions exert a momentous effect on the world economy as a whole.[14] While significant attention has been devoted to explaining the differences between the policy choices in the United States and Europe,[15] the purpose of the current analysis is to highlight the common trajectory that led these two very different monetary institutions to adopt policies that mark a similar and significant deviation from monetary orthodoxy.

Two major findings emerge from the comparative analysis, which impart a partly reassuring and a more concerning message for the role of central banks in domestic societies. What is reassuring is that central banks do not solely care about and heed financial market interests. Specifically, although the book concurs with the one of the key insights of the critical political economy scholarship, namely the insight according to which central bank independence does not depoliticize monetary policymaking,[16] the book shows that central banks respond to the expectations and demands of various audiences (including political and public audiences) based on the challenges these audiences pose to the reputation of the central banks. While this finding is far from negating the influence that financial markets command or solving the problems of democratic oversight over independent monetary institutions,[17] it nonetheless indicates the existence of a political space that citizens and their political representatives can use to engage in a dialogue on the future direction of central banking.

What is more concerning is the finding about the limits to central banks' power to address policy challenges other than inflation. In particular, central banks did not unproblematically switch from their traditional inflation-fighting role to the new deflation-fighting one—even as central bankers might think otherwise, as the quote at the beginning of this chapter from the former Fed chair, Ben Bernanke, implies. Rather, central banks accepted that new role only under specific conditions, namely in coordination with fiscal authorities and on the back of public contestation. When these conditions were absent, central banks were pushed to subordinate monetary accommodation to the preservation of their conservative and politically neutral reputation, thereby shying away from measures that might have compromised their public institutional image. To put it differently, despite the transformations that occurred since 2008, central banks often resisted growing into the role of deflation fighter in order to safeguard their reputational capital. The time has come to recognize that central banks cannot have it "both ways" (meaning that they cannot fight policy challenges other than inflation as vigorously as they fight inflation, lest they disrupt their reputational capital), and they "cannot do it alone" (meaning that they need political and public support to risk their reputational capital).

The Puzzling Break from Orthodoxy

Central banks have never been static institutions, ever since the first central banks were established in Sweden and later in England in the seventeenth century. Rather, "the central bank is a body that has developed over time, progressively acquiring new and increasingly complex functions, duties and features, establishing more and more intricate and delicate relations with the rest of the banking and financial system and with the political system and the economy in general."[18] In particular, at different points in time, central banks have usually placed more weight on different policy objectives, including price stability, financial stability, and economic stabilization.[19] Their relationship with domestic governments has also taken on differing forms over time, with central banks operating under varying degrees of political control. For instance, whereas the first central banks were chartered as clearinghouses for commerce and buyers of government debt, those created at the turn of the twentieth century came to prioritize price and financial stability, especially under the framework of the gold standard. In the aftermath of World War II, government control over central banks' policies significantly increased. At the same time, central banks' role in stabilization policy became much more prominent, with policy priorities shifting to high employment.

It is exactly the post-WWII period that set the stage for the rise of modern central banking—that is, for the rise of central banks as we know them. Indeed, the increased focus on active economic stabilization contributed to the buildup of inflationary pressures that became particularly pronounced in the 1970s, during the macroeconomic period known as the Great Inflation.[20] The battle to fight inflation reached its apex with the painful disinflation of the 1980s, brought about by Paul Volcker, the then US Fed chair. The Fed's ability to vanquish inflation became a watershed moment in central banking around the world and especially across high-income countries. In particular, the lessons drawn from the Volcker's Fed in the 1980s nurtured the development of a solid consensus in monetary economics that guided central banks and justified their policy choices for the subsequent three decades. This consensus revolved around a tidy institutional and operational setup that centered on independent central banks and on price stability as the overriding objective to be achieved through interest rate policy.

As figure 0.1 shows, the new monetary consensus was highly successful: inflation was firmly brought under control. A corollary of central banks' newfound ability to ensure macroeconomic stability was the celebration of monetary policy as a "science" and the relegation of controversial issues to the sidelines of the policy debate. The issue of what policies central banks should adopt if their interest rate became too low to stimulate the economy out of a recession was exactly one of those issues that was regarded "as merely a theoretical curiosity."[21] As a result, at least before 2008, "monetary policy in a deflationary environment largely remained the subject of historical inquiries."[22]

This is not to say that monetary economists were unaware of the challenges that central banks have to confront in a deflationary context, including those related to their independence. Ever since the Great Depression of the 1930s, the question of whether central banks can lose control over price levels and economic activity when nominal interest rates are too low—which is widely known as the liquidity trap—has been lively debated in the economics profession. The Japanese experience of fighting deflation in the early 2000s also renewed the amount of

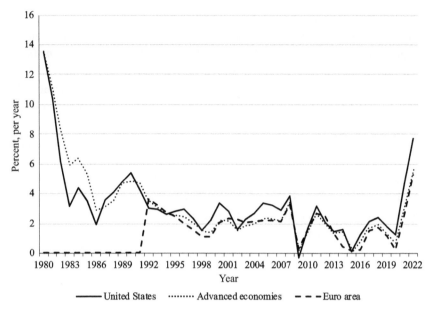

FIGURE 0.1. Inflation rate, 1980–2022

Source: IMF World Economic Outlook Database, April 2022

attention given to central banks' policy tools in a low inflation environment and revived scholarly interest in deflationary dynamics.[23] As a result, already before the crisis period that started in 2008, it was understood that, in a disinflationary context, the major challenges to central banks stem from the speed with which deflationary expectations take root and from the severe economic costs on domestic societies that sustained price declines impose in terms of output losses and financial stability.[24]

In spite of these analyses, however, before 2008, inflation was so prominent in practitioners' minds that "there was no real policy concern about deflation."[25] As one review of the state of monetary policy concluded back at the beginning of the millennium, "although the recent literature has tended to emphasize the deflationary risks arising in a low inflation environment . . . those risks do not seem as serious as often claimed."[26]

The crises that started in 2008 and 2020, however, fundamentally brought into question this conclusion; the economic disruptions brought about by the collapse of the financial sector (especially in 2008) and by the confinement measures that governments around the world adopted to contain the spread of the coronavirus (in 2020) unleashed potent recessionary and deflationary forces. For instance, ten years after the start of the 2008 crisis, output losses were still persistent in several countries, especially in countries that also experienced banking crises, while inflation had declined in all major economies, including the United States, the euro area, the United Kingdom, and Japan.[27] Secular stagnation—a situation of sluggish growth, low interest rates, and feeble inflation—thus became the buzzword in policy circles.[28] The COVID-19 crisis deepened these ongoing trends, at least initially.[29] The contraction in global output was so severe that it elevated the crisis aftermath to the worst recession since the Great Depression, even far worse than the one experienced after the 2008 global financial crisis.[30] By the end of 2020, inflation was well below the target in all high-income countries; however, it started to pick up and accelerate from mid-2021 onward (figure 0.1).

Given the change in the macroeconomic context, it is not surprising that deflation made its way to the top of the list of policymakers' concerns. These concerns have been especially elevated for central banks. Indeed, the deflationary scenario revived memories associated with the Great Depression of the 1930s and alerted central banks to a well-known but (up to that moment) unfamiliar policy challenge—namely, the situation where real interest rates are too high to boost economic activity, with monetary policy at risk of "pushing on a string."[31] With the prospect of disinflation and even deflation looming, central banks were confronted with issues that had not been at the center of monetary theory and operational practice for a very long time.

Central banks initially responded to the recessionary and deflationary forces through their conventional policy tool: the interest rate. In general, by lowering borrowing costs and reducing the incentives to save, central banks can stimulate the economy and accelerate the end of recessions and deflations. However, once interest rates reached the zero-lower bound, most central banks in high-income countries scrapped their policy playbook. Specifically, central banks experimented with largely unknown and unconventional policies, such as large-volume liquidity provisions to banks and non-banks alike and the purchase of long-term government bonds and private securities.[32] The central banks' balance sheets thus supplanted interest rates as the key tool with which to set the monetary policy stance in virtually all major central banks. Furthermore, rather than consistently targeting price stability, central banks started targeting, more or less explicitly, employment and financial stability objectives.[33] After 2020, the Fed and the ECB even revised their official monetary strategies in such a way that signaled their renewed focus on employment and even "inclusive" growth and the fight against climate change.[34]

According to a central banking veteran, "This [transformation] was something historically unprecedented and would simply have been unthinkable until then."[35] This is not meant to gloss over the cross-country differences that do exist in terms of the specific design of unconventional policies. However, these differences simply "do not invalidate [the] general picture,"[36] That is, these differences do not undermine the observation that profound transformations have taken place in central banking and in the macroeconomic regime centered around independent, price stability-oriented monetary authorities.

For institutions that are commonly described as the embodiment of the dominant monetary regime, the adoption of policies that directly challenged the very essence of that regime cannot be regarded as either automatic or unproblematic. These considerations thereby raise some fundamental questions. For example, why and how did central banks respond to the changed economic conditions by breaking with orthodoxy and sustaining this course of action over time? How did the unthinkable become thinkable?

Reputation and the Political Foundations of Monetary Policy

There are few doubts that the key feature of modern central banks is independence from politics.[37] The rise and diffusion of independence as the key characteristic of central banks' institutional design is closely associated with the quest for policy effectiveness or *credibility*, in central banking parlance.[38] In the simplest form, the conventional rationale for independence can be summarized as follows: if elected policymakers control monetary policy, then they have an incentive to fuel the economy to satisfy their constituencies and win elections without worrying about the long-term costs of inflation. Given this time inconsistency problem, monetary policy will not be credible unless the inflationary bias of discretionary policymaking is addressed.[39] Here is where the delegation of monetary policy to an independent, technocratic central bank becomes key: entrusting central banks with monetary policy responsibility came to be regarded as the almost universal solution to the (alleged) distortions associated with the democratic political cycle.[40]

Although independence is a key ingredient for the purposes of credibility, it is not the only one. The experience of the Great Inflation in the 1970s and, especially, the successful taming of inflation under the leadership of US Fed Chair Paul Volcker since the early 1980s also led to widespread recognition of how important it was for central banks to consistently signal their policy stance to manage actors' 'rational' expectations and win societal support.[41] The modality by which central banks sent these *signals* was the projection of a distinct organizational image that I refer to as reputation. Indeed, from the late 1980s onwards, central banks had significantly invested in cultivating a distinct reputation.[42] This reputation was built around two planks: conservativeness and political neutrality. Conservativeness refers to the importance that central bankers assign to low inflation in relation to other macroeconomic objectives. Political neutrality refers to the primacy of "science" over discretion, as central banks' decisions were presented as being almost exclusively driven by available economic information interpreted through the most updated macroeconomic knowledge. As a result, distributional considerations, including those regarding the state of a governments' finances, were regarded as simply alien to monetary policymaking.[43]

If reputation has served central banks very well for almost three decades, it came under threat as economic conditions veered to the unfamiliar deflationary context set in motion by the 2008 crisis and exacerbated by the 2020 crisis. In particular, the economic imperatives of the new deflationary context openly clashed with the reputational tenets that monetary authorities had so carefully developed. Indeed, fighting deflation required central banks to commit to high inflation and step into distributive decisions to increase credit and revive economic activity. In practice, deflation fighting required central banks to act *irresponsibly*—that is, to act against the conservative and neutrality principles that had been the hallmark of their reputation.[44]

Recognizing the reputational problems that central banks confronted in such a deflationary environment leads to distinct expectations about the transformation path of monetary policy. Indeed, if a favorable reputation among political and public audiences is a valuable asset for central banks, the key to explaining central banks' behavior under changed external circumstances ultimately lies in reputation protection.[45] In other words, the institutional evolution of central banks is a function of their attempts at preempting and managing the reputational threats associated with the changes in the economic and political context where monetary authorities operate. These attempts materialized in a sequence of unconventional policy responses that ultimately cumulated in a profound transformation of the role and functions of central banks in domestic societies.

First, central banks moved into unconventional terrain when the conditions to preempt reputational damages were in place. These conditions materialized in the form of policy fixes, such as limitations in the scope and duration of the new policies or repeated calls for policy normalization. That is to say, at the beginning of the crisis period, central banks deviated from orthodoxy but did so with "caveats." Importantly, domestic governments offered a reputation-protection cover for new monetary interventions in the form of (more or less explicit) political support for central banks' actions. As the empirical analysis that follows is going to show, this developmental dynamic characterized not only the ECB, which has often been criticized for its "too little and too late" approach in dealing with the 2008–2010 crisis and its deflationary aftermath.[46] However, even what is often considered the most resolute deflation-fighting central bank, the US Fed, often resorted to policy caveats and coordination with government to move away from monetary orthodoxy.

Second, central banks stayed and even deepened their deviation from monetary orthodoxy as a way to manage the rising and unusually visible discontent about their activities. Indeed, the difficulties in reviving economic activity and the distributive effects of unconventional policies, which largely benefited powerful financial interests, ultimately contributed to significant changes in the political conditions within which central banks are used to operating. In particular, central banks found themselves at the center of an unprecedented politicization process, meaning an elevated level of public attention and contestation.[47] Faced with increased contestation, central banks redirected their public image by emphasizing employment, growth, and climate objectives as a strategic way to shore up public support and mitigate public backlash. For instance, at least before the return of inflationary pressures in early 2022, both the Fed and the ECB tried to manage their public image by committing to policy actions geared at attaining a "high-pressure economy" (i.e., an economy with stronger-than-average economic growth and low unemployment).[48] Both central banks also became involved in policy issues that would have been an anathema to the observers of any central bankers just ten years ago. In particular, both central banks signaled that fighting social inequality (for the Fed) and climate change (for the ECB) had become part of the monetary mandate.

Some commentators have gone as far as suggesting that central banks' new focus on social issues and climate change has sapped their independence and distracted them from the inflationary risks that emerged after the pandemic.[49] In other words, central banks have been accused of having failed to react adequately to the new changes in economic conditions and, in particular, to the return of inflation after a decade of persistent deflation.

While the debate is still open on the failures of central banks, these criticisms make an important point that resonates with a key finding of the book: central banks cannot automatically switch from one role to another, whether such a switch is from fighting inflation to fighting deflation, as seen at the beginning of the crisis period, or from fighting deflation to fighting inflation, as seen in the post-COVID world. The reason is that central banks are not just technocratic institutions whose decisions are driven by expert ideas developed within a politically insulated epistemic community. Central banks are first and foremost *political* institutions, meaning they need political support to survive over time and actively look for that support by sticking to their existing reputation. As such, central banks cannot be unproblematically rewired in the face of changed environmental conditions. Instead, their adaptation confronts the problems that stem from the legacy of past institutional development.

The Plan of the Book

By affecting output, inflation, and employment, the decisions made by central banks are among the most influential policy decisions for the economic and political trajectory of domestic economies. The power assigned to central banks becomes even more discernible during financial and economic crises. The policy record of the 2008 and 2020 crises is a testament to the fact that central banks' liquidity operations and bond-buying programs were not only crucial for managing the crises and mitigating their recessionary aftermath but also functioned as distributive decisions that worsened the inequality present in domestic societies. This historical period was thus a moment in time when central banks critically affected the course of history in advanced capitalist economies and beyond, especially given the influence that the central banks of high-income countries have in global markets. It is therefore not surprising that this crisis period revived the debate on the principle of central bank independence and on how to make unelected technocrats account for their decisions.[50]

This book contributes to the debate on the role of central banks in democratic societies by shedding light on central banks' choices in the recent past. Since 2008, central banks have indeed taken unprecedented decisions that have called into question what used to be regarded as the tenets of monetary orthodoxy. According to the orthodoxy that developed since the 1980s, central banks have avoided claiming overt responsibility for financial stability or real economic objectives, including job creation. Their mantra was that monetary policy can influence only the level of inflation, while long-run employment and economic growth are determined by structural policies. Monetary dominance was the other revered mantra.[51] Central banks jealously guarded their capacity to achieve their price stability mandates and vowed to never adjust monetary policy to take account of the government's fiscal actions. A decade of unconventional policies, however, have shaken the adherence to these precepts. From today's perspective, central banks have become routinely enmeshed with financial stability, have often claimed responsibility for economic growth and social objectives, and blurred the boundaries of monetary dominance by working alongside fiscal policymakers to address pressing economic and social challenges. Understanding how this transformation came about and what its implications are for the future role of central banks in domestic societies are the questions that this book sets out to explore.

By examining central banks' responses to the crisis period, this book also sheds light on an important scholarly gap in the international political economy literature. Specifically, the bulk of the existing scholarly works in the fields of political science and economics (both mainstream and critical) have largely focused on central banks' performance in taming inflation.[52] That is, the bulk of the existing scholarship has been interested in establishing whether independence brings about *low* inflation and, if so, under what conditions. This scholarship has yielded enormously important insights but at some significant costs. In particular, the focus on inflation has somewhat overly narrowed the behavior of central banks to inflation fighting and has thus obscured the question of whether independent central banks are similarly able to reflate domestic economies if the condition is so needed.[53] Examining the extent to which central banks can successfully address both inflation and deflation is a crucial gap that this book aims to fill.

Investigating the evolution of monetary institutions is not just a scholarly question, though. Determining which economic authorities, especially with what policy levers and within what limits, can support domestic societies is one of the most fundamental issues for the functioning of contemporary democracies. This issue is also particularly complicated because macroeconomic stability is deeply intertwined with issues related to financial stability and even climate risk management. A careful analysis of how central banks take on new functions and who they respond to in doing so is thus necessary to issue any sensible conclusion about the role that these important institutions can—or cannot—play in our domestic economies as well as their democratic accountability.

The policy performance of the central banks analyzed herein, however, should be of interest not only to those interested in central banking and macroeconomic governance but also to anyone concerned with the broader relationship between economics and democratic politics.[54] During the crisis period that spanned from 2008 and 2020, central banks made consequential decisions about the distribution of wealth within democratic societies, contributing to the political conflicts that pit creditors against debtors. Examining central banks' decisions and their drivers thus provides insights into the extent to which these non-majoritarian institutions have contributed to the emergence of new political cleavages in democratic societies and restructured the patterns of electoral competition.[55] The comparison between crisis management in the United States and in the European Union, as well as the resulting aftermath, might also be of interest to those interested in comparative politics and in explaining the commonalities and differences in countries' economic trajectories.

Chapter 1 begins charting this research agenda by discussing the transformation that has occurred in central banking and articulating the theoretical arguments developed in this book. The chapter starts by positioning the reputational argument vis-à-vis the major available explanations for the behavior of central banks. It then introduces the concept of reputation, applies the concept to the study of central banks, and explains the logics of reputation protection with the attendant empirical expectations.

Chapter 2 moves into the empirical analysis by providing a historical reconstruction of the buildup of central banks' reputation and economic orthodoxy. Specifically, the chapter offers a historical reconstruction of the way in which conservativeness and political neutrality became the tenets of modern central banks' reputation. The analysis is organized into three major historical junctures and the institutional developments that spanned each of them. The first juncture is the period of the Great Inflation, which gave rise to central banks' reputation as conservative institutions. The second juncture is the period broadly associated with the era of the Great Moderation, which ranged from the late 1980s until the beginning of the 2000s. In this period, the reputation of central banks was cemented, and the notion of monetary neutrality was clearly engrained in the institutional image of monetary authorities. Finally, the analysis focuses on Japan's "lost decade." The Japanese experience in the 1990s is particularly important because, up to that point, Japan was the only high-income country to experience deflation since the 1930s. The Japanese experience thereby provided a glimpse into the problems that independent and reputable central banks might have confronted in the context of low inflation.

Chapter 3 brings the reader up to the most recent historical period. In particular, the chapter illustrates the economic and political changes that central banks have been confronted with since 2008, as well as the curious convergence of monetary policy away from orthodoxy, despite the different timing and circumstances that led to the adoption of unconventional policies. To start with, the chapter examines the new economic problems that central banks have confronted since 2008—namely, the collapse of the financial system, secular stagnation, and a global pandemic that has disrupted both domestic demand and global supply chains. The chapter then examines the changes in the political context in which central banks operate. In particular, the chapter analyzes the causes and consequences of the politicization of monetary policy—that is, the increasing public visibility and contestation of the distributive effects of the decisions taken by central banks.

After delineating the general picture of the transformation in central banking, the analysis turns to the two central banks whose policy and institutional trajectories are closely examined: the US Fed and the ECB. Chapters 4 and 5 investigate how the Fed and the ECB broke with orthodoxy in the wake of the 2008 crisis and continued sustaining this break throughout the 2020 crisis and its aftermath.

In the concluding chapter, the book goes back to the technocratic versus political nature of central banks and examines the empirical evidence against the tenets of the reputational argument that I have advanced. The chapter also elaborates on my main findings and connects them to policy and scholarly debate on the role of central banks in domestic societies. In particular, the conclusion reflects on the institutional capacity of central banks to deviate from their inflation mandate and so stimulate economic growth and take on a more active role in other policy areas, including the one related to the fight against climate change. The conclusion also engages with the debate in political economy on which political and societal actors lend their support and legitimize central banks and the neoliberal macroeconomic regime centered around price stability.

CENTRAL BANKS AS POLITICAL INSTITUTIONS

How do institutions respond to external challenges, and how do they evolve over time? These are probably the most widely asked and debated questions in social science research. Given the extensive and excellent scholarship that has investigated questions related to institutional and policy change, here I narrow the focus by connecting these broader scholarly debates with the studies that have analyzed the development trajectory of the institutions under examination—namely, central banks.[1]

Central banks are indeed particularly interesting institutions to study to get at questions related to institutional transformation. Ever since the seventeenth century, when the first central banks were established in Sweden and England, the roles of the banks have evolved. In particular, the balance between the objectives of price stability, financial stability, and support for the real economy has shifted over time, usually in response to major economic and financial challenges.[2] Originally chartered to lend government funds and to act as clearinghouses for commerce, by the turn of the twentieth century, several central banks were created to provide financial stability or to manage the gold standard.[3] On the heels of both the Great Depression and the experience of World War II, central banks refocused their activities on helping domestic governments keep borrowing costs low or on financing national development projects, especially in emerging market countries. The Great Inflation of the 1970s served as the catalyst for another major shift in central banking, which led to central banks becoming guardians of the monetary orthodoxy centered on the achievement of price stability (as will be extensively discussed in chapter 2). Starting from 2008, the role of the central banks has shifted again. In particular, central banks confronted persistent deflation and secular stagnation by adopting (unconventional) policies that, as discussed in the introduction, led them away from previous monetary orthodoxy and significantly transformed their institutional profile.

This chapter offers an analytical framework within which to investigate this process of institutional transformation. The analytical framework proposed herein extends beyond explaining single monetary policy decisions; rather, it is meant to shed light on the overall political dynamic that led central banks in high-income countries to move away from the standards of monetary orthodoxy by revising their tools and expanding the remit of monetary policy beyond the objective of price stability into issues such as inequality and climate change.

In charting this transformation, this book starts with a crucial but often underestimated observation. In particular, the book recognizes that the transformation in central banking could not have been taken for granted when the crisis period started in 2008 and continued into the 2020s. In other words, although central banks' policy responses to economic and financial disruption may be read as "obvious" in hindsight, this was far from being the case. Central banks might have either responded differently to the challenges at hand or not responded at all. This means that central banks' departure from orthodoxy was far from automatic, thereby raising the question of what factors and mechanisms stand behind the process of policy and institutional development.

This chapter begins by situating the central banks' transformation within the scholarship of political economy. In particular, I discuss the literature that helps shed light on the policy choices of central banks and the evolution of macroeconomic regimes. In doing so, I bring to the forefront a fundamental distinction between explanations that emphasize the technocratic nature of central banks (the standard view) and those that emphasize their political nature instead. Next, I introduce the book's analytical framework based on the notion of reputation and its importance to the maintenance of political support for public institutions. I apply the notion of reputation to central banks and then elaborate on the empirical expectations that will be assessed in the ensuing empirical analysis.

The Standard View: Central Banks as Technocratic Institutions

The transformation of central banking has been so momentous that it has attracted significant attention. This attention is justified because of the implications that the transformation entails. For instance, central banks' involvement with policies that entail unequal distributive effects across society raises serious questions about the legitimate basis on which monetary authorities take their decisions.[4] As central banks' mandate expands, it calls into question the continuing validity of the principle of central bank independence as well as the relationship between independence and accountability.[5] The transformation of central banking has also been puzzling because of the conventional wisdom about central banks— that is, they are not ordinarily regarded as revolutionaries but rather as the guardians of the macroeconomic regime that has been in place since the late 1980s.[6] The fact that central banks have become agents of change and heralds of policy experimentation has taken more than a few observers by surprise.

Two major narratives have become the dominant explanations of the process that has led central banks away from orthodox monetary theory and practice: the "only game in town" narrative and the "learning" narrative.

According to the "only game in town" narrative, central banks' transformation was forced on them because of a political void in domestic societies.[7] More precisely, the argument is that when the crisis period started in 2008 and continued throughout the decade-long aftermath, central banks were the only economic policymakers with the institutional capacity to respond to the new economic and financial challenges. In particular, while fiscal policymakers failed to act because they were either polarized or ideologically averse to intervention, monetary policymakers possessed a key institutional feature that made them well positioned to act—namely, independence. Being above the political fray by virtue of their legal independence, central banks could make difficult decisions that fiscal policymakers were either unable or unwilling to make.[8] From this perspective, the transformation in central banking was basically a side effect of central banks acting as good citizens by filling in the void that other policymakers had left open.

The second common narrative used to account for central banks' developmental trajectory says that the central banks had learned the lessons of the 1930s.[9] Whereas at the time, many central bankers concluded that monetary policy could not be used to stimulate economic activity with an interest rate essentially at the zero level, by the 2000s, they had learned that the consequences of such inaction might be dire.[10] From this perspective, central banks evolved by overcoming ideational constraints. That is, central banks overcame monetary orthodoxy because new policy ideas gained currency among central bankers; namely, new ideas about the objectives and tools of monetary policy.[11] In other words, it took the development of new ideas and economic models to replace the old ones. In the case of the European Central Bank (ECB), for instance, the switch away from a discourse of "credibility" to one of "stability" is regarded as the pivotal condition that allowed the ECB to take unconventional actions that it had previously resisted.[12] The epistemic community character of central banks was key in this process; the expertise that characterizes the community of central banks allowed them to reconsider precrisis monetary ideas, after which they adjusted and implemented them.[13]

Although the "only game in town" and "learning" narratives build on different social logics of action, they ultimately share a common flaw. Specifically, by emphasizing independence and expertise, both narratives basically advance a *technocratic* dynamic of the process of change at the cost of marginalizing politics in the analysis. In other words, both narratives basically view the momentous transformation in central banking narrowly, as either a process of the functional adaptation of an independent agent to changed economic circumstances or the outcome of a "battle of ideas" among monetary technocrats.

What this technocratic interpretation masks, however, is that "economic policy-making is a quintessentially political process." That is, "even in a field where the correct choice of policies depends heavily on expertise and the instruments for policy implementation, policy is driven by a dynamic that is as much political as economic."[14] Recovering this political dimension is a key goal that this book seeks to achieve. In particular, my purpose is to shed light on the fact that even if they are formally independent and made up of monetary experts, central banks, as public institutions, need political support to implement monetary policy and survive under changed external conditions.

In making the case for the political bases of the post-2008 evolution in central banking, the book builds on a well-established tradition in critical political economy literature that has long emphasized the political foundations of monetary policy and regimes. In this tradition, "all monetary phenomena are fundamentally political" because they reflect the outcome of political conflicts and ideological struggles (see Table 1).[15] From this perspective, the monetary regime that prevailed from the late 1980s, with its prioritization of low inflation as the ultimate economic objective, is not a reflection of a technocratic process mostly driven by an independent institution or by new economic ideas positing the benefits of low inflation. Rather, the late-1980s monetary regime provides evidence of a distinct political outcome: the victory of a "deflationary bloc" led by financial interests.[16] A similar reasoning applies to central bank independence. The fact that monetary policy decisions have been almost universally delegated to independent central banks is ultimately the reflection of the institutional victory of both a distinct neoliberal ideology and the particular groups that benefit from the policies that this ideology recommends.[17]

Importantly, these groups have lent the necessary political support for the new regime to be *credible* and thus to be *reproduced* over time. As Ilene Grabel put it starkly, "Credibility . . . is founded on politics, not metaphysics." This "view is no less true of policies implemented by politically insulated institutions purporting to promote the national interest."[18] Indeed, the credibility of the policies

TABLE 1.   Explanations of central banks' behavior and of policy and institutional change

EXPLANATION	CONCEPTION OF CENTRAL BANKS	DRIVERS OF CHANGE
Only game in town	Technocratic institutions	Independence
Ideational	Technocratic institutions	Ideational innovation and learning
Critical political economy	Political institutions	Political conflict
Reputational	Political institutions	Reputation protection (preempting and managing reputational threats)

implemented by independent central banks has been secured through the mobilization of the financial sector's political and economic power.[19] In other words, independence has not automatically brought about credibility and low inflation. Rather, it has been "the success of the signaling effect" (i.e., the positive response of financial sector actors to the policies adopted by independent central banks) that has secured the reproduction of the low inflation regime centered on independent central banks since the late 1980s.[20]

In what follows, I build on the fundamental insight that macroeconomic policies and regimes always need politics. In particular, I share the view according to which the policies that central banks choose are meant to "signal" a distinct policy stance to secure political support beyond them. However, I also move away from critical political economy scholarship in two important respects. First, absent major political realignments in domestic societies, this scholarship is much more attuned to explaining stability and reproduction rather than change. Thus, a primary objective of the theoretical framework suggested in the following pages is that of explaining change, even when the underlying balance of power among groups in domestic societies has not been significantly altered. Second, while critical political economy scholarship has elevated the relationship between independent institutions and financial markets as the key relationship by which to explain specific macroeconomic policies and regimes, the theoretical framework proposed herein suggests that the audiences whose political support is necessary for particular policies and regimes may change over time. In other words, the political foundations of credibility and monetary policy are larger and more varying than those investigated thus far. In this sense, my theoretical approach subsumes the critical international political economy (IPE) one.

To advance these arguments, it is therefore necessary to start from the channels through which technocratic institutions such as central banks construct their credibility and thus their political support. In particular, I argue that a key—but underexamined—channel through which central banks have secured support is based on *reputation*. In what follows, I unpack the concept of reputation before applying this concept to central banks.

From Technocracy to Politics: Reputation and Political Support

The importance of reputation as a driver of institutional behavior has been considerably investigated in the study of public bureaucracies. According to Daniel Carpenter's widely used definition, bureaucratic reputation refers to "a set of symbolic beliefs about the unique or separable capacities, roles, and obligations of an organization, where these beliefs are embedded in audience networks."[21] Reputation can thus be regarded as an "organizational claim to uniqueness" in that its construction and social acceptance pertain to the distinctive *traits* of the institution, as shaped by its history, mission, capacity, and actual performance.[22]

Based on this definition, reputation can be analytically examined based on two mutually related traits or dimensions: an internal dimension, which pertains to the "construction" of reputation, and an external dimension, which pertains to the "acceptance" of reputation and thus to social and political support.

The internal dimension of reputation refers to the buildup of the public image of an institution as "developed endogenously by the internal character of the administrative organization."[23] That is, reputation is deliberately built by the members of the institution with the aim of shaping audiences' expectations about the institution's goals and performance. This suggests that, in performing the functions delegated to them, institutions retain the room to maneuver to areas outside their audiences' attention toward certain aspects of their mission, especially if the bureaucracy is assigned multiple goals.[24] For instance, public agencies customarily calibrate their actions "to construct the way in which their audiences judge their success or failure."[25] The projection of a distinct reputation usually reflects the dominant beliefs within the institution about what tasks the institution can and cannot perform and with what means. Of course, these aspects may change over time, especially if recruitment brings in members with different professional backgrounds.[26] In general, however, bureaucratic reputations are quite stable because institutions heavily invest in them and adopt policies that reproduce them. Furthermore, although it is understandable that not all staff members will agree with the institutional image that the bureaucracy projects of itself, bureaucratic reputations ultimately reflect the dominant view within the institution—namely, the one that emerges after internal political battles.[27]

The external dimension of reputation pertains to the "receiving end" of the image crafted and projected by an institution. Indeed, for reputation to exist, a set of beliefs about the institution's history, mission, and capacity needs to be "embedded in audience networks."[28] Audience is thus the "animating concept" of reputation-based accounts.[29] That is, reputation needs to be recognized and accepted by the diverse groups that interact and are affected by the institution's decisions. These groups are necessarily heterogeneous. For instance, audiences generally include elected officials, interest groups, market actors, the media, and citizens. Audience heterogeneity entails that the institution is unlikely to satisfy all audiences simultaneously, which requires the institution to prioritize some audiences over others (as discussed below). However, audience acceptance is crucial for the institution to obtain the necessary social and political support that provides the foundations of an institution's power and independence.

Indeed, a key insight of the reputation-based literature is that an institution's power and independence are based on more than the function of the contract that it holds with its political principals, as principal-agent accounts have it. That is, the power and independence that an institution commands do not solely reflect the letter of its formal mandate and the control mechanisms that principal actors put in place in their delegation contracts. In contrast, power and independence are significantly shaped by reputation. That is, a favorable reputation underpins and protects an institution's power and independence. Once possessed, these factors are used and managed in ways that maintain the institution's reputation and thus its power and independence.[30] It is also worth stressing that reputation not only helps secure power and independence but also may serve other purposes for the institution to thrive and survive over time. For instance, reputation has been found to provide a protective shield in the presence of opposition from hostile external audiences, and it is an asset with which to assert control over policy issues that are under public debate.[31]

Institutional reputation is thus a crucial resource for an institution. However, it is also a resource that the institution cannot entirely produce on its own because it is dependent on the interplay between the signaling institution and the multiple audiences that characterize its operating environment. Reputation-seeking institutions can thereby be conceived as "politically conscious actors" that actively seek to protect their (favorable) reputation before their key audiences to maintain political support.[32] In what follows, I show how these insights can be extended to central banks and the consequences for their behavior and their path of institutional transformation.

The Importance of Reputation to Central Banks

While reputation is a key political asset for most public institutions, few institutions have made the construction of reputation as crucial to their activity as central banks have done. The importance of building and sustaining a distinct reputation is closely associated with the notion of credibility, which has become the dominant intellectual prism that guides the behavior of central banks since the experience of the Great Inflation in the 1970s.[33] In particular, after the 1970s, monetary theory and practice achieved a solid consensus about the conditions that allow a central bank to be credible—with credibility referring to central banks' ability to convince economic and financial actors *to believe* in its policy pronouncements to steer investment and consumption decisions.[34] Specifically, two conditions were identified: legal independence and, importantly, a reputation based on conservativeness and political neutrality.

A Conservative and Apolitical Reputation

To understand how conservativeness became a key organizational trait for central banks around the world, and certainly for central banks in high-income countries, it is necessary to recall that modern central banking was forged during the Great Inflation that spanned the 1960s–1980s.[35] At that time, the scourge that confronted economic policymakers was that of rising prices and growing unemployment. In the United States, for instance, between 1964 and 1974, inflation rose from 1 percent to over 12 percent, and unemployment rose from 5 percent to over 7 percent. By the summer of 1980, inflation was near 14.5 percent, and unemployment was over 7.5 percent.[36] Then, Paul Volcker became the head of the US Federal Reserve (the Fed). Under Volcker's leadership, the US Fed started a disinflationary process that eventually vanquished inflation, although this success came at the cost of high unemployment and a deep recession (see chapter 2).

Volcker's success in taming an extended period of inflation was probably the most influential episode in the development of central banks' organizational image around the world; it was also a defining moment for the development of macroeconomy theory. Indeed, Volcker came to epitomize a distinct view of the mission of central banks—namely, the view that "central banks can and should use monetary policy to maintain *low* inflation over time."[37] The image of central banks as guardians of low and stable inflation was also supported by concomitant developments in macroeconomic theory. The lessons of the Great Inflation indeed invalidated the supposed long-term trade-off between inflation and un-employment, as theorized by the Phillips curve. The notion that the economy gravitates to some natural rate of unemployment in the long run—no matter what the rate of inflation is—became the new standard in macroeconomic thinking.[38] This conclusion had important consequences for the development of central banks' institutional image. Indeed, absent a long-run trade-off between inflation and unemployment, the best contribution that central banks could make to eco-nomic activity in the long run was to keep inflation low. That is, "the central banker has to be conservative, where conservativeness refers to the importance that he or she assigns to price stability in its relation to other macroeconomic objectives."[39]

Building and sustaining a reputation for conservative, inflation-averse behav-ior has thus come to orient the practice of central banking. As central banker officials explain it, "For a central bank, earning a reputation as a guardian of price stability is of paramount importance."[40] In particular, central banks regard con-servativeness as important for increasing the success of monetary policy and thus for justifying their independence.[41] Even when legal statutes have assigned cen-tral banks multiple policy goals, monetary authorities have often developed a clear policy hierarchy in which the price stability objective has pride of place. The case of the US Fed is an apt case in point; even though the Fed is assigned the "dual mandate" of seeking maximum employment and stable prices, the em-phasis on which objective should be paramount has shifted over time, with the former mandate being more paramount in the period before 2008.[42]

The primacy that central banks came to attribute to low and stable inflation had been underpinned by the widespread adoption of inflation-focused mone-tary frameworks. Since the late 1980s, central banks around the world have come to adhere to some form of inflation targeting to signal their commitment to fight inflation.[43] Indeed, "inflation-targeting central banks have a single goal—low in-flation; and they are normally given precise numerical targets by their govern-ments."[44] This means that central banks raise or lower interest rates based on above-target or below-target inflation, respectively. The importance of inflation targeting for the establishment of central banks' reputation as conservative, inflation-averse institutions can further be gleaned from the fact that before the crisis period that started in 2008, even those central banks that did not consider themselves formal inflation targeters (including the US Fed and the ECB) had nonetheless incorporated key features of the inflation-targeting regime in their monetary practice, including the prioritization of the low inflation objective and greater transparency in communication to achieve it.[45]

In addition to conservativeness, central banks have nurtured a reputation as politically neutral institutions whose actions are almost exclusively driven by available economic information interpreted through the best macroeconomic knowledge. That is, central banks have been keen on projecting an image as technocratic, apolitical institutions, where expertise trumps political discretion. As a former US central banker stated, "Monetary economists have developed a set of basic scientific principles, derived from theory and empirical evidence, that now guide thinking at almost all central banks."[46] It is not by accident that references to "monetary science" have been abundant over the past decades, especially to distinguish the realm of monetary policy from the much messier and distributive area of fiscal policy.[47]

The alleged distance between monetary policy and distributive policy has been further underpinned by the notion that money is neutral. That is, the mantra present in monetary economics had been that changes in the supply of money affect only prices and not the real economy. The implication was that "the idea that central banks achieve their narrow objective of price stability without much in the way of distributive consequences."[48] One way in which central banks signaled their neutrality was also by severing their relationship with fiscal authorities.[49] That is, central banks embraced the principle of monetary dominance according to which monetary authorities pursue the price stability objective without being constrained by the governments' fiscal needs. In other words, central banks were keen on projecting an institutional image aimed at signaling that deficit-financing and debt-servicing issues played no role in monetary policy decisions. The idea of monetary financing (i.e., financing fiscal deficits through money creation) thus came to be seen as "a mortal risk to hard-won central bank credibility."[50]

It is fair to say that central banks' efforts to project an organizational image of themselves as technocratic institutions have largely been successful. Central banks are routinely regarded as "a conservative bunch" or as the typical example of epistemic communities whose members share policy views that closely reflect the state of knowledge in the field of macroeconomics and common professional and educational backgrounds.[51] Expert knowledge informs central banks' decisions by helping them navigate the "pervasive" uncertainty that characterizes monetary policymaking.[52] As a result, even if faced with these informational constraints, central bankers "aren't throwing darts at a decision tree"; instead, they use "the technical apparatus of empirical and theoretical macroeconomics to reach a consensus that creates a policy conclusion."[53] As Juliet Johnson aptly stated, "Central bankers built their community's legitimacy by presenting themselves as seers who could be trusted to conduct the complex, arcane, and delicate task of guiding monetary policy."[54] The problem is that the economic and financial challenges that have emerged since 2008 have shown the limits of the reputation that central banks so carefully cultivated in the previous three decades.

Reputation in a Changed Context

Before 2008, central banks' reputation was perfectly attuned to the economic and political conditions of the times. The macroeconomic environment of the Great Moderation, which was characterized by low inflation and sustained economic activity, justified what central banks had been doing—namely, placing relatively more weight on achieving the inflation objective as a way to tame, or even put an end to, the business cycle (see chapter 2). At the same time, the behavior of central banks basically "coincided with what the consensus among the political classes and in the polity at large wanted them to do," which is what William Buiter has called the "cosmic coincidence."[55] That is, central banks' reputation seemed to be attuned to broad political and societal demands and expectations.

The transition from the Great Moderation to the post-2008 deflationary context, however, has served as a challenge to the reputation to which central banks have been previously upheld. This challenge has occurred because fighting disinflationary forces calls for reputable central banks to act *irresponsibly*—that is, to behave in ways (i.e., adopt policies) that directly conflict with the image of conservative and politically neutral institutions. Specifically, a deflationary context challenges the reputation that central banks have been carefully cultivating for over three decades in two major respects.

First, a disinflationary context challenges central banks' conservative resolve by requiring a potentially prolonged period of monetary accommodation. As Paul Krugman explained with regard to the irresponsibility that reputable central banks must confront: "The simplest way out of the slump is to give the economy the inflationary expectations it needs. This means that the central bank must make a credible commitment . . . that it will *not* reverse its current monetary expansion when prices begin to rise!"[56] The problem is that such commitment risk undermines central banks' investment in a reputational image centered on inflation-averse behavior. A group of ECB high officials summarized the problem that central banks confront in a disinflationary context as follows: "While the central bank can most of the time maintain composure in the face of [economic] disturbances, . . . it needs to demonstrate anti-inflationary action if inflation ultimately challenges its credibility."[57] In other words, central banks' attempts at reflation will ultimately hit the limits of having to preserve central banks' reputation as inflation fighters.

The risks to central banks' reputation as conservative institutions are further magnified by the fact that the policy measures aimed at countering disinflationary forces often take time to wind down; the time lag creates the risk of unanchoring longer-term inflation expectations that central banks have so successfully tamed over the past decades. The use of quantitative easing (QE) programs well illustrates this risk for central banks' conservative reputation. QE entails the buying of different types of financial assets with the intention of lowering their yields and thus directing investors to higher-risk financial assets. However, should inflationary pressures emerge, removing the QE stimulus would take time; unlike simply raising the target for the policy rate using the interest rate tool, the removal of the QE stimulus requires either selling assets or waiting for them to mature. The problem is that inflationary pressures may become unanchored, thus eroding central banks' reputational investments in inflation fighting. It is therefore not surprising that central banks' experiments with QE programs over the past decade have generally received cold acceptance among conservative policymakers. From their perspective, central banks' asset purchase programs are a risk for "currency debasement and inflation," as a group of Republican political strategists accused the Fed back in 2010.[58] Although both the 2008 and 2020 crises show that these concerns were overly exaggerated, if not largely unfounded, the experience of the past decade shows that the central banks whose actions are analyzed in this book were deeply aware of the reputational risks they were facing by adopting unconventional policies over the past decade (see chapters 4 and 5).

An additional risk for central banks' conservative reputation arises from the interaction between the measures needed to counteract disinflationary forces and financial markets. Indeed, monetary expansions tend to fuel financial stability concerns. That is, central banks' anti-disinflationary actions contribute to creating an environment of ultralow interest rates, ample liquidity, and low volatility that increases the incentives for investors to search for higher yields. As a result, the prices of equities and other risky assets rise; at the same time, these assets become highly vulnerable to changes in the monetary policy stance. The abundance of liquidity may also lead banks to delay balance sheet adjustments and writing off nonperforming loans.[59] Ultimately, central banks that are confronting financial stability risks may be forced to accept a higher rate of inflation than they would ordinarily accept, at the cost of undermining their conservative reputation, though.[60]

Second, the policies needed to counteract deflationary pressures conflict with the other major tenet of central banks' reputation—namely, their political neutrality. Indeed, one of the major side effects of most unconventional measures is that these measures affect the distribution of income and wealth, thus advantaging some sectors and individuals over others.[61] Stressing the distributive effects of unconventional policies is not meant to neglect those associated with conventional monetary policy or to deny the intrinsic political quality of money.[62] However, most unconventional policies explicitly conflict with central banks' reputation as politically neutral institutions because the distributional effects are much more visible than is the case for interest rate policy decisions (see also chapter 3). This is particularly evident in what is probably the most controversial measure that central banks have adopted to counteract deflationary forces: the purchase of public and private securities under QE programs.[63] As already hinted at previously, QE affects the economy by influencing the price of assets of all types and maturities (i.e., QE purchases increase asset prices and decrease yields). Theoretically, lower yields should imply lower borrowing costs for both firms and households. However, QE is likely to be implemented during a period where the credit channel is impaired, meaning that the main channel that these policies are likely to work through is capital market funding. Since capital funding is only accessible for larger companies, the policy is likely to have more favorable outcomes for this group of actors than for smaller firms and households.[64] In addition, QE benefits holders of assets such as hedge funds, traders, and high-wealth individuals. Given the distributional impact of such unconventional policies, their systematic use in response to disinflationary prospects contrasts with the image of central banks as politically neutral technocrats.

The policies needed to fight deflationary forces may also conflict with central banks' reputation as politically neutral institutions through another channel: the relationship with domestic governments. For instance, their purchases in the public sector reduce yields on government bonds, thereby decreasing the cost of borrowing for governments. Lower financing costs for governments, however, can be read as central banks caving into political pressures, as central banks' actions ultimately give domestic governments the possibility of adopting a fiscal policy stance that could help increase their reelection prospects. Furthermore, central banks' purchases of sovereign debt can be seen as an opportunity for governments to postpone fiscal consolidation on the expectation that the central bank will be accommodative. Although it is difficult to detect any real, systematic moral hazard effects of central banks' unconventional policies, at least as a result of the 2008 financial crisis, the reputational costs that the specter of monetary financing entails for central banks have been made abundantly clear. [65] The more central banks have tried to respond to deflationary forces by stepping into sovereign debt markets, the more intense the criticisms are about monetary authorities venturing into political, distributive terrain, which unelected institutions should not impinge on (see chapters 3–5).

In short, deflation fighting requires central banks to act "irresponsibly"—that is, to act against the tenets of the conservative and politically neutral reputation that have been the trademark of modern central banking since at least the 1990s. Indeed, fighting deflation would require central banks to tolerate inflation and make open distributive decisions, which is precisely the opposite of the image that central banks have carefully sponsored and that has provided them with solid societal and political support for years. Recognizing the reputational threats that central banks confronted as the economic context flipped to a deflationary scenario is thus the crucial starting point to make sense of their behavior and their institutional development. In particular, explaining the transformation in central banking cannot help but start with understanding why and how central banks have dealt with those reputational threats, thereby setting in motion the chain of decisions that have led them away from the monetary orthodoxy of the recent past. It is exactly these "why" and "how" issues that I turn to in the next section.

Signaling Reputation

I have thus far argued that central banks care about their institutional reputation not just because of their past investments in reputation building but also because the social acceptance of reputation has long supported central banks' power and independence. In other words, reputation has been instrumental in nurturing societal and political support around central banks' activities and their independent governance. In the previous section, I have also argued that central banks found themselves in a very uncomfortable position when the economic conditions changed because the prolonged monetary accommodation required to fight deflationary forces risked compromising their image as conservative and politically neutral institutions before their audiences.

Recognizing the reputational risks for central banks helps shed light on the developmental trajectory of central banks in response to the 2008 and 2020 crises. The reputational logic indeed suggests that the transformation can be read as the result of central banks' calibrated attempts to cultivate a positive reputation under changed external circumstances. In particular, central banks' decade-long transformation is the cumulative effect of central banks' responses to the reputational threats that have emerged from their external environment—namely, from the audiences whose support underpins their power and independence. Indeed, "the reputation-based power of any organization rests in the judgment of its audiences; those audiences have a form of power, too."[66] Audiences can thus influence the behavior of an institution by threatening its reputation. For instance, several studies have indicated that when faced with audience criticisms, public institutions change their behavior to avoid being negatively perceived and thus retain political support. In particular, institutions modify their performance or adopt behaviors to reduce blame, among other actions.[67] The basic idea behind these insights is that institutions have to *signal* specific organizational traits as a way in which to assuage criticisms and retain necessary political support.[68] In short, if we want to understand how an institution behaves, it is necessary to "look at the audience, and look at the threats."[69]

Which Audience Matters

Stressing the importance of reputational threats brought about by the audiences of an institution raises an important question: Who are the key audiences whose criticisms and expectations an institution attends to or prioritizes? As already mentioned above, institutions usually face heterogeneous audiences, spanning from political principals to experts and the media. These audience groups generally hold different and competing views about the distinct traits of an institution.[70] For instance, financial interests are likely to judge central banks based on their capacity to achieve the low inflation objective, while trade unions' assessment could weigh the unemployment objective more heavily. If both objectives cannot be achieved simultaneously, it is often the case that satisfying one audience may dissatisfy and even alienate the other.

Given audience heterogeneity, an institution that attempts to tailor its policies to specific audiences has to decide which audience(s) to prioritize.[71] That is, reputation-seeking institutions do not necessarily attend to the demands and expectations of the same audience group over time. The decision to respond to one set of audiences often depends on the consequences that the specific audience group can bring to bear on the organization should their demands and expectations be disappointed. For instance, citizens are generally considered less powerful than business or governmental actors in applying pressures on reputation-seeking institutions because they do not directly threaten the institutions' financial resources or bureaucratic turf. However, it is also recognized that citizens' influence on reputation-seeking institutions can increase significantly if they mobilize in the form of protests, vote for parties whose political agendas threaten the institution's turf, especially vis-à-vis competitors, or increase the level of media attention placed on the institution.[72]

What about central banks' audiences? In the previous sections, I already stressed the "special" relationship that central banks have with financial markets. The special attention that financial markets receive from central banks could be justified based on the way in which monetary policy works. Indeed, markets work as the transmission belt through which monetary policy decisions are passed on to households and firms through market pricing and financing conditions. Central banks thus rely on banks and other financial intermediaries to transmit the impulse of monetary policy decisions to the broader economy.[73] However, the relationship between central banks and markets goes beyond the workings of monetary policy; it is also rooted in the adherence to the same set of ideological beliefs.[74] In addition to financial markets, the literature on central banks has also often pointed to monetary experts as another key constituency for central banks. That is, as technocratic institutions, central banks try to legitimize their actions before the professional community made up of monetary economists in academia and in policy centers.[75] This community is particularly important for central banks because it is the one that lends them professional prestige and esteem.[76]

While financial actors and monetary experts are certainly important audiences for central banks, they are not the only ones whose negative reactions may undermine central banks' reputation, thereby eliciting a response. Political audiences—including both political principals (governments and legislatures) and the public—are important audiences, too. Under some circumstances, they could even be more important in explaining changes in central banks' behavior.

The rationale underlying this claim is threefold. First, even if central banks are legally independent, their independence can always be undone. That is to say, independence is not something akin to a natural right and consequently inalienable. Instead, independence is entrusted on an agency and can always be repealed.[77] The authority to repeal independence lies with political audiences. Specifically, governments and legislatures hold the key to reversing central bank independence. This reversal risk increases in crisis times when central banks may become an easy scapegoat for both politicians and the public to blame. Second, even if the threat to independence is not imminent because of foolproof legal design, as is the case for the ECB, whose independence is enshrined in an international treaty (discussed in chapter 5), central banks may still feel the need to accommodate political audiences to maintain their support in the future and thus secure their independence. As John Goodman explains this observation. "The extent to which central banks must give ground [i.e., accommodate political requests] . . . hinges upon their success in building support among key societal actors."[78] The lower the level of support is, the higher the expectation of a central bank to "give ground." Finally, while financial markets and monetary economists can channel criticisms behind closed doors, the criticism coming from political audiences is usually much more vocal. Politicians have a strong incentive to raise criticisms so that their constituencies can hear them, while public criticism usually takes the form of mass protests and negative public opinion. This is exactly the politicization dynamics that central banks have been confronted with in the aftermath of the 2008 and the 2020 crisis periods analyzed herein, as discussed at greater length in chapter 3. In short, the reputational threats that emerge from political audiences are serious. Central banks cannot dismiss these threats, meaning that their emergence is likely to be met by attempts by the central banks to protect their favorable reputation.

Preemption and Management

The reasoning developed thus far leaves open the issue of *what* signals the central banks will choose. To put it differently, the issue is how central banks respond to the reputational threats coming from their political environment. Indeed, in responding to negative reactions from audiences, central banks, like other public institutions, have a variety of choices. For instance, central banks may opt for strategic silence or inaction if the type of reputational threats they confront affect secondary aspects of the institution's reputation or when their reputation is particularly strong.[79] That is, an institution with a strong reputation can afford to ignore the criticisms or, at best, to opt for cosmetic changes to realign audiences' perceptions with the internal vision of its mission. In contrast, institutions tend to change their policies and behavior in a more profound way if the reputational threat they confront touches on the core aspect of the institution or if the threat comes from audiences that are key to the institution's survival.[80] In short, the type of reputational threat presented generally affects the institutional response to that threat.

To explain central banks' responses to the reputational threats coming from their political audiences, I build on this theoretical insight. In particular, I argue that to explain central banks' responses to changed external conditions and thus their institutional evolution, it is necessary to distinguish whether the reputational threats that central banks confront are potential or whether they are actual, which leads to two distinct pathways of reputation protection: reputation preemption or reputation management, respectively.

In the preemption scenario, the reputational threats an institution confronts are potential, meaning that they may (or may not) materialize in the future based on the institutions' behavior. In this scenario, it is plausible to expect institutions to engage in preemptive behavior—that is, to adopt actions that attempt to preserve their past reputation while mitigating the materialization of future reputational risks. This behavior was evident early in the crisis periods analyzed herein, at the moment when the reputational risks were still potential. Indeed, both the US Fed and the ECB moved into unconventional terrain only under specific conditions (i.e., when it was possible for them to align their past reputation to the changed economic circumstances). Two conditions were particularly important to this end.

First, central banks moved away from monetary orthodoxy when they could signal their new policies as being aligned with their past reputation. This signal worked through the operational design of unconventional policies—in other words, through the use of policy "caveats." In particular, unconventional policies were carefully designed to signal central banks' continuing adherence to the tenets of their conservative and politically neutral reputation. Provisions such as the limits placed on the scope of monetary interventions, premature withdrawals of policy measures, and calls to policy "normalization" serve central banks' signaling purpose. As the empirical analysis that follows is going to show, this strategic approach in responding to deflationary forces characterized the ECB, which has often been criticized for its "too little, too late" approach in dealing with the crisis and its deflationary aftermath.[81] However, even what is often considered the most resolute deflation-fighting central bank, the US Fed, has often resorted to policy caveats as a way to mask the transformation in its policies—at the cost of diluting the strength of the monetary response.[82]

Second, central banks' action preempted reputational risks by subordinating their interventions to the policy interventions from other economic policymakers. In particular, policy coordination—by which I mean that the decisions made by distinct economic policymakers are taken in ways that reduce conflicts or produce synergies among their different sets of decisions—offered central banks political cover for actions that could have potentially threatened their reputation.[83] Indeed, coordination and fragmented governance structures help distribute the burden of responsibility among multiple public agencies and thus obscure the attribution of blame on just one of them, especially in the event of policy failures.[84] Hence, coordination offers potential political cover against negative audience reactions when central banks overstep their reputational boundaries. As Deborah Mabbett and Waltraud Schelkle have noted regarding central banks' management of financial risks, "If forced to act alone to maintain financial stability, the central bank will be subject to adverse assessments from audiences which judge the expansion of liquidity excessive and criticize the apparent accommodation of the financial sector."[85] This insight can be extended to central banks' unconventional policies at large. That is, coordination with fiscal authorities helps central banks mitigate adverse reactions from their audiences, who may judge that unconventional interventions are not aligned with the central banks' reputation as conservative and neutral institutions. As the empirical analysis that follows is going to show (especially chapters 4 and 5), the importance of coordination can also be gleaned by the active stance that central banks take to build it. That is, central banks actively sought coordination and even forced it when confronted with the adoption of measures that openly challenged their reputation.

In addition to the preemption scenario, there is the management scenario. Here, the reputational threats that an institution confronts are no longer potential but actual. In this scenario, it is plausible to expect institutions to engage in an active managing behavior—that is, to adopt actions that attempt to win back support by signaling the institution's willingness to meet the demands and expectations articulated by its audiences. In other words, when faced with serious and actual reputational threats, the institution is likely to signal "responsiveness" and to adopt measures that reflect those articulated by the relevant audiences. Evidence of this behavior can be found in the reaction to the politicization challenge that the two central banks analyzed herein confronted at the start of the crisis period. Indeed, both the US Fed and the ECB reacted to the increased public contestation of their policies by signaling that employment would be given more attention over price stability considerations. Both central banks also signaled an increased amount of attention to new social goals, including the pursuit of inclusive growth (in the United States) and climate change (in Europe), by revising their monetary strategies.

It is difficult to assess whether central banks' attempts at managing the reputational threats emanating from politicization have been successful and whether they have managed to win back political and public support. What is possible to conclude is that in responding to reputational threats, central banks have progressively departed from the monetary orthodoxy of the past. Indeed, similar to what happened with the adoption of the unconventional policies during the 2008 and 2020 crises, the adoption of new strategy reviews has expanded both the scope of monetary policy beyond price stability and the tools needed to achieve the new social goals. The following chapters explore the transformation of central banking in detail, as well as the implications of these transformations.

CONSTRUCTING REPUTATION AND MONETARY ORTHODOXY

Reputation is a key political asset for most public institutions, but it is particularly so for central banks. Since the early 1980s, central banks around the world have indeed invested in cultivating a well-defined reputation regarding their role in domestic societies. This reputation is centered on conservativeness and political neutrality.[1] The rise of modern central banks' reputation has been closely associated with the widespread acceptance of the neoclassical economic theory of policy credibility.[2] That is, building and sustaining a reputation as an inflation-averse and neutral institution came to be regarded as *one* of the crucial ingredients of increasing the effectiveness—or credibility—of monetary policy in both good and bad times.

This chapter focuses on the construction of central banks' reputation and of monetary orthodoxy in the decades preceding the tumultuous crisis period that started in 2008. In particular, the chapter examines the process of reputation building and reputation consolidation by focusing on the key historical moments that have spurred the emergence of an organizational image based on conservativeness and political neutrality. In particular, the chapter focuses on the "formative years" of central banks' reputation that took place in the wake of the Great Inflation. It then moves on to the "success years" of the Great Moderation— namely, the period in which the reputation of central banks was established and consolidated. Finally, the chapter discusses the challenges to reputation that loomed under the aura of the Great Moderation. In particular, the chapter discusses the origins of the "lost decade" in Japan and the policy debate about mistakes made in the country with regard to monetary policy.

The Formative Years: The Great Inflation

There are few doubts that the origins of modern central banks' reputation are to be found in the critical decades from the 1960s to the 1980s. In particular, reputation building was significantly shaped by the experience of the Great Inflation and the concomitant shift away from Keynesianism and toward monetarism as the dominant paradigm in economic theory.

The Great Inflation refers to the macroeconomic era characterized by a generalized "deviation from a period of stable prices and output growth" across many developed countries.[3] Starting with the inflation dimension, as figure 2.1 shows, prices started to pick up across all major high-income countries in the second half of the 1960s. However, it was in the 1970s that inflation basically became a "fact of economic life" experienced throughout the industrial economies.[4] Two inflation peaks are clearly detectable in this period. The first occurred in the first half of the 1970s, following the 1973 oil price shock. The Arab oil producers' decision to impose an embargo to boycott the United States and punish the West for their support of Israel in the Yom Kippur War led to the price of crude oil quadrupling from $3 per barrel to $12 by 1974. The rise in oil prices quickly translated into higher inflation across all high-income countries. The second inflation peak started in the latter part of the 1970s and reached its peak at approximately 1980. Similar to what had happened with the previous inflation peak, an energy shock was the most proximate driver of the generalized upward price pressures. Indeed, the political turmoil in Iran at the end of the 1970s disrupted oil production in the country, contributing to higher global oil costs. To provide a measure of price pressure, between December 1978 and March 1980, the average cost per barrel of imported crude oil to US refiners rose from approximately $15 to over $33.[5] In contrast to the first inflation peak, however, this second inflation peak was followed by sustained disinflation, as discussed below.

In addition to the upward price pressures, the period of the Great Inflation was also characterized by a deterioration in both economic growth and unemployment rates—as figures 2.2 and 2.3 show—for the United States and the United Kingdom, respectively. The poisonous combination of high prices and poor economic growth popularized the term "stagflation."

The causes of the Great Inflation and stagflation have been the object of lively academic debates in the economics profession.[6] Thorough explanations for this complex historical period need to take into account the impact of a variety of factors, including adverse energy supply shocks and the end of the Bretton Woods system, with its consequences for the balance of payments and currency values.[7] Despite the complex combinations of several events, two factors regularly appear in what has become the dominant narrative for the generalized price in-

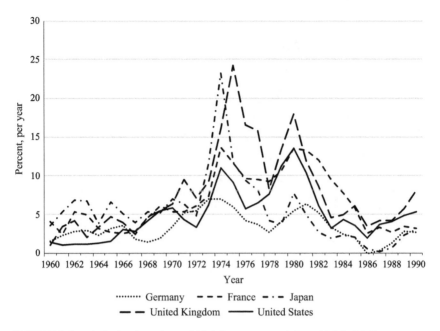

FIGURE 2.1. Inflation in selected high-income countries, 1960–1990

Source: World Bank data

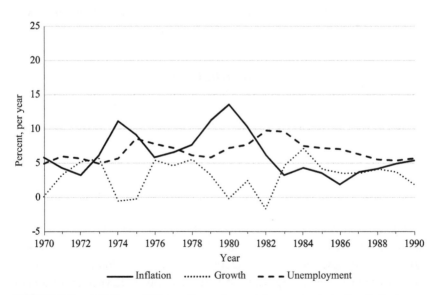

FIGURE 2.2. Inflation, GDP growth, and unemployment rate in the United States, 1970–1990

Source: World Bank data

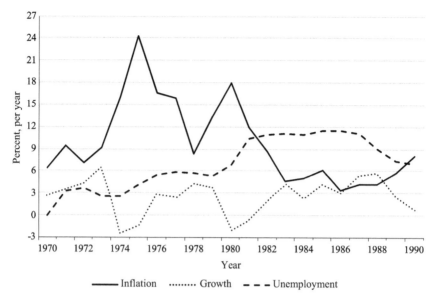

FIGURE 2.3. Inflation, GDP growth, and unemployment rate in the United Kingdom, 1970–1990

Source: World Bank data

crease recorded across advanced economies: politics and an intellectual economic consensus, according to which governments had the responsibility of managing aggregate demand.

The Origins of the Great Inflation

The US experience is often used as the quintessential example of the impact of politics and economic ideas on inflation malaise. In particular, according to what would have become the dominant narrative used to explain the rise of the Great Inflation, US politics during the 1960s actively contributed to setting in motion persistent price rises by relying on the trade-off between inflation and unemployment as an instrument to alleviate domestic social tensions. That is, US policymakers were willing to accept inflation in exchange for lower levels of unemployment as a way to heal the societal divisions that were brought to the surface by the civil rights movement and the Vietnam War.[8] The political priority attached to employment was in turn supported by the then-dominant Keynesian consensus that had been forged after WWII. According to Keynesian economics, governments were expected and encouraged to pursue an activist policy of aggregate demand management to ensure steady growth and low unemployment.[9]

The mutually reinforcing combination of political priorities and the Keynesian intellectual apparatus came to be regarded in hindsight as the ultimate cause of the deep economic malaise and the failure of monetary policy to deal with it.

Central banks were indeed not immune to the political and intellectual dynamics of the time. That is, the political climate and the intellectual consensus revolving around aggregate demand management also shaped monetary policy. The case of the US Fed is once again useful to illustrate the stance of monetary policy in the run-up to the 1980s. In particular, according to what has become the dominant interpretation of the events that underpinned the Great Inflation, the US Fed ultimately elevated low, stable unemployment as the key objective of its monetary policy.[10] Operating in line with the idea that inflation could be traded off for lower unemployment, as the Keynesian interpretation of the Phillips curve suggests, the US Fed, similar to other central banks in industrial economies, tolerated rising inflation levels. As a result, "the Fed tended to justify periodic actions to contain inflation against an implicit objective for low unemployment."[11] This monetary stance translated into what became known as discretionary monetary policy or stop-and-go policy. Under this policy framework, inflation would rise as monetary policy targeted employment in the go phase of the policy cycle. Then, when inflationary concerns became pressing, the central bank raised interest rates in the stop phase of the cycle. However, the policy window for the stop phase was narrow, as a tighter monetary policy had a negative impact on economic activity and employment.

The difficulties that the Fed confronted in tightening policy in the face of rising unemployment were made abundantly clear under the tenure of Fed Chair Arthur Burns. Appointed in February 1970 by President Richard Nixon, Burns initially agreed to a gradual approach to lower inflation with the view of limiting the deterioration in the labor market—that is, with the view of limiting the impact of tighter monetary policy on unemployment. However, by the end of the 1970 recession, the unemployment rate had climbed to 6 percent, well above the 4.5 percent rate that the Burns Fed had initially agreed to tolerate.[12] Against this backdrop, the US Fed ultimately retreated from an anti-inflation policy stance to instead support the Nixon administration's attempts to control inflation through the imposition of wage and price controls that followed the abandonment of the Bretton Woods system in August 1971. Although these measures initially stoked inflationary pressures, inflation ultimately reared its head again and even accelerated following the 1973 oil shock. By the summer of 1980, inflation was near 14.5 percent, and unemployment was over 7.5 percent.[13]

In his 1979 Per Jacobsson Lecture, aptly titled "The Anguish of Central Banking," Burns later reflected on the failures of monetary policy in regard to controlling inflation.[14] In particular, Burns highlighted a paradox that extended well beyond US monetary policy. In his words,

> By training if not also by temperament, they [central bankers] are inclined to lay great stress on price stability, and their abhorrence of inflation is continually reinforced by contacts with one another and with like-minded members of the private financial community. However, despite their antipathy to inflation and the powerful weapons they could wield against it, central bankers have failed so utterly in this mission in recent years. In this paradox lies the anguish of central banking.[15]

Burns identified the key to this paradox in a "fundamental factor." Specifically, he stressed that the causes of the persistent inflationary bias that had emerged since the 1960s were to be found in "the philosophical and political currents that have been transforming economic life in the United States and elsewhere since the 1930s." From this perspective, if "viewed in the abstract, the Federal Reserve System had the power to abort inflation at its incipient stage fifteen years ago [1964] or at any later point, and it has the power to end it today [1979]." Although the Fed could have used its power, it ultimately failed to do so because it was "caught up in the philosophical and political currents" of the time.[16] In other words, the Fed, similar to other central banks, was politically and intellectually "captured," which is a circumstance that, according to Burns, stands at the heart of the monetary policy failures in the run-up to the 1980s.

Burns's interpretation of the ultimate causes that led to the Great Inflation would resonate with the lessons that were about to be drawn from the disinflationary strategy initiated in the 1980s, as will be discussed below. Indeed, the continuous deterioration in the macroeconomic outlook ultimately set the stage for the transformation in monetary policy and for the reversal of the inflationary bias that anguished central banks. This development is strongly associated with the lessons learned from the actions that the US Fed took under Paul Volcker's leadership and the attendant rise of a key tenet of modern central banks—namely, their reputation as inflation fighters.

The Volcker Shock

In 1979, President Jimmy Carter appointed Paul Volcker at the helm of the US Fed. Under this leadership, the Fed moved much more decisively than it had done up to that point toward tightening monetary policy in the attempt to tame inflationary pressures.

Volcker arrived at the Fed with some solid anti-inflation credentials. Before being appointed, Volcker had signaled his preference for "stronger policy" and

vocalized his skepticism toward exploiting the alleged trade-off between inflation and unemployment.[17] Nonetheless, financial markets initially questioned
the Federal Reserve's resolve to tighten policy. Indeed, on September 18, 1979, the
Federal Reserve Board approved a discount rate hike of 50 basis points to accom-
pany a decision made by the Federal Open Market Committee (FOMC) to tighten
policy. However, the close vote and the dissent present among US monetary policymakers "engendered the perception that the Federal Reserve's resistance to inflationary forces would be insufficient and discomfited financial markets."[18]

At the next policy meeting, on October 6, 1979, Volcker decided that the Fed
needed "to change the playbook."[19] As the historical reconstructions of the policy debate within the FOMC show, US monetary policymakers came to recognize that "the new plan had to break dramatically with established practice, allow
for the possibility of substantial increases in short-term interest rates, yet be politically acceptable and convince financial markets participants that it would be
effective."[20] The question was how to achieve these objectives.

As Volcker himself later recollected, "We threw everything we could into the
October 1979 announcement."[21] In particular, the Fed announced a profound
change in the conduct of monetary policy. Whereas the US central bank traditionally aimed to control interest rates (i.e., the price of money), the central bank
now aimed to start controlling the supply of money (i.e., the quantity of money).
In other words, the Fed started targeting the aggregate quantity of money instead of the short-term federal funds interest rate in the Treasury repo market.
By limiting the money supply, the Fed no longer aimed for a specific interest rate
increase. Rather, the central bank committed to determining how much money
was available, leaving markets to set the price.

Given the emphasis on the money supply, the Fed's October decisions are
widely regarded as one of the most emblematic examples of the takeover of monetarist theory over postwar Keynesianism. The idea that there is a link between
the money supply and inflation is one of the key foundational principles of monetarist thinking. Although different views exist on the extent to which the Fed's
decisions made under Volcker were driven by monetarist ideas rather than mere
political convenience, an overwhelming consensus exists on the effects of the
October decisions.[22] Indeed, the Fed's new monetary framework, along with Volcker's determination, are widely regarded as the ingredients that ultimately
allowed inflation to be brought under control. In particular, core consumer price
index inflation, which had surpassed 11 percent in 1979, fell to under 5 percent
by 1982. However, the success at taming inflation was bought at high social
and economic costs. Markets pushed interest rates much higher than Volcker and
Fed policymakers had anticipated, jumping as high as 20 percent in January 1981
and pushing the US economy into the double-dip recession of 1980 and 1982.[23]

Unemployment reached 10.8 percent in November 1982, and an infuriated Congress put forward a host of proposals for reining in the Fed.[24]

It is important to note that the United States was not the only country that managed to tame inflation throughout the 1980s. As already mentioned, the Great Inflation was generalized to basically all advanced economies. During the 1970s, inflation reached double digits in the United Kingdom, Italy, France, and Canada, and although more contained, it was high even in inflation-averse Germany.[25] The monetary policy shift that took place in the United States was followed by similar shifts in other high-income countries. Most notably, the United Kingdom adopted a monetary targeting framework in March 1980, a move that was facilitated by the political context in which Prime Minister Margaret Thatcher and her political advisers had endorsed monetarism as "a matter of faith."[26]

The Volcker shock thus initiated a decade of generalized disinflation across high-income countries. In the 1990s, even high inflation economies in Latin America and Eastern Europe joined the club of countries that had been able to control inflation.[27] The advent of low inflation coincided, by and large, with important changes being made to the monetary policy framework and, in particular, with what came to be known as the most important legacy of the Volcker shock: the delegation of monetary policy to independent central banks whose primary objective was pursuing price stability.

The Volcker Legacy

Volcker's success in taming inflation had enormous and long-lasting consequences for the theory and practice of monetary policy that extended well beyond the United States. Indeed, it is fair to say that Volcker's pushback against inflation was probably the most influential episode in the development of central banking until the crisis period that started in 2008. In particular, one of the key lessons that monetary policymakers drew from the measures that the Fed under Volcker adopted since October 1979 centered around the importance for central banks of building and sustaining credibility.[28]

As discussed in the previous session, one of the major problems that the Volcker Fed confronted with regard to controlling inflation was convincing the public (and especially financial markets) of the central bank's resolve. The negative reaction of the markets to the initial monetary tightening that Volcker supported on taking office, for instance, was a clear signal of the Fed's poor credentials in its fight against inflation. As Volcker himself later recollected, when the FOMC met in October 1979 to adopt what would later become the symbolic measures of the fight against inflation, the Fed's challenge was "to convince people we were really serious" about controlling inflation.[29]

The importance of restoring public confidence or credibility was supported by a key insight of monetarist theory and, in particular, the notion of rational expectations. As popularized by Robert Lucas's work, the theory of rational expectations suggests that people adjust their behavior in anticipation of the consequences of future governments' economic policies. In doing so, they can undermine or even offset the outcome that economic policies intend to achieve.[30] In other words, people's expectations of the future, especially future economic policy, are able to influence what the future state of the economy will become.[31]

Seen from this theoretical prism, the difficulties that the Fed confronted in taming inflation lied in the fact that public expectations were not aligned with the central banks' actions; rather, the public anticipated more inflation down the road and acted accordingly by demanding higher wages and higher interest rates to protect their investments. In the wake of the Volcker experience, the credibility problem did not only come to be seen as a major hindrance to inflation fighting. The lack of credibility also came to be blamed for the economic and societal costs of fighting inflation. In other words, the painful recession and unemployment that followed the Volcker shock were attributed to the central bank's lack of credibility, which required higher interest rates to convince the public of the central bank's resolve to combat inflation.[32]

The experience of the Volcker Fed, as filtered through the neoclassical theoretical lenses, thereby established the case for the importance of credibility. As former Fed chair Bernanke summarized this view, Volcker's disinflation "was undoubtedly a major catalyst for an explosion of fresh thinking by economists and policymakers about central bank credibility."[33] However, the lessons that the policy community extracted from this historical period went beyond the recognition of the importance of credibility. In particular, the policy community turned to Volcker's disinflation to identify which conditions are needed for a central bank to be credible. Two major conditions were identified.

The first condition is independence. Volcker's disinflation was largely interpreted as the success of a central bank that had managed to operate independently from political pressures—the same pressures that Fed chair Burns had so eloquently identified as having held back central banks from controlling inflation in the 1970s. To put it in another way, the difficulties that central banks had confronted in regard to taming inflation in the run-up to the 1980s were now largely ascribed to the coordination between monetary and fiscal policy and how subservient monetary policy had become toward the latter. The policy conclusion drawn from the Volcker experience was thus straightforward: rather than engaging in coordination with fiscal authorities, central banks should operate at an arm's-length distance from them and should be legally protected from political pressures. Delegating monetary policy to legally independent central banks "to solve the problem of inflation purportedly caused by political involve-ment in monetary policy making" thus became one of the most successful ex-amples of policy diffusion across developed and developing countries alike.[34] Indeed, Volcker's disinflation set off a wave of reforms that increased the level of legal independence granted to central banks.[35] Interestingly, the newfound legal independence has not abated ever since.[36]

The second condition necessary to ensure credibility that the policy commu-nity extrapolated from the Volcker experience is conservativeness. That is, cen-tral banks need to establish a conservative reputation—that is, a reputation as an inflation hawk—to convince the public about the seriousness of their com-mitment.[37] Indeed, Volcker and his successful fight against inflation came to epitomize a distinct view of the central banks' mission: "the view among cen-tral bankers that *lower* inflation is always better."[38] Again, this view was closely intertwined with the transformation in economic theory and, in particular, in the dismissal of Keynesianism. Indeed, the stagflation experience and the atten-dant invalidation of the trade-off between inflation and unemployment, as theorized by the Phillips curve, led to a specific conclusion about the goals (or, better, the goal) that monetary policy should pursue. The underlying reasoning has been summarized as follows: "If, in the medium and longer term, an econ-omy could not grow faster by accepting a somewhat higher rate of inflation, then the optimal monetary policies must be to maintain price stability" and, specifi-cally, low inflation.[39] In other words, in the wake of the Volcker shock, central banks came to rethink the weights attributed to inflation and employment in their reaction function. During the 1960s and 1970s, the Fed and other central banks had prioritized employment as the primary objective that monetary pol-icy should pursue in coordination with governments; after the Great Inflation, central banks reshuffled the weights they assigned to the two macroeconomic variables. In particular, central banks came to assign more weight to low and stable inflation. Developing a reputation for conservativeness thus became a key task for central banks to pursue.

It is important to stress that, in principle, a conservative reputation was not meant to achieve the single-minded objective of low inflation or to deflate the economy at lower output costs. A conservative reputation could also come in handy had the central bank needed to reflate the economy. In this scenario, a conservative reputation would have allowed the central bank greater space to counteract a recession at lower inflation costs—that is, without deanchoring in-flation expectations. It was argued that the credibility for low inflation similarly "strengthens the power of monetary policy to counteract recessions."[40]

A corollary of the importance of being conservative is the rise of more pre-cise, rule-based monetary frameworks. Indeed, the implicit logic here is that the public will believe that central banks are committed to low inflation if the standards against the which the central banks adopt its policy are clear. As will be discussed in the next section, this development became particularly prominent in the 1990s with the diffusion of inflation targeting, which was meant to circumscribe the discretion of monetary policy and sustain its alleged depoliticization; in other words, the understanding was that monetary policy does not have real distributional effects.[41] Although it was in the 1990s that the rise of depoliticization and neutrality became widespread, their origins are to be found in the Volcker era. As former Fed chair Bernanke has summarized with regard to Volcker's disinflation, "This new thinking [on credibility] has contributed to a wave of changes in central banking, particularly with respect to the institutional design of [the independence of] central banks and the establishment of new frameworks for the making of monetary policy."[42]

In conclusion, Volcker's success in taming an extended period of inflation was probably the most influential episode in the development of modern central banking not only in the United States but around the world. The largest legacy of Volcker's disinflation has undoubtably been the consensus in monetary policy circles about the importance of central banks being conservative. That is, Paul Volcker's leadership came to epitomize the importance of directing central bank independence toward the goal of low inflation. Crafting and sustaining a reputation for conservative, inflation-averse behavior thus came to orient the practice of central banking over the decades that followed, namely through the 1990s and into the 2000s.

The Success Years: The Great Moderation

If the 1980s were marked by the rise of central banks' organizational image centered on conservativeness, the following decades were characterized by the consolidation of central banks' reputation as guardians of low and stable inflation. The consolidation of reputation was accompanied by a period of extraordinary economic performance that has come to be known as the Great Moderation. From the mid-1980s until 2007, high-income countries recorded low inflation associated with significant improvements in economic growth and productivity. At the same time, economic volatility was markedly reduced; recessions became less frequent and milder, while output and employment volatility declined.[43] Stressing the economic success of the Great Moderation is not meant to gloss over the serious economic and financial challenges that economic and monetary policymakers confronted in this period. These challenges included the 1987 stock market crash; the savings and loan crisis of the 1980s and early 1990s; the 1994 Mexican peso crisis; the Asian financial crisis and the Russia debt default in 1997 and 1998; the dot-com bubble and crash in the early 2000s; and the 9/11 terrorist attacks. Although these events were serious economic challenges that shook the world economy, they did not substantively undermine the positive economic record that is associated with the Great Moderation.

The experience of the Great Moderation is important to the purposes of the present analysis because it lent additional support to the lessons that central banks had drawn from the Volcker era. Specifically, the economic success of the Great Moderation was largely attributed to the conduct of monetary policy and, in particular, to the improved control of inflation. Although other factors have certainly contributed to the change in global inflation dynamics, including globalization and financial deregulation, the merits of monetary policy were elevated to center stage. In particular, the consensus view on the reasons why monetary policy was to be praised for the Great Moderation rested on the observation that "monetary policy has been much more focused on achieving low inflation, and less on exploiting short-run output gains." In doing so, central banks had achieved the holy grail of credibility. "Increased credibility has, in turn, anchored inflation expectations at a low (and constant) rate of inflation."[44]

Similar to what happened during the 1970s, the US experience starting in the mid-1980s is particularly emblematic of the evolution of monetary policy and the consolidation of central banks' reputation. Indeed, it is not by accident that the period of the Great Moderation is also often referred to as the Greenspan era, named after then Fed chair Alan Greenspan, who that took over the reins of the US central bank in August 1987.

The Greenspan Era and the Rise of Central Banks

During Greenspan's eighteen-year tenure as chair of the Federal Reserve System, the US economy grew steadily with low and stable inflation. Although the United States experienced two recessions, one in 1990–1991 and the other in 2001, both lasted less than one year; furthermore, in both cases, the decline in output was negligible.[45]

The Greenspan economic record not only cemented the view that monetary policy was at the heart of the strong economic performance of the period; the lessons that the policy community drew from the Greenspan era also helped consolidate the tenets of central banks' reputation that had already emerged in the wake of Volcker's disinflation: conservativeness and neutrality.

Although different views exist on the "formula" that allowed the Fed under Greenspan to successfully steer the US economy, the importance of its reputation as an inflation fighter stands out.[46] The words of well-known monetarists best capture this conclusion. In a retrospective on the legacy of the Greenspan era, Alan Blinder and Ricardo Reis comment on their list of reflections about the success of the Great Moderation: "Two principles that clearly were important in guiding Greenspan's decisions do *not* appear on our list: the concern for price stability and the importance of establishing and maintaining credibility."[47] Interestingly, the reason that Blinder and Reis omitted these principles is not because they thought of them as unimportant but rather "because they are so obvious and widely shared that they cannot reasonably be said to define the specific legacy of Alan Greenspan" or the practice of most central banks around the world.[48] In other words, by the time of the Great Moderation, conservativeness had become a key and widely accepted tenet of central bank reputation.

The consolidation of a reputation for conservativeness was further reinforced by important transformations that were made in regard to the operational conduct of monetary policy. In particular, central banks' attempts at cementing a reputation staked on conservativeness led to two developments for the practice of monetary policy: the widespread diffusion of inflation targeting frameworks and the progressive narrowing of the scope of monetary policy on the low inflation objective.

First, inflation targeting (IT) refers to a distinct monetary policy framework for the conduct of monetary policy. Under this framework, the central bank estimates and makes public a projected ("target") inflation rate. It then attempts to steer actual inflation toward that target in the medium term using interest rate changes. What IT implies is the importance that monetary policymakers attribute to the inflation objective and the rise of interest rate policy as the main technology through which central banks steer domestic economies. Although focused on the inflation objective, the IT framework was also introduced with the view of guaranteeing the policy space for central banks to support output in the event of economic or financial shocks, especially in the short run. In practice, however, central banks came to adopt some form of inflation targeting mostly as an instrument to signal their commitment to low and stable inflation.[49] This is especially the case for central banks in emerging and developing countries where central bank credibility was still being established.[50] Considering the adoption of inflation targeting as an instrument for the consolidation of central banks' reputation as conservative, inflation-averse institutions can further be gleaned from the fact that even those central banks that did not consider themselves formal inflation targeters at the time (including the European Central Bank and the US Fed) nonetheless adopted key features of the IT framework in their operational practice, "including a numerical definition of price stability, a central role for communications about the economic outlook, and a willingness to accommodate short-run economic stabilization objectives so long as these objectives do not jeopardize the primary goal of price stability."[51]

The second development for central banks' operational conduct that took place during the Great Moderation was the narrowing of the scope of monetary policy. In particular, central banks' reputation as conservative institutions contributed to downgrading any policy objective other than price stability, which could have interfered with the primary inflation objective. The influence of Greenspan's monetary policy is again evident here. Indeed, Greenspan has come to be associated with a peculiar manner of thinking (which has come to be known as the Greenspan doctrine), according to which monetary authorities cannot "limit the size of a bubble and, hence, its destructive fallout."[52] In other words, central banks cannot—and should not—target financial stability by "leaning against the wind" of potential asset price bubbles. What monetary policy could do, if necessary, was "to mop up after"—that is, to protect the economy and the banking system from the fallout of a speculative bubble that burst.[53]

The implication of the Greenspan doctrine is that price stability should be the only needle guiding monetary policy. This principle is evident in the institutional design frameworks for the conduct of monetary and financial stability policy. In particular, from the mid-1990s, the two functions were increasingly assigned to separate authorities, with financial stability being explicitly lodged in ad hoc regulatory authorities.[54] In short, financial stability was not a key policy concern for central banks, and central banks' best contribution to financial stability was conceived as the attainment of price stability. Claudio Borio, head of the monetary and economic department at the Bank for International Settlements, summarized the consensual view of the time by stating that "the prevailing pre [2008] crisis consensus had gravitated towards a 'narrow' view of central banking, heavily focused on price stability."[55]

In addition to conservativeness, the Great Moderation also attested to the consolidation of the other tenet of central bank reputation that had already emerged in the wake of Volcker's disinflation. This tenet revolved around the projection of monetary policy as a scientific exercise that left no space for discretionary decisions or decisions guided by distributive goals. In short, central banks came to project an image as politically neutral institutions.

The adoption of monetary strategies like inflation targeting underpinned the reputation-building efforts. Indeed, IT frameworks were meant not only to signal the importance that central banks attached to price stability but also to limit their policy discretion.[56] By presenting (and justifying) monetary policy decisions as a function of a predefined numerical inflation target or well-identified economic indicators, central banks could effectively claim to respond to science rather than discretion. That is, "the adoption of a monetary policy strategy is an attempt to characterize to the best possible extent, given the imperfect knowledge of the economy, the way in which the central bank will respond to the arrival of information" while minimizing judgment.[57] The adoption of a predictable policy strategy has thus been regarded as a critical tool "for a reputable central bank."[58]

Along with signaling limited discretion through monetary strategies, central banks were also keen on proving their political neutrality by claiming that their decisions did not have real distributional economic effects. Indeed, according to the notion of monetary neutrality, interest rate policy affects only nominal variables (i.e., price and inflation) and not real economic variables (i.e., employment and output) in the long run.[59] This does not mean that central banks were or are unaware of the distributional impact of short-term interest rate decisions on relative prices and income distribution, as discussed at length in chapter 3. However, during the 1990s and through the early 2000s, central banks have been consistently projecting an organizational image of themselves as being as distant as possible from these distributional issues. One way in which central banks have signaled the distributional neutrality of their decisions has been the breakup of any form of explicit coordination with fiscal authorities. In particular, one of the key principles of independent central banks has been the view that governments' fiscal policies are exogenous. As a depoliticized institution, a central bank is merely concerned with its own monetary policymaking and not with the potential consequences of fiscal decisions.[60] "The idea of financing fiscal deficits via money creation thus came to be seen as a mortal threat to central bank independence."[61] Monetary policy should simply not be enmeshed with government policy and the attendant distributional consequences.

In short, the Great Moderation cemented central banks' reputation as conservative and politically neutral institutions. This institutional image found supportive audiences outside central banks, too. Evidence of broad-based political and societal support can be found in the diffusion of central bank independence as the almost-universal governance arrangement for the conduct of monetary policy. Indeed, the diffusion of central bank independence can only partly be explained by the shift in the dominant macroeconomic paradigm, which led monetarism to supplant Keynesian ideas. For instance, one cannot discount the fact that the spread of central bank independence since the 1990s has also reflected the broad agreement among leading public officials—finance ministry staff, central bankers, and international organizations officials—over the desirability of establishing monetary stability.[62] Support for central banks and their activities has not been confined to political elites. After having conquered inflation, central banks have drawn strength from broad societal support for their policies focused on low and stable inflation. This support has sometimes been referred to as a "stability culture" and is most associated with Germany; however, it has also influenced the popular discourse about economic policy in many countries.[63]

In conclusion, against the backdrop of the Great Moderation, "it seemed as if the world's economic problems had become more or less solved."[64] Central banks became the institutions that took the most credit for the unusual economic success. As one central banker stated in the early 2000s, "reputation has never been higher," thereby securing monetary authorities "in a position of power and responsibility unrivalled in their history."[65] The aura and reverent respect that surrounded central banks at the time is clearly detectable in the titles of books and commentaries that refer to central banks as "lords" or "priests" of a special and exclusive congregate.[66] The appellative of "maestro" being reserved for Fed chair Alan Greenspan is the emblem of the spirit of the time.[67]

Despite the economic success, this period already harbored the signs of the problems that central banks might soon be confronted with. In particular, while inflation had basically been tamed, what was happening in Japan was a stark reminder that central banks might be asked to bring down prices as well as to prop them up.

Not All Bright under the Sunshine: The Cautionary Tale of Japan

Despite the huge success of monetary policy in stabilizing inflation, the period of the Great Moderation brought to the surface some uncomfortable issues for reputable central banks. In particular, the Japanese experience with stagnation and deflation in the 1990s shed light on problems that had basically disappeared from the radar screens of academic and policy debates. Interestingly, the Japanese experience represents a largely unheeded cautionary tale. The most influential analyses have dismissed the failures of the Bank of Japan (BoJ) as a distinctively Japanese problem and a case of domestic monetary policy mismanagement rather than a more general case of the problems that a central bank with a reputation for inflation fighting might confront in a deflationary context.[68] To understand what lessons can be drawn from the Japanese experience and how this experience speaks to what was about to happen following the 2008 financial crisis, it is first necessary to revisit the problems that bedeviled Japan.

From Bubble to Burst

The origins of the Japanese economic problems are to be found in the financial market bubble of the latter part of the 1980s. In this period, land and equity prices escalated, while the characteristics of the Japanese banking system, which tied equity price increases to increased bank lending, supported a cumulative upward process in both prices and credit creation.[69] What happened next is the classic story of a speculative bubble: the rise in asset prices was followed by a dramatic fall, which was initiated by the BoJ's decision to raise the discount rate in May 1989. The Nikkei 225 Index peaked at the end of 1989 and contracted by over 50 percent during the next two years. The stock market has since never returned to the precrisis peak.[70]

An economic recession followed the financial market crash, which furthered the strains on domestic banks that started accumulating massive nonperforming loans in their balance sheets. Financial losses pushed many financial institutions toward bankruptcy. This process culminated with the failures of two of the largest financial institutions in Japan: Hokkaido Takushoku Bank and Yamaichi Securities Company. These failures rang a deeply alarming bell. In particular, "the failure of these two large institutions challenged the basic principle of Japan's financial system based on mutual support and a policy of no failures of large institutions. It was now clear that no bank or institution was too large to fail in Japan."[71] The situation was further exacerbated by the Asian financial crisis, whose shockwaves were felt both around the region and beyond. The international market turbulence triggered by the Russian government's default added to the Japanese woes as risk premiums and liquidity demand increased sharply across financial markets.[72]

Financial stress quickly translated to the real economy. The collapse of asset prices generated a negative wealth effect on spending and investment and dented consumer confidence and business investments. The deterioration in banks' balance sheets also took its toll on lending volumes, thereby reinforcing the economic contraction. The Japanese economy thus came to experience a long spell of economic stagnation and declining output, which came to be known as the "lost decade." The unemployment rate soared, while the inflation rate declined to zero and crossed into negative terrain starting in 1999.

As deflation took center stage, the policy debate brought back memories of the 1930s. That is, Japan's problems were often compared to the problems experienced by many countries during the Great Depression, although the scale of the contraction, especially in terms of unemployment, was much deeper during the 1930s than in the post-1990s Japan. The comparison with the 1930s was nonetheless particularly evocative because of the risk of a liquidity trap.[73] Indeed, the Bank of Japan became the first central bank of a high-income country since the Great Depression to deal with near-zero interest rates and expectations of declining prices. How did the BoJ respond to these challenges?

Lessons from Monetary Policy in Japan

At the beginning of the crisis cycle, the BoJ reacted to the financial market bubble by raising the discount rates.[74] In particular, the BoJ reversed its prior monetary accommodation from May 1989 by raising the discount rate by a full percentage point from 2.5 to 3.5 percent. Over the next fifteen months, the BoJ continued tightening, and the discount rate reached 6 percent. Lending limits were also introduced for real estate companies. This tighter monetary policy was instrumental in stopping the speculative bubble. The subsequent decline in asset prices and the attendant economic stagnation, however, led the BoJ to change its course of action. After the 6 percent peak in 1990, the interest rate was cut down quickly and repeatedly; it reached 0.50 percent in 1995 and has been basically close to zero ever since, with the exception of an interest rate rise in August 2000.

In this tumultuous period, the Bank of Japan Law was revised in 1997 and became effective on April 1, 1998, following the appointment of Governor Yujiro Hayami. Economist Takatoshi Ito captured the essence of the legislative change by stating that "the Bank of Japan Law of 1998 is in every sense a state-of-the-art modern central banking law."[75] Indeed, the BoJ was given a clear mandate to pursue price stability, with no mention of aggregate demand or full employment as part of the central bank's objective. The new law also strengthened the BoJ's legal independence by revising the terms of the appointment and dismissal of the members of the monetary policy setting committee—namely, the Policy Board.[76]

The new Policy Board confronted a very challenging situation in which major financial institutions had just collapsed (as discussed in the previous section) and economic growth was extremely low. With the official discount rate already at a historical low of 0.50 percent, the BoJ ultimately moved beyond the interest rate policy script. In the spring of 1999, the BoJ attempted to manage expectations by committing to maintain the zero interest rate policy until deflationary concerns had been dispelled. To support this decision, the central bank also expanded the scope of its repo operations and revised its collateral policy to include corporate bonds and asset-backed securities in the list of assets eligible to be used in the BoJ's market operations.[77]

From March 2001 until 2006, the BoJ also launched what was then an unprecedented monetary policy experiment that came to be referred to as quantitative easing. In particular, the BoJ adopted a new monetary policy framework that changed the main operating target for money market operations from the uncollateralized overnight call rate to the amount outstanding on financial institutions' current account balances (i.e., reserves) at the BoJ. The target amount was initially set at 5 trillion yen, and the BoJ used purchases of Japanese government bonds as the main instrument with which to reach their operating target of current account balances.

Despite the unprecedent nature of the BoJ measures, the impact on economic activity and inflation fell behind the BoJ's intentions. In particular, "there is little evidence that [BoJ] actions have been sufficiently aggressive to dent deflationary pressures."[78] As a result, before the start of the 2008 crisis, the Japanese economy had been stagnant for more than twenty years, and deflationary expectations had largely become entrenched.

What factors explain the Japanese "lost decade"? This question has attracted significant attention in policy circles, not least because no other high-income economy has experienced similar economic problems since the 1930s.

One of the key conclusions of the debate on the Japanese malaise places the blame for what went wrong right at the door of the Japanese central bank. Takatoshi Ito and Frederic Mihskin summarized this view as follows: "Many problems have been pointed to as contributing factors that explain the 'lost decade' in Japan. . . . However, the most likely cause for deflation in Japan is a failure of monetary policy, since inflation or deflation is ultimately a monetary phenomenon."[79] Former Fed chair Ben Bernanke went even further. He attributed the recession to "exceptionally poor monetary policy making" because the BoJ failed to use all the weaponry at its disposal to counteract the deflationary spiral, including a depreciation of the yen, ceilings on long-term interest rates, and central bank-financed tax cuts.[80]

In short, the widespread conclusion in policy circles is that the BoJ failed to convincingly commit itself to monetary easing. In other words, similar to one of the major lessons learned from the Great Inflation, the lesson drawn from the Japanese experience is that monetary policy confronted a credibility problem, although it was a credibility problem that was the "reverse" of the problem that Volcker and his peers confronted back in the 1970s and 1980s. In the Japanese case, "the markets and the public did not expect the BoJ to pursue expansionary monetary policy in the future which would ensure that deflation would end."[81] In other words, the markets and the public did not believe in the BoJ's commitment to stick to and sustain reflationary policy. As Paul Krugman forcefully argued, private agents viewed zero interest rate policies as temporary and reversible. "And that is why monetary policy [was] ineffective!"[82] In short, the BoJ lacked credibility. "These mistakes in the management of expectations are a key reason why Japan found itself in a deflation that it is finding it very difficult to get out of."[83]

While most analyses concur with the credibility diagnosis, more disparate views exist about the reasons for the BoJ failing to establish trust in the central banks' resolve to combat deflation. In other words, why did the BoJ fail to establish credibility? Answers to this question are particularly important in light of the increased independence granted to the BoJ by the 1998 law. Indeed, as discussed previously, after the Great Inflation, legal independence came to be widely regarded as a necessary condition to ensure the credibility of monetary policy.

Among the factors that might have hampered the BoJ's resolve, some scholars have emphasized the weaknesses in the Japanese banking sector, which impaired the transmission of the BoJ accommodative policies.[84] Others have pointed to the problems in the monetary framework. For instance, the BoJ has been criticized for not having adopted an inflation targeting framework that might have provided a bulwark against inflation rates that were too low.[85] Criticisms have also been raised about the way in which the central bank communicated its unconventional policies, which ultimately undermined their effects.[86]

Although the problems present in both the financial sector and the design of the monetary framework are certainly important factors in accounting for the credibility problem with which the BoJ was confronted—despite the fact that establishing the causes of the BoJ credibility problems are outside the scope of this work—the problems stemming from the BoJ's attempts to preserve its conservative reputation also figure prominently. For instance, scholarship on Japanese monetary policy shows that members of the Policy Board may have been overly concerned that the BoJ's reputation as a conservative central bank would be jeopardized if they had followed a more expansive monetary policy in the late 1990s and early 2000.[87] As a result, they tended to discount the dangers of deflation by emphasizing the dangers of inflation instead, "even when the problem for Japan was the opposite."[88] This behavior contributed to the credibility problem that confronted the BoJ because the public came to believe that the central bank was basically and solely "committed to price stability as a long-run goal."[89] These insights are consistent with the works of scholars who have drawn attention to the ideational apparatus that informed the BoJ's policymakers since the early 1990s. For instance, the ideas informing the BoJ's closed policy community are regarded as having hindered the acceptance of more aggressive policy measures to deal with deflation and economic stagnation.[90]

In short, the problems that the BoJ has confronted since the 1990s offer a glimpse into the problems that central banks in high-income countries would be confronted with after 2008. The BoJ's experience in combating deflation and economic stagnation shows that the credibility problems that a central bank confronts are not confined to an inflationary scenario. That is, central banks need to convince the public of their commitment to support prices and economic activity in a deflationary context as much as they need to convince them of their resolve to keep the interest rate high if prices rise in an inflationary scenario. The BoJ's experience has also foreshadowed the difficulties of navigating between safeguarding a reputation staked on conservativeness, on the one hand, and adopting expansive monetary interventions on the other hand. However, the BoJ's experience was largely regarded as a Japanese anomaly. The policy community conceded that deflation represents relatively unfamiliar territory for central banks, and a deflationary environment can hinder the ability of central banks to pursue countercyclical monetary policies once interest rates are close to the zero lower bound. Despite these problems, the policy conclusions were upbeat. Even if a central bank faces serious problems in a deflationary environment, for a smart and reputable central bank, "most of the complications might prove to be *transitory* as the central bank [becomes] accustomed to the new policy environment."[91] The crisis period that started in 2008 would soon provide a hard test for this rosy and bold conclusion.

CHALLENGING MONETARY ORTHODOXY IN A NEW CONTEXT

The crisis period that started in 2008 threw "a large rock into the calm waters of central banking."[1] Central banks were soon confronted with economic and political conditions that were significantly different from those that provided the background for the rise in their public stature during the Great Moderation era.

This chapter zooms in on the changes that central banks were confronted with in the crisis period that spanned from 2008 to 2020 and highlights the challenges to orthodox monetary policy. First, the chapter focuses on the economic changes and, in particular, on three major policy problems that central banks had to grapple with: the collapse of the financial system, secular stagnation, and a global pandemic that disrupted both domestic demand and global supply chains. Second, the chapter examines the political changes that materialized in the context in which central banks operate. In particular, the chapter traces the rise of the politicization of central banks—that is, the increasing visibility of the distributive effects of monetary policy and the attendant public contestation of central banks and their decisions.[2] In examining how monetary authorities coped with these new economic and political challenges, the chapter aims to bring to the surface the common trends in the institutional trajectory of central banks in high-income countries. In particular, the chapter chronicles the embrace of unconventionality and the progressive departure from orthodoxy.

Before entering into the details of the economic and political changes that characterized the period from 2008 through 2020, a note of caution is needed. The analysis that follows emphasizes the commonalities in the problems that central banks confronted as well as the commonalities in terms of the policy responses. The purpose is not meant to gloss over the important differences in the specific problems that different countries confronted or in the timing and design of policy responses across countries. While these differences exist and are important, what emerged at the end of the crisis period was that, despite these differences, central banks converged on a set of policies that, as discussed in previous chapters, marked a substantial deviation from the monetary orthodoxy that had been in place since the 1980s. Before focusing on why and how this transformation materialized and was sustained over time in the United States and Europe (chapters 4 and 5), this chapter introduces the overall evolutionary trajectory of central banks over a very tumultuous decade.

On the Brink of Financial Collapse

The crisis that started in 2008 marked a critical turning point for the global economy.[3] The dynamic, scale, and spread of the crisis led several commentators to compare it to the 1930s and the Great Depression and refer to its aftermath as the Great Recession.[4] Indeed, similar to the Great Depression, the financial sector was the epicenter of the shockwaves that threatened the stability of the global financial system and caused a decade of stagnant economic growth.

The most proximate cause of the crisis was the financial panic that followed the downturn in the US housing and mortgage markets. In the run-up to the crisis, banks and other private financial institutions had accumulated large portfolios of mortgage-backed securities (MBS)—that is, securities made up of a bundle of home loans bought from the banks that issued them. The MBS market represented the perfect example of the promises of securitization: pooling mortgages in liquid securities allowed freed up capital for the originating banks while offering creditors a mechanism to lower their investment risk through the division of ownership of the underlying debt obligations.

It all went well until the housing boom ended in 2006 and 2007. As housing prices fell and an increasing number of homeowners began to default on their mortgages, investors determined that mortgage-backed securities (like any other asset-backed securities) is only as sound as the asset (in this case the mortgage) that backs it up. Indeed, on the back of mortgage defaults and declines in house prices, the MBS market lost value, which negatively affected the portfolios of the many banks and investment firms that had bought those securities. The deterioration of the MBS market set in motion a familiar spiraling effect. With lenders no longer able to fund loans, especially subprime loans, through the sale of MBS, banks stopped lending to customers. The contraction in lending volume, in turn, led to further home sales and price declines, which further depressed sales and prices. These negative effects were not confined to US markets and investors. Securities based on US mortgages had been bought and sold in other countries, most notably in Europe. The seeds of global contagion had already been planted.

The early signs of global financial stress were already visible in the spring of 2007, when New Century Financial Corporation, one of the largest subprime lenders in the United States, filed for bankruptcy and was soon followed by other subprime lenders. By the summer, France's largest bank, BNP Paribas, announced billions of dollars in losses, citing US subprime mortgage sector woes.[5] In September, the UK bank Northern Rock, increasingly unable to fund itself by selling its securitized loan books, sparked the first depositors' run in the United Kingdom since 1866.[6]

In a context where mortgages had been included in securities of different types, however, even financial institutions that were not fundamentally affected by the losses in MBS portfolios were no longer immune from risks. Indeed, investors could no longer assess credit losses and discern safe assets from those at risk. As former Fed chair Ben Bernanke stated regarding the gravity of the situation in financial markets, "Pervasive uncertainty about the size and incidence of losses in turn led to sharp withdrawals of short-term funding from a wide range of institutions; these funding pressures precipitated fire sales, which contributed to sharp declines in asset prices and further losses."[7] Financial markets virtually froze in September 2008 following a number of events from that year that sent markets into a tailspin. This chain of events started on March 16, when JPMorgan Chase took over of the global investment bank Bear Stearns with US Federal Reserve support. On September 7, the US government placed into conservatorship the two big mortgage government-sponsored enterprises, Fannie Mae and Freddie Mac. In the early morning of September 15, Bank of America announced the takeover of the insolvent Merrill Lynch brokerage.[8] An hour later, investment bank Lehman Brothers declared bankruptcy, heralding the most dramatic phase of the crisis. The Lehman collapse led markets to scramble for liquidity and ultimately panic. The prices of all structured finance basically fell, and credit stopped flowing. Even money markets, which were traditionally regarded as the safest segments of the financial system before the crisis, came under stress. The entire global financial system found itself on the brink of collapse.

The economic consequences of the financial crisis were dire. The year 2009 was witness to the largest economic contraction in seven decades. According to the International Monetary Fund (IMF), ninety-one economies, making up a combined two-thirds of the global gross domestic product (GDP), experienced a fall in output in 2009.[9] In particular, the United States saw a 2.6 percent drop in GDP in 2009, the largest decline in the postwar era. In the European Union, the GDP decrease was 4.3 percent in the same year. Between the third quarter of 2008 and the first quarter of 2009, the economic downturn also spread rapidly to countries that were initially not affected by the financial and banking crisis. Emerging market economies saw a real output decline of approximately 4 percent.[10] The economic effects of the financial crisis were not solely profound but also prolonged. As will be discussed at greater length below, output deviations from precrisis trends persisted over time.

To address the crisis, the majority of advanced economies initially introduced sizable expansionary fiscal packages to help offset the effects of the financial shock, including through measures such as government guarantees of banking sector liabilities, purchases of toxic assets from banks, and capital injections. These policies have been found to be effective at shortening the length of recession.[11] Austerity, however, progressively took over the initial fiscal support, because of both the financial underpinnings of the crisis and policymakers' ideational orientations favoring balanced budgets.[12] Explaining the shift from expansionary to contractionary fiscal policy would deserve an analysis on its own. What is relevant for the purpose of the present analysis is that, in this changed macroeconomic policy context, central banks were on the frontline addressing financial market dysfunctions and restoring the foundations necessary for sustained economic growth.

In doing so, central banks converged on a policy playbook that pushed the boundaries of monetary policy well beyond interest rate policy. "Unconventional" became the adjective to describe the new monetary policy.

Although there are several ways to classify the unconventional policies that central banks adopted, two sets of policies are particularly relevant because of their deviation from previous practices and the visibility they accrued to central banks: *liquidity support* to a wide range of financial institutions and market segments and *monetary policy support* through asset purchases.[13] With no attempt to provide an exhaustive overview of all the policies that central banks in high-income countries have adopted since 2008, in what follows, I provide some of the most emblematic examples of what measures the policies entailed.

To ensure that financial institutions that needed liquidity had access to it, several central banks broadened the list of counterparties and eligible collateral to accede to standing facilities. Additional facilities were created to channel funding to institutions or markets that did not have access through existing facilities. Examples of such programs include the US Fed's Term Securities Lending Facility and Primary Dealer Credit Facility, which were meant to offer access to funding for nonbank financial institutions, and the Bank of England's Special Liquidity Scheme, which swapped temporarily illiquid assets for UK gilts.[14] Nonstandard liquidity was also complemented with a set of measures of "market-making of last resort." These policies involved extending credit to financial institutions to purchase specific assets or the outright purchase of assets by the central bank in an attempt to support the liquidity of key markets for short-term funding for financial institutions. Examples of these policies include the US Fed's Asset-Backed Commercial Paper Money Market Mutual Fund Liquidity Facility and the Commercial Paper Funding Facility, which were introduced in September and October 2008, respectively. The covered bond purchase program of the European Central Bank was introduced in June 2009. Central banks also stretched their lender-of-last-resort function by extending liquidity to institutions that were too large and important (or "too big to fail"), suggesting that their failure could have widespread consequences for the global financial system. Northern Rock in the United Kingdom was the first example of a systemically important bank that was extended a line of credit and eventually nationalized in February 2008 after attempts to restructure the institution failed. This first episode was shortly followed by the Fed's actions to extend loans to Bear Stearns in March and American International Group (AIG) in September (see chapter 4).

In addition to liquidity support, central banks also focused on providing monetary policy support once interest rates hit the zero lower bound. The central bank's balance sheet became the key critical tool to this effect. The US Fed was one of the first central banks to use its balance sheet to ease monetary conditions with the launch of the MBS purchase program in November 2008. The asset purchase program was extended in March 2009 to include the purchase of Treasuries to help stimulate lending to the real economy in general (see chapter 4 for more details). Shortly after the Fed's initial moves, the Bank of Japan increased the size of its asset purchase program, which had been unchanged since October 2002. Around the same time, the Bank of England introduced its quantitative easing program, which was overwhelmingly focused on the purchases of UK government bonds but included the purchases of private-sector assets as well.[15] The European Central Bank started its purchase programs in May 2010. Named the Stability Market Program, this initial program was expanded over time with new and more ambitious asset purchase programs (as discussed in chapter 5).

In short, central banks in high-income countries basically converged on a common policy script to respond to the 2008 global financial shock. This policy script marked a significant departure from precrisis standard macroeconomic theory and policy practice. Indeed, before the crisis, standard monetary theory doubted that monetary policy could provide an additional stimulus at the zero lower bound. The logic was simple: if interest rates would have become negative, individuals would have just held cash, thereby disempowering monetary policy. Although additional policy measures that may be used to provide monetary stimulus at the zero lower bound have been discussed in theory (as discussed in chapter 2), these policies have been largely untested in practice. In the wake of the 2008 crisis, however, central banks significantly expanded the tools available for conducting monetary policy, most of which were focused on either central bank liquidity or on policies that changed the size and composition of central banks' balance sheets. In doing so, central banks also expanded the remit of monetary policy by prioritizing financial stability and employment objectives. Despite the innovative policy response, the scars of the crisis became deep and prolonged.

Secular Stagnation

In November 2013, economist Larry Summers delivered a speech at the annual IMF research conference that popularized the concept of "secular stagnation."[16] In referring to this concept, Summers echoed the thinking of economist Alvin Hansen, who first warned of the risks of secular stagnation following the experience of the Great Depression. Summers maintained that the global economy was facing the prospect of a chronic excess of savings relative to capital investment, similar to the post-1930s context. This dynamic was forcing long-term interest rates down and threatening a persistent shortage of demand.

Several economic indicators seemed to support the secular stagnation hypothesis. At the time of Summers's speech writing, economic recovery was anemic in many parts of the world. Precrisis GDP levels had been surpassed, but few high-income countries had returned to precrisis growth rates, despite prolonged ultraloose monetary policy.[17] Ten years after the peak of the crisis, the IMF estimated that 85 percent of the twenty-four economies that had experienced a banking crisis still showed negative deviations from the precrisis growth trend.[18] Output losses relative to precrisis trends were persistent even in those economies that had not experienced a banking crisis in the 2008–2009 period, largely because of weaker external demand stemming from trading partners that did suffer banking crises. These persistent recessionary effects were accompanied by increasing inequality. In particular, "economies with larger output and employment losses in the initial aftermath of the crisis registered greater increases in income inequality compared with their precrisis average."[19]

Inflation risks, in turn, had clearly switched to the downside. Having remained stable at the height of the financial crisis, inflation in advanced countries started falling around 2012 and had remained substantially below target since. These developments had already led the IMF to flag the risk of an incipient global deflation in 2014.[20] Deflationary risks were all the more disturbing in light of the increase in the level of debt; the median public debt-to-GDP ratio rose from 36 percent to 56 percent in the ten years after 2008.[21]

The economic risks on the horizon inevitably focused policymakers' minds on what policies were needed to combat recessionary and deflationary challenges. Standard economic theory would suggest that anything that can be done to reduce real interest rates and boost investment and consumption is a good policy strategy. From this perspective, turning to central banks was still the most obvious policy solution. However, serious doubts were mounting about the effectiveness of central banks' actions in the economics profession. As Summers and Stansbury eloquently wrote ten years after the start of the global financial crisis, "There are strong reasons to believe that the capacity of lower interest rates to stimulate the economy has been attenuated—or even gone into reverse."[22] Two reasons in particular cast doubt on central banks' ability to effectively respond to recession and deflationary forces.

The first reason is self-evident: central banks' traditional policy tool had basically reached its limits. As figure 3.1 shows, since 2008, policy rates in major high-income countries have been steadily declining; even before the 2020 crisis, the nominal interest rates of all major economies were hovering around the zero lower bound. This means that most central banks—and indeed the major central banks in high-income countries—were in principle too poorly positioned to deliver an effective countercyclical stimulus. In other words, central banks lacked sufficient policy space to boost domestic economies. To provide a measure

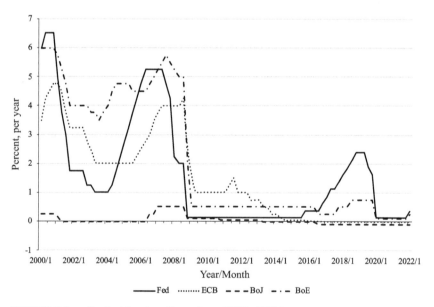

FIGURE 3.1. Central bank policy rates, 2000–2022

Source: Bank for International Settlements data

of the problem that central banks confronted, a typical peak-to-trough policy rate cycle in the United States would see the rate cut by just over 500 basis points. However, just before the COVID-19 crisis started, the target range for the federal funds rate was approximately 150 to 175 basis points.[23]

Concerns about the limitations of monetary policy in a recessionary context were widely acknowledged in central banking circles even before the COVID-19 virus started taking a huge toll on global economic activity. As former Fed chair Bernanke noted in his 2020 presidential address to the American Economic Association, "In the presence of an effective lower bound on nominal interest rates . . . persistently low nominal rates constrain the amount of 'space' available for traditional monetary policies."[24] Bernanke's successor, Janet Yellen, voiced a similar concern. Low interest rates, she said, have "put central banks in a position where they don't have a lot of ammunition. If we have a serious recession, we're probably not going to be able to count on central banks to offer up a significant response."[25]

The second reason that cast doubt on central banks' ability to effectively counteract disinflationary forces was the interaction between monetary policy and financial stability. In particular, as already noted in preceding chapters, one of the key problems of ultraloose monetary policy lies in its repercussions on financial markets' behavior; an excessively accommodative monetary policy increases risk taking, delays balance sheet adjustments, and encourages irresponsible "zombie" lending. By preventing the default of nonviable companies, however, "zombie" lending creates excess capacity in the economy and thereby downward pressures on prices. Rather than helping economies counteract recessionary and disinflationary forces, an accommodative monetary policy risks producing the opposite outcome. Again, monetary policymakers were acutely aware of the perilous side effects of their loose monetary policy. In a number of reports, the analysis carried out at the Bank for International Settlements (BIS) raised the point that prolonged accommodative policies fuel financial and price instability, risk taking, and debt accumulation. Rising debt burdens, in turn, make future normalization progressively harder. Moreover, the BIS warned about spillovers to emerging markets in the form of undesirable exchange rates and capital flow volatility.[26]

In short, a decade after the start of the global financial crisis, the specter of secular stagnation was hanging over the economies of high-income countries. This economic context was testing the ability of central banks to fight recessionary and disinflationary forces. In particular, the aftermath of the 2008 crisis brought to the forefront the limits of monetary policy in regard to stimulating domestic economies without generating further financial instability. By 2020, central banks were still struggling to return economic activity to its full potential when a new deflationary shock appeared on the horizon: the economic crisis induced by the spread of the COVID-19 virus. The resulting health emergency crisis and its dramatic socioeconomic consequences placed central banks in the spotlight again.

COVID-19: A Crisis Like No Others

On January 11, 2020, China reported the first death from an unknown coronavirus that tragically came to be known as COVID-19. One month later, the death toll in China had reached 1,113, while the total number of confirmed cases had reached 44,653.[27] In the hope of containing the contagion, the Chinese authorities imposed sweeping controls on the movement of persons, basically sealing off Wuhan, the city of 11 million inhabitants where the coronavirus outbreak emerged.

In a globalized world, however, viruses have no frontiers. In a matter of weeks, the virus was no longer only a Chinese problem. By mid-February, there were 393 cases outside China in twenty-four countries. Asian countries were initially the most affected, including Taiwan, Japan, Thailand, and South Korea. It was only when Europe and later the United States started recording a major surge in infection numbers that the world woke up to the uncomfortable reality: what we were witnessing was not just a pandemic, with immense human costs, but also an economic crisis of historical proportions. Indeed, countries hit by the virus were forced to shut down a large part of their economies in the hope of stopping the contagion chain. However, with citizens in lockdown, the economic system basically came to a halt. Production and supply chains went disrupted, and firms struggled to cope with the resulting loss of income and spending power.

The first chilling signs of the health emergency's dramatic economic costs came from the financial sector, bringing back memories of the previous 2008 crisis. As investors started fretting about the economic consequences of the inevitable confinement measures, the usual panic dynamic settled in: investors started selling assets and rushed into the safety of US Treasuries. The liquidity squeeze further exacerbated the pain of firms whose revenues were shrinking quickly. The surging US dollar, in turn, spread the pressure worldwide and especially to developing and emerging market countries that borrow in US dollars.

In April 2020, IMF forecasts certified that the world was experiencing the worst economic crisis since the 1930s, a crisis far more profound than the 2008 crisis.[28] By the end of April 2020, more than 30 million US citizens had already filed claims for unemployment benefits, and over 30 million workers in Europe had turned to the state for wage support. The economic consequences were pro-

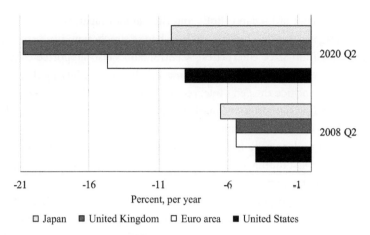

FIGURE 3.2.   Real quarterly GDP growth, 2008 Q2 and 2020 Q2 compared

Source: Federal Reserve Economic Data (FRED)

found. As figure 3.2 shows, the real GDP growth rate collapsed in the worst quarters of the 2008 crisis, hovering around the –5 percent mark in major economies. In comparison, the COVID-19 shock brought about a more dramatic fall: approximately –10 percent in the United States and Japan, –15 percent in the euro area, and around –20 percent in the United Kingdom. In the wake of lockdowns, unemployment also rose sharply, peaking at 13 percent in the United States and 8 percent in the euro area. Inflation remained subdued until early 2021 and only started sharply rising after this point.

Faced with the economic shock of the COVID-19 crisis, governments stepped in to mitigate the impact of economic fallout for households and firms, especially in high-income countries where fiscal resources were easier to mobilize than in several developing countries. In particular, although significant variation exists across countries, government-supported measures usually include some variants of wage subsidies, tax relief and extension, postponement of debt repayments, loan guarantees for firms' bank funding, and even cash transfers. These necessary measures led to a significant increase in fiscal deficits and public debt ratios, thereby straining governments' capacity to continue supporting domestic economies right when this support was needed the most.[29]

Central banks were also on the frontlines of crisis management. Building and expanding on the 2008 policy script, central banks responded on a "massive and unprecedented" scale to the collapse of economic activity and disinflationary forces.[30] Indeed, as in the wake of the 2008 crisis, virtually all major central banks designed policies to channel liquidity and support economic activity. For instance, central banks, including the US Federal Reserve, the European Central

Bank (ECB), Bank of England (BoE), and the Bank of Japan (BoJ), launched or activated targeted lending facilities to help banks supply liquidity, especially to small and medium-sized enterprises.[31] Central banks also supported companies that finance themselves through capital markets by directly buying their securities. Examples include the Fed's interventions to shore up the commercial paper market by lending support to the markets for corporate debt and municipal debt, among others. The Fed also launched a Main Street Lending Program to lend directly to firms under strain. In Europe, the ECB increased corporate bonds' purchases under outstanding facilities and pledged to buy additional corporate bonds under its revamped balance sheet policies. In a similar spirit, the BoE designed its COVID Corporate Financing Facility, while the BoJ basically doubled its purchases of equity exchange-traded funds to support domestic firms.

Central banks also adopted measures designed to provide expanded monetary policy accommodation. For instance, the Fed and the BoE used their remaining policy pace to further cut the main policy rate. Beyond conventional interest rate cuts, basically all central banks in high-income countries provided monetary accommodation by expanding existing asset purchase programs and designing new ones. Among others, the Federal Reserve scaled up the purchases of US Treasury debt, dwarfing the purchases conducted in the wake of the global financial crisis; the ECB launched a new Pandemic Emergency Purchase Program to buy private and public securities; the BoE expanded its Asset Purchase Facility, thereby increasing the stock of UK gilts and nonfinancial investment-grade corporate bonds; and similar moves were made by the BoJ, which in the wake of the crisis increased the amount of purchases of government and corporate bonds, commercial paper, and exchange-traded funds. The overall result of this new round of quantitative easing (QE) is clearly detectable in the size of central banks' balance sheet, as well as in the speed with which it increased. As figure 3.3 shows, although balance sheet expansion had already been sizable in the wake of the 2008 crisis, the pace at which central banks used their balance sheets in the aftermath of the COVID-19 crisis was remarkable.

The Politicization of Monetary Policy

Post-2008, commentaries often likened central banks to heroic characters. Central banks have often been credited with having "helped the world pull back from the precipice of another Great Depression."[32] This positive view of central banks has many followers.[33] However, the actions of central banks during the crisis have also attracted many critics. One of the major criticisms leveled at central banks concerns the distributive implications of their unconventional policy

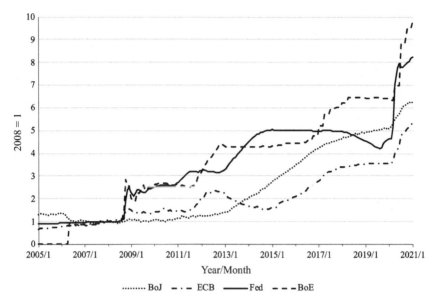

FIGURE 3.3. Total assets of major central banks, 2005–2021

Source: Federal Reserve Economic Data (FRED), Bank of England

decisions. In particular, central banks have come under fire from across the political spectrum based on the allegation that their policies have ultimately benefited the few at the expense of the many in domestic societies.[34] In what follows, this chapter thus sheds light on the way in which central banks' new policy "normal" has led them into distributive terrain that unelected technocrats are not expected to encroach upon.

The Distributive Consequences of Monetary Policy

Monetary policy is always distributive. That is, even the conventional policy of lowering (or raising) interest rates entails distributive effects. For instance, when a central bank raises interest rates to restrain demand, there are typically some costs to debtors and some gains to savers. In other words, there is always somebody who benefits more than others.[35] While always distributive, the effects of conventional policy are generalized; interest rate policy affects credit conditions, economic activity, and prices for all agents in the economy. Contrary to the effects of interest rate policy decisions, the distributional effects of unconventional policies are much more targeted and thus more visible to outside audiences.[36] In particular, policies such as lending to banks and nonbank institutions and the purchase of assets imply that central banks decide which actors and sectors

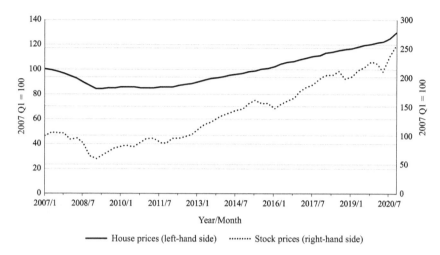

FIGURE 3.4. Evolution of house and equity prices, 2007–2020

Source: Bank of International Settlements (Annual Economic Report 2021)

in the economy to support. In other words, central banks end up picking winners and losers. The purchase of public and private securities under QE programs
is helpful in illustrating this dynamic.

As discussed above, policies aimed at influencing financing conditions and
ultimately economic activity have ultimately translated into a significant expansion of central banks' balance sheets. Although necessary to counter the economic downturn and the attendant deflationary forces, the purchase of financial
securities has ultimately created the conditions for disproportionate gains among
those who already have a greater portion of wealth. Indeed, asset purchases influence wealth inequality primarily through their effect on asset prices—that is,
by boosting asset prices and encouraging borrowing for their acquisition. For
instance, with accommodative policies in the background, housing prices and
stock market indices have been rising steadily since the global financial crisis
(figure 3.4). The problem is that households that hold more equity in their
portfolios—typically the very wealthy (i.e., the top 1 percent or even the top
0.1 percent of the wealth distribution)—have made large capital gains.[37]

Another key channel through which accommodative monetary policy has exposed central banks' distributional footprint is the rise of indebtedness levels. As
already anticipated, asset purchases influence wealth not only by boosting asset
prices but also by encouraging borrowing for their acquisition. It is therefore not
surprising that over the last decade, indebtedness has increased markedly. In advanced economies, total nonfinancial sector debt rose from 261 percent of GDP

in 2011 to 289 percent in 2021. Emerging market economies (which were less affected by the 2008 crash and thus by the ensuing deleveraging pressures) saw an even steeper rise, from 136 percent of GDP to 229 percent in the same period.[38] One major consequence of higher indebtedness levels has been the growing public perception of central banks as caving into financial market pressures. The former head of one of the world's largest fixed-income investors, PIMCO Mohamed El-Erian, captured how central banks have repeatedly intervened or adjusted their policy stance to support markets by noting that "whenever central banks have tried to pursue a path independent of markets, markets have forced them to do a massive U-turn. . . . What has developed over the years is an empowerment of markets to believe that they can lead central banks."[39]

The distributive implications of monetary policy have also become more visible with regard to the relationship between monetary and fiscal policy. The reason for the growing visibility is to be found in one of the major legacies of the crisis period: the increase in public debt. For instance, by the end of 2020, the US fiscal deficit was on track to reach levels not seen since World War II. In the eurozone, the deficit-to-GDP ratio was expected to balloon from 0.6 percent in 2019 to 10.1 percent in 2020 and 5 percent in 2021.[40] Since the start of the crisis period, monetary policy has basically supported public finances. That is, central banks have massively intervened to lower government funding costs. For instance, by the end of 2020, the four major central banks in the group of high-income countries (the BoE, the Fed, the ECB, and the BoJ) had ultimately bought more than half of government debt issued since the start of the pandemic in February 2020. Similar to what was noted already regarding the rise in private-sector debt, the rise of public-sector debt and the attendant central banks' support has come to clearly expose the distributional footprint of monetary policy.

The distributional impact of postcrisis monetary policy—or better yet, its increased visibility compared to precrisis policy—has raised new and serious challenges for central banks. Indeed, "whenever monetary policy's distributive outcomes are immediately plain to see and create clear winners and losers . . . central bankers will find it hard to take shelter behind the claim to technocratic legitimacy."[41] This is exactly the path through which central banks and their policies became increasingly contested.

The Contestation of Monetary Policy

As discussed in chapter 2, in the precrisis period, central banks generally benefited from a sort of "permissive consensus" among political elites and the public.[42] In particular, politicians and public opinion, at least in high-income countries, had generally implicitly supported central banks, their activities, and ultimately, their independence. In the wake of the crisis period, this benign political context changed.

Central banks soon became the target of criticism from across the political spectrum. At the more conservative end were those blaming central banks because of the alleged inflationary and currency debasement implications associated with the use of unconventional policies.[43] At the other, more progressive end of the spectrum, critics lashed out at central banks because their unconventional policies had unduly redistributed wealth and ultimately led them into quasi-fiscal policy terrain that is not up to technocratic policymakers to encroach upon.[44] The rise of populism, fueled by the social costs of the economic crises, has also added to the widespread politicization of central banks.[45] In particular, an increasing number of politicians, most notably former US president Donald Trump, have made central banks the target of public criticism mostly for their failure to support the real economy.[46] Populist disdain toward central banks also stems from the main features of modern central banks. As one central banker stated regarding the challenge that populism entails for monetary authorities: "With their PhDs, exclusive jargon, and secretive meetings in far-flung places like Basel and Jackson Hole, central bankers are the quintessential rootless global elite that populist nationalist love to hate."[47]

Several long-standing observers of central banking have thereby argued that the rise of populism constitutes a powerful threat to the support that has historically underpinned central banks and their independence from the late 1980s onward.[48] Populist politicians, however, are not the only policymakers who have put open pressure on central banks. The accusations made about central banks have been quite common across countries and across party lines.[49]

In addition to political elites, social attitudes toward central banks changed, too. In particular, the recent crises and how central banks responded to them have shed light on the weakening of public support toward central banks. The two central banks whose development trajectories are going to be analyzed in great detail in the next two chapters (chapters 4 and 5) offer some of clearest examples of this politicization process. In Europe, for instance, citizens' trust in the ECB reached all-time lows in the wake of the 2008 crisis and the ensuing euro crisis, and it has not fully recovered ever since.[50] In the same period, the ECB even became the target of an unusual string of mass protests, with protesters surrounding its buildings and even interrupting a press conference to articulate their dissent and opposition to the ECB and its policies.[51] Similarly, favorable views of the US Fed have oscillated with the business cycle, hovering at approximately 40 percent in the aftermath of the 2008 crash and then climbing up to over 60 percent by early 2020. Polls from early 2021 showed a net negative favorability again, with 53 percent of Americans saying they do not trust the central bank.[52] At the same time, ever since the start of the global financial crisis, the number of congressional proposals to curb the Fed's powers has increased markedly.[53]

The weakening of public support is particularly alarming for central banks. Indeed, at least in democratic societies, public support is key for central banks because, ultimately, "it is the general public that gives central banks their democratic legitimacy, and hence their independence."[54] A supportive public is also a "referee of some sorts in the event of a public conflict" between central banks and governments threatening to reverse their independence, hence the guarantor of said independence.[55] Central banks thereby cannot easily shrug off the possibility of an unfavorable political reaction.[56] If public opinion becomes increasingly negative, then democratically elected policymakers could be expected to become less likely to respect central bank independence.

Central banks have not been blind to the risks that eroding levels of public support entail. Rather, they have been fighting back to rekindle their public image. Revising their communication with the public has been a crucial strategy. In particular, central banks have increased their level of public engagement both in terms of communicative practices and issues covered in their communication. The Fed was one of the first central banks to venture into this terrain. As the long-serving economic editor at the *Wall Street Journal* recalled, "Communicating beyond markets and Congress to the broader public was never a priority for Federal Reserve chairmen Paul Volcker or Alan Greenspan"; however, since the global financial crisis, the Fed has felt compelled to review its communication priorities, as attested by Ben Bernanke's TV appearances in which he aimed "to talk to ordinary Americans."[57] All major central banks have followed similar steps. For instance, in a notable shift for an institution that has consistently justified its accountability through the achievement of the price stability objective rather than through disclosure to the public, the ECB started publishing accounts of its internal deliberations in January 2015, increased the frequency of communication with the European Parliament, and expanded the issues it addresses in its external communication in an attempt to appear more responsive to EU citizens' concerns.[58] Generally, central banks in high-income countries have also engaged more broadly with key societal issues, as attested by the rising share of central bankers' speeches on issues such as "inequality" and the "distributional" impact of monetary policy.[59]

In conclusion, the crisis period that started with the 2008 global financial crisis and continued through the 2020 COVID-19 crisis confronted central banks in high-income countries with new and difficult challenges—namely, the meltdown of the financial sector, the risk of secular stagnation, and the prospect of prolonged and deep recession. Although cross-country differences exist in terms of policy responses and their timing, two common trends emerge out of the crisis period. First, central banks basically converged on a new policy normal. That is, central banks moved away from interest rate policy to venture into unconventional policies that mark a significant deviation from precrisis monetary theory and practice and challenge central banks' cherished reputation, as will be examined in more detail in the following chapters. Second, central banks' responses to the new economic challenges have made the distributive consequences of monetary policies much more visible than was previously the case for conventional interest rate policy. Against this backdrop, the contestation of central banks' policies and independence has increased. In other words, central banking has become increasingly politicized. After identifying the broader transformations that have taken place from 2008 onwards, chapters 4 and 5 focus on the specific path through which these transformations came about in the United States and Europe, respectively.

THE US FEDERAL RESERVE

If we were to rank central banks according to the attention they attract, the US Federal Reserve System (hereafter, the Fed) would undoubtedly occupy one of the top positions. As one scholar has stated, "The Fed, and the holders of the chairmanship of the [Federal Open Market Committee] in particular, have probably prompted the writing of more books and articles than possibly for any other central bank."[1] Few central bankers have their words as closely scrutinized by financial investors as US monetary policymakers do, and one of the oldest adages in the financial community is the one prescribing the listener to "never fight the Fed."

There are good reasons for the attention the Fed attracts. The Fed serves as the central bank of the world's reserve currency that provides liquidity to international markets. Changes in US monetary policy have significant global consequences: by influencing investors' risk appetite, the Fed's interest rate decisions affect international capital flows and foreign bond yields. The Fed's key role in international financial stability was reasserted during the market stress that escalated in both 2008 and 2020. Then, the Fed acted as a global lender of last resort by establishing swap lines with selected foreign central banks in advanced and emerging market economies as a way to ensure emergency dollar liquidity.

It is in the pursuit of its domestic dual mandate, however, that the Fed's actions have probably attracted the most scholarly and public attention. This attention largely stems from the fact that the Fed's actions in response to both the 2008 and 2020 crises were unprecedented in several ways. Not only did the Fed's policy responses often entail the activation of powers not seen since the Great

Depression of the 1930s, but its actions also involved creating innovative instruments that assisted nonbank financial institutions, facilitated bailouts of major firms, and even intervened in distressed corporate and municipal debt markets, among others. Arguably, the most tremendous actions that the Fed has undertaken involve its balance sheet policies, through which the Fed has purchased a trillion dollars of assets, including US Treasuries, corporate bonds, and mortgage-backed securities. However, by 2020, the transformation in the Fed's monetary practice took a further turn, as the central bank committed to tolerating higher levels of inflation than it used to tolerate in the past to support employment and dispel deflation. The Fed even reframed its views on maximum employment, stating that the goal the Fed pursues is "broad-based and inclusive" employment.

Explanations for the Fed's actions to counter the economic downturn and the attendant threats of deflation usually stress the importance of learning from the Great Depression and financial market power. For one thing, the Fed is often portrayed as a bold and quick responder to crises because of the opening of its political leadership to the lessons of the 1930s.[2] The fact that Ben Bernanke, a scholar of the Great Depression, was at the helm of the Fed when the crisis period started is often regarded as playing a pivotal role in the technocratic learning process that led the Fed to break away from orthodox monetary policy. Likewise, the continuation of these unprecedented policies in the wake of the COVID-19 crisis can, in principle, be traced back to the lessons that the Fed learned from during the 2008 crisis, which led the central bank to repeat a script that had proved successful in quelling financial instability and supporting economic activity.[3] In addition, the Fed's actions are also often attributed to the peculiar circumstances of the US political economy. In particular, the Fed's policy responses, especially to the 2008 financial panic, are read as a reflection of the influence that financial markets exert on the US economy and on its political institutions, including the US central bank.[4] That is, the Fed's policy responses are largely interpreted as the result of the pressures exerted by financial market actors, which have benefited enormously from the monetary support the Fed has provided since 2008.

The narrative that follows dilutes these well-established views. In particular, based on a close examination of the Fed officials' key decisions from 2008 to 2020, the empirical evidence that follows shows that, at the beginning of the crisis period, the Fed's policy responses were significantly shaped by the Fed's attempts to preserve the institution's past reputation. In particular, Fed policymakers were reluctant to engage in policies that would have tainted the institution's anti-inflation and politically neutral reputation. This reluctance translated into cautious policies and untimely attempts at policy "normalization" that weakened the Fed's departure from monetary orthodoxy and probably had the same level of effectiveness on its anti-deflation fight.[5] The Fed's break away from orthodoxy thus did not happen overnight and did not solely happen because monetary authorities had learned the "right" lessons from the Great Depression or because financial markets forced its hand. A key condition that allowed the Fed to venture into unconventional policies lies instead in its relationship with US elected policymakers and the US public and the influence that these political audiences exerted on the Fed through reputation protection. In particular, as the following analysis shows, the Fed's responses to recessionary and deflationary challenges were significantly dependent on supportive actions from US administrations and Congress, which offered the Fed political cover for the adoption of policies that challenged its established conservative and neutral reputation. As time wore on, the reputational threat posed by the politicization of monetary policy among the US public encouraged the Fed to sustain and even deepen its deviation from orthodoxy. For instance, the Fed rebalanced the focus it devotes to the employment objective compared to the price stability objective and even started paying attention to social objectives such as "inclusive" growth and inequality. Memoirs of top Fed officials, public statements, and transcripts of the Federal Open Market Committee (FOMC) reveal this political dynamic and the extent to which Fed officials felt beholden to the need to secure political support to consent to actions that might have disrupted the Fed's reputation.

The Fed before the Crises Struck

Although currently the Fed is arguably one of the most powerful institutions in the US political system, its creation and evolution have often been challenged.[6] A chief reason (among others) is the fact that the Fed's architects and supporters have had to repeatedly confront deep-seated opposition to the concentration of economic power in a single institution. For example, the Fed was created in 1913 only after several failed attempts that were eventually overcome by virtue of the decentralized institutional design on which the central bank was modeled. Indeed, the Federal Reserve Act created an institution consisting of twelve regional (district) Federal Reserve banks and a seven-member Federal Reserve Board, which was renamed the Board of Governors of the Federal Reserve System in 1935. The FOMC, the Federal Reserve's centralized policymaking body, was not created until 1933. Although the presidents of all twelve district banks attend and participate in FOMC deliberations, only the members of the Board and five regional presidents may vote on policy decisions: namely, the president of the Federal Reserve Bank of New York and four other district bank presidents who serve on a rotating basis.

Although the Fed was founded in 1913 largely in response to the periodic episodes of banking panics that had plagued the US economy during the nineteenth and early twentieth centuries, today's Fed is accountable to Congress for two macroeconomic objectives: maximum employment and price stability.[7] Since the Monetary Accord with the Treasury in 1951, a number of statutory arrangements have guaranteed that the Fed pursues these objectives independently from political interferences. In particular, the Fed enjoys operational independence, meaning that the central bank can choose the instruments it deems fit in order to achieve the mandate assigned to it by Congress. The Federal Reserve is also structured to ensure that its policy decisions do not become subject to political pressures. Hence, the members of the Board of Governors are appointed for fourteen-year terms, and the Board chair is appointed for a four-year term.

Although the Fed is accountable to Congress for its dual mandate, the balance between the two objectives of price stability and employment started tilting in the early 1980s, paving the way for the emergence of the Fed's distinct bureaucratic reputation. As extensively discussed in chapter 2, the rebalancing of the Fed's dual objectives was closely associated with the Fed's experience in combating inflation. During the 1960s and the 1970s, the Fed struggled to control inflationary pressures, and under the leadership of Paul Volcker as Fed chair, it initiated a "major transformation—akin to a paradigm shift," as one former Fed top officials stated.[8] In particular, the Fed eventually succeeded in taming inflation and kept it under control. This policy success was pivotal for the Fed's institutional development till basically the start of the 2008 crisis. In particular, it provided the building block for its anti-inflation reputation. As former Fed chair Ben Bernanke explains the implications of the Volcker years for the Fed's understanding of its role, that experience "entailed a changed view about the dual mandate, in which policymakers regarded achievement of price stability as helping to provide the conditions necessary for sustained maximum employment."[9] That is, although the letter of the Fed's mandate did not change, the Fed's reputation was reoriented by instilling "a focus on controlling inflation and inflationary expectations as an enduring aspect of Federal Reserve monetary strategy."[10] Importantly, the shift in the Fed's interpretation of its mandate and, consequently, in its public image was initially supported by the decision made by the Fed under Volcker's leadership to use bank reserves as the operating procedure for the conduct of monetary policy. One of the critical turning points in the battle against inflation was the Fed's decision to target the aggregate quantity of money instead of the short-term federal funds interest rate in the Treasury repos (repurchase agreements) market as a way in which to control the money supply (see chapter 2). However, the change in the way in which the Fed balanced its inflation and employment objective—namely, the shift favoring the former over the latter—outlasted Volcker's monetarist experiment and "endured even after the Federal Reserve resumed its traditional use of the federal funds rate as the policy instrument."[11]

In addition to the Fed's new willingness to respond more vigorously to inflation than to employment risks, the Fed has also progressively narrowed the scope of monetary policy. Although created to deal with recurrent financial crises as discussed above, financial instability receded to the background of the Fed's responsibilities. This development is the most evident in the "Greenspan doctrine," named after Alan Greenspan, the former chair of the US Federal Reserve, according to whom monetary policy should not "lean" against a growing bubble, either in equity or real estate markets (chapter 2 and references therein). In other words, the Fed came to project the image of a technocratic institution focused on price stability whose attainment was carefully protected from the interferences of other policy issues, including those related to financial stability. As Fed Chair Janet Yellen put it, "Financial stability became a 'junior partner' in the monetary policy process, in contrast with its traditionally larger role."[12] So it was, at least until the start of the 2008 global financial crisis.

The Fed in a Changed Economic Context

If the 2008 and 2020 crises proved to be extraordinary tests for most central banks around the world, the problems faced by the central bank of the world's reserve currency were no less taxing. Actually, the problems that the Fed confronted at the start of the decade-long crisis period were particularly elevated because the United States found itself at the epicenter of the financial crisis that engulfed the world starting in 2008. Indeed, as discussed in chapter 3, the trigger that set off the 2008 global crisis was the turn of the US housing cycle and the associated rise in delinquencies on subprime mortgages.[13]

Starting in the summer of 2007, declining housing prices and rising rates of foreclosure imposed substantial losses on many financial institutions and raised serious concerns about the values of mortgage-backed securities. As a result, mortgage lenders, structured investment vehicles, and commercial and investment banks started experiencing difficulties rolling over commercial paper that was backed by subprime and other mortgages. As uncertainty mounted about who would bear the costs of such financial losses, a generalized loss of confidence led to a sharp contraction in the market for asset-backed commercial paper (ABCP), which in the United States is a critical and very large market. The country's major banks, such as JPMorgan Chase, Citigroup, and Bank of America, all relied heavily on ABCP sales. Similar pressures were felt even in the repos market; this was an exceptional development given that, until that time, short-term repos had always been regarded as risk-free instruments. Faced with severe disruptions in funding markets, financial intermediaries were forced to sell their assets, thereby setting in motion a particularly adverse dynamic: asset sales drove prices further down, which in turn fanned investor concerns about counterparty credit risk, which, in turn, intensified funding pressures. Financial stress reached its apex in September 2008, following the collapse of the fourth-largest investment bank in the United States: Lehman Brothers (more below).

The turmoil in financial markets quickly transmitted to the real economy following a pattern similar to that of the panic induced by traditional "bank runs": financial intermediaries, unable to fund themselves, cut down their lending to households and firms, taking a huge toll on economic activity.[14] This is what happened as commercial paper markets and the markets in the debt and securitization instruments basically stopped working. Unable to borrow, US households and businesses became increasingly wary to spend, consume, and invest. Recession took hold of the US economy starting in December 2007.

The economic consequences of the financial crisis were not only serious but also quite persistent. For instance, six years after the start of the crisis, US output was still far short of where its potential was expected to be as of 2007. Importantly, unemployment was still higher than at the beginning of the crisis period, while inflation levels had not fully recovered even before the start of the COVID crisis (figure 4.1).

The COVID-19 crisis aggravated the weaknesses present in the US economy. The restrictive measures taken to limit the spread of the virus and the global supply chain disruptions took a huge toll on US economic activity; the drop in real gross domestic product (GDP) was 3.04 percent from 2019 to 2020, while employment contracted by 5.8 percent (both figures exceeded the 2008–2009 figures).[15]

Although different in their origins and dynamics, both the 2008 and 2020 crises unleashed potent recessionary and deflationary pressures. Both crises also attested to important and innovative monetary interventions that aimed to stabilize the financial sector and support economic activity. Without aiming to be exhaustive, the Fed adopted measures that focused on expanding the scale and scope of its lending to financial institutions and even stepped into providing liquidity to nonfinancial institutions.[16] The Fed also directly intervened in a number of markets as a backstop to prevent them from seizing up. These interventions are sometimes referred to as *market maker of last resort* or even *buyer of last resort* because in such situations, the Fed extended credit to financial institutions to purchase specific assets or directly purchased assets that neither the banks nor private investors wanted. The Fed also engineered new policies to

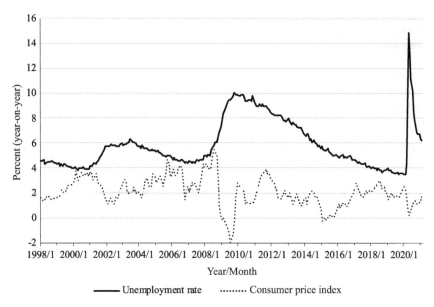

FIGURE 4.1. US unemployment rate and consumer price index, 1998–2020

Source: Federal Reserve Economic Data (FRED)

make broader financial conditions more accommodative and counter the threat of deflation. The most prominent among these accommodative measures has been the purchase of public and private-sector securities (i.e., Fed quantitative easing programs). In particular, the Fed launched several rounds of asset purchase programs, which resulted in an almost *tenfold* expansion of the Fed balance sheet compared to that present at the start of the recessionary cycle in December 2007.

The Fed's policies related to the 2008 and 2020 crises have been extensively scrutinized, especially when attempting to ascertain their actual impact. The debate is still open as to the extent to which the Fed's unconventional policies have supported economic activity instead of stoking financial excesses and growing inequality.[17] However, a preliminary and crucial question about the *process* that led the Fed to choose among policy alternatives is all the more important in light of the fact that the unconventional policies the Fed took in response to these crises represent a significant departure from traditional monetary policy. In particular, the Fed responded to the crises by significantly expanding the scope and tools of monetary policy in a way that challenged orthodox theory and practice. In what follows, I focus on the process and conditions that allowed the Fed to step into action.

The Fed's Journey Away from Orthodoxy

Reconstructing a decade-long decision-making process inevitably entails a degree of subjective judgment about what policy decisions to focus on. Since 2008, the Fed's monetary policy has indeed been variegated and tailored to different circumstances, and individual decisions were often revised over time. To shed light on the institutional development of the US Fed, the analysis that follows cannot investigate all the important decisions that the Fed made from 2008 to 2020. The analysis is instead organized around three major types of policy actions whose adoption has marked the Fed's departure from monetary orthodoxy. These policies are the expansion of liquidity support to banks and nonbanks alike, the adoption of quantitative easing, and the revision of the monetary strategy.

Bringing Financial Stability Back In

Given the financial sector origins of the 2008 crisis, it is not surprising that re-establishing financial stability quickly became a top priority on the Fed's to-do list. The Fed's interventions to stabilize financial markets, however, were far from standard practice. If conventional monetary wisdom holds that in a panic, a central bank should lend freely against good collateral, as Bagehot's dictum would have it, then the Fed interpreted the dictum in an extensive way. In particular, the Fed expanded its support to a broad range of financial counterparties and against considerably expanded collateral.[18] A further extension of the Fed's traditional activity as lender of last resort took place through the provision of liquidity assistance to nonbank financial institutions, which normally do not have access to the Fed's discount window operations. Indeed, the Fed created a range of emergency liquidity facilities to meet the funding needs of key nonbank market participants by invoking section 13(3) of the Federal Reserve Act, which permits a five-member majority of the Federal Reserve Board to authorize a Reserve bank to lend to individuals, partnerships, or corporations in "unusual and exigent circumstances." For instance, the Federal Reserve invoked section 13 (3) to extend a bridge loan to the investment bank Bear Stearns through JPMorgan Chase on March 14, 2008. After the collapse of Lehman Brothers, the Fed intervened to prevent the failure of the American International Group (AIG) by extending an $85 billion line of credit to the insurance company.

In hindsight, the Fed's interventions aiming to stabilize financial markets, particularly the decisions to bail out some of the major US financial firms, could be interpreted as a foregone conclusion given the adverse developments in the

US financial markets and the attendant risks to the real economy. That is, the Fed was simply responding to "realities on the ground" and, as the only institution not caught up in a political gridlock, was able to marshal financial resources quickly, as proponents of the only-game-in-town argument suggest.[19] Although the Fed certainly enjoyed a favorable institutional position from which to act, this does not mean that it did not face important hurdles to taking action on its own. In particular, the Fed's resolve to counter the threat of deflation was often diluted by the awareness of the reputational risks the central bank confronted in deciding to act. In other words, several Fed officials and especially then Fed chair Bernanke acknowledged that the central bank had to intervene to support financial institutions to stop the vicious cycle leading to a full-fledged deflationary crisis.[20] However, they were also aware that political audiences might react negatively to the Fed's interventions, thus weakening the central bank's reputation and the independence staked on that reputation.

In his memoirs, Bernanke spells out these concerns clearly. For instance, in reflecting on the message received from Larry Summers, in which the former Treasury secretary warned the Fed about the moral hazard implications of saving Wall Street giants, Bernanke recalls the awareness of the reputational risks among the members of the Board of Governors: "Larry's point about moral hazard was a good one. But he didn't need to explain it to us. (Nor did he need to explain that, if we failed, our credibility would be in tatters. We knew that.)"[21] In other words, Fed policymakers were looking at their audience and gauging their potential reactions should the Fed have decided to expand its traditional lender-of-last-resort role to stabilize the financial system.

The perception of the risks to the Fed's organizational image was also magnified by the uncertainty surrounding the impact of the Fed's potential interventions. As one of the highest officials in the Board of Governors stated, "Before the crisis, emergency lending by the Federal Reserve was almost never discussed. If it was discussed, it was always viewed as implausible, and it would be noted that the Federal Reserve had not made an emergency loan since the 1930s."[22] The uncertainty surrounding the Fed's liquidity assistance became particularly elevated as the Fed confronted the challenge of stabilizing systematically important financial institutions. Donald L. Kohn, then vice chair of the Board of Governors, recalled the policymaking context when such momentous decisions were made as follows: "We were well aware that we were possibly assuming a risk of loss when we lent to stabilize the systemically important firms of Bear Stearns and American International Group."[23] Fed officials were not just concerned about potential short-term reputational costs to their institution. They were also concerned about the long-term implications. Specifically, monetary policymakers fretted that undermining the Fed's reputational capital would have made the institution vulnerable to political pressures—statutory independence notwithstanding. Again, as Bernanke stated in his memoirs, Fed officials were making decisions in the shadow of congressional politics. "If we failed, an angry Congress might eviscerate the Fed."[24]

In this context, support from fiscal authorities has often proved crucial for the Fed to justify the adoption of actions that openly clash with its established reputation and risk damaging the institution's future. In particular, Treasury support has often provided the Fed with political cover for such actions that would inevitably conflict with the Fed's reputation.

The importance of political support for the Fed to spring into action can be gleaned from several sources, but it is probably most clearly illustrated in the decision making surrounding the controversial rescue of a major Wall Street bank: Bear Stearns. By March 2008, confidence in Bear Stearns had been fast eroding, culminating in a full-fledged bank run by its clients. As the Fed was considering various policy options to help Bear Stearns and avoid further market stress, including fostering its acquisition by a rival bank, Bernanke drew a clear line in the sand for the Fed's intervention. In Bernanke's words, "The Fed could go no further without the administration's agreement."[25] Former Treasury secretary Henry Paulson similarly recalls in his memoirs that the Fed chair declared himself "prepared to go ahead here only if Treasury [was] supportive and prepared to protect [the Fed] from any losses."[26] Although Paulson could not provide full-fledged fiscal support absent congressional approval, he ultimately provided the Fed with the political support the central bank had been seeking by promising a letter expressing the administration's support.[27] The letter was made public on March 17, 2008.[28] It was not by coincidence that the Board of Governors committed $30 billion to back Bear Stearns assets to facilitate its acquisition by JPMorgan Chase only after the agreement with Secretary Paulson was reached.[29] As Bernanke wrote in his memoirs, after the agreement was reached with the Treasury, the Fed could show it "had the president's support" in extending its financial support to Bear Stearns.[30] Similarly, the Board of Governors' decision to provide temporary support to the two government-sponsored enterprises, Fannie Mae and Freddie Mac, through the Federal Reserve Bank of New York on July 13, 2008, was taken only after the US Treasury secretary reassured Bernanke that the Treasury had enough support from Congress to pass legislation to sustain the two companies; this legislation was enacted at the end of July under the title of the Housing and Economic Recovery Act.[31] A similar dynamic was at play in the decisions pertaining to Fed interventions in disrupted markets. For instance, Kohn explicitly admitted that the Fed accepted the risks of intervening in the securitization markets because of coordination between monetary and fiscal authorities. In his words, "The Federal Reserve supplied the liquid funding, while the Treasury assumed the credit risk."[32] For instance, the Fed's credit risk exposure to the Term Asset-Backed Securities Loan Facility (TALF) program, created in November 2008 to provide a backstop to the asset-backed securities market (including student loans, auto loans, credit card loans, and loans guaranteed by the Small Business Administration), was minimized by the commitment of $20 billion of Troubled Asset Relief Program (TARP) funds in the form of credit protection for the Federal Reserve's interventions in those markets.

In short, some of the most controversial yet key measures taken to stabilize financial markets and counteract the attendant deflationary pressures were crucially dependent on political support rather than independent, technocratic decision making. From the Fed's perspective, political support was key to justifying the central banks' forays into unorthodox terrain and thus shielding the central bank from negative audience reactions, be they from financial markets or congressional policymakers. As Timothy Geithner, 'former New York Fed president, stated when discussing Paulson's letter declaring the Treasury's support for the Fed's actions in the Bear Stearns affair: "While it merely stated fiscal facts, I thought it gave us some *cover,* implicating Treasury in the risks we were taking."[33] In this light, it is possible to read the Fed's consistent calls for the involvement of the Treasury in addressing the problems in financial markets. As one scholar of the Fed's crisis responses eloquently wrote, "The phrases, 'with the full support of the Treasury department' and 'in close consultation with the Treasury department' became standard language in Fed press releases and Congressional testimony by Bernanke and others."[34]

When Lehman and AIG Got into Trouble

The importance of political support for the Fed to counteract the economic downturn can also be gleaned in the *inaction* of the Fed in the face of Lehman Brothers' collapse, which triggered the most severe market dislocation during the crisis.

By mid-2008, the financial stability of Lehman Brothers, the fourth-largest investment bank in the United States at the time, had been severely damaged by the large losses the bank had been experiencing in its real estate investments. As confidence in the firm evaporated, the usual financial panic set in: Lehman's share price collapsed while customers and counterparties fled away. In the first week of September, Lehman's liquidity was basically wiped out. Over the weekend of September 13–14, 2008, Treasury and Fed officials tried to broker the sale of Lehman to a stronger firm, similar to what had been done with Bearn Stearns earlier in the year. Eventually, however, these attempts failed as the potential buyer, the British bank Barclays, walked out of the negotiations. Lehman had no choice but to file for bankruptcy on September 15.

Several analyses have focused on the motivations that led the Fed to decide not to extend financial support to Lehman as it had done with Bear Stearns just some months earlier and was about to do with AIG.[35] For instance, a number of commentators have argued that an adequate loan from the Fed would have kept Lehman in business by giving it time to survive a traditional liquidity crisis.[36] The Fed's decision to let Lehman fail—irrespective of the fact that the Federal Reserve Act gave it the sole authority to decide on the rescue—is also puzzling in light of the expressed preferences and economic ideas of its key policymakers. For instance, from the statements and memoirs of top officials of the time, it is possible to infer that, at least at the beginning of the cycle that led to Lehman's collapse, the Fed was in principle willing to prevent Lehman's failure, cognizant of the knock-on and deflationary effects that a financial market collapse entailed. As Bernanke wrote in his memoirs, "We [at the Fed and the Treasury] had little doubt a Lehman failure would massively disrupt financial markets and impose heavy costs on many parts other than Lehman's shareholders, managers, and creditors, including millions of people around the world which would be hurt by its economic shockwaves."[37] Therefore, why did the Fed decide not to act in this episode?

The Fed's official answer to this question is that the central bank lacked the legal authority to intervene, especially absent adequate collateral to secure a loan. However, detailed analyses based on the record of policymakers' deliberations before the bankruptcy show that there is "no evidence that [Fed officials] examined the adequacy of Lehman's collateral, or that legal barriers deterred them from assisting the firm."[38] Other accounts draw attention to influence of personalities in this episode and, in particular, to Bernanke's deference to Treasury Secretary Paulson, who, according to many accounts, refused to help Lehman because of the strong political opposition to the Bear Stearns rescue and the government takeovers of Fannie Mae and Freddie Mac.[39] "I can't be Mr. Bailout," Paulson was notoriously reported as saying.

Beyond personalities, however, the Fed's decision about Lehman cannot fully be explained without taking into account the Fed's concerns for its reputation. Indeed, in deciding to intervene, the Fed's officials were deeply concerned about the implications of the Fed's policies to the integrity of the Feds' institutional image as a politically neutral institution. In particular, Fed officials were deeply aware that if they decided to lend to Lehman, they "would have to do so in the face of bitter criticism" from the public and Congress.[40] The image of a Fed that was no longer able to stay above the political fray, however, seriously threatened to undermine the apolitical, technocratic credentials that the Fed had long cultivated.

Building on the Bear Stearns episode, the Fed attempted to minimize the perceived reputational risks that would have stemmed from its intervention by seeking out coordination with the Treasury. Geithner's suggestion during the Lehman negotiations that he might "talk [Paulson] into another Bearn" implicitly suggests that the Fed felt beholden to the Treasury's simultaneous intervention to assist Lehman. When support from the Treasury did not materialize, however, the Fed was no longer willing to rescue Lehman in anticipation of the political backlash that would have followed. In Bernanke's words, "The ability of the Fed to keep rescuing major financial firms, alone and without support from Congress, was fast coming to an end."[41]

In short, the Fed's decision not to rescue Lehman was significantly influenced by more than legal and technical considerations of how insolvent the firm was. Fed policymakers' perception of the reputational risks that the US central bank was exposed to, absent political support, ultimately tipped the balance in favor of the dramatic decision to let Lehman Brothers fail. As Bernanke commented in his memoirs, "Even if it had somehow been possible for the Fed on its own to save Lehman . . . we would not have had either the capacity or political support to undertake any future financial rescues."[42] That is, the Fed under Bernanke was aware that what was at stake with the Lehman rescue was not just financial stability but also the institutional image of the Fed and thus its future. Absent the necessary political cover for its reputation, the Fed walked away from actions that might have reduced the deflationary forces associated with a financial crash.

The collapse of Lehman Brothers and its attendant shockwaves contributed to altering the political climate in Washington. As several observers have noted, the dramatic consequences of the Lehman collapse, which basically drowned the US stock market, heightened the pressure placed on other financial firms, and exacerbated the economic recession, also somehow softened the general opposition to bank bailouts in Congress. "Lehman had to die so that the rest of Wall Street could live," so wrote the New York Times.[43] Bernanke similarly noted that Congress would have never approved TARP absent the failure of a systemically important financial institution.[44]

These changes in the political context are crucial for understanding another momentous decision that the Fed made in the fall of 2008—namely, the decision to extend a loan not to a bank but rather to the insurance firm AIG. Indeed, Lehman's fate was closely interlinked with AIG's. Lehman held billions of dollars in credit default swap contracts with AIG, and AIG had extended similar protection to the largest global banks. Lehman's failure thus suddenly raised serious pressures on AIG to honor its enormous outstanding insurance contracts.

The Fed was once again at the center of the negotiations to find a solution to AIG's troubles, which ultimately led to the decision to extend AIG a $85 billion loan to keep the insurance company running. This decision was certainly motivated by the quick deterioration in market conditions that followed the collapse of Lehman and the severe deflationary waves that were plausibly expected to occur after the failure of another large financial player. For instance, in his audition before the Financial Crisis Inquiry Commission, Bernanke justified the decision to lend to AIG by noting that "if we let it fail, . . . the probability was 80 percent that we would have had a second depression."[45] Geithner, who was president of the Federal Reserve Bank of New York in 2008, put it more colorfully by commenting that the Fed rescued AIG because "it was our only hope of avoiding unimaginable carnage."[46]

Although market conditions certainly influenced the Fed's decision to rescue AIG, politics also mattered. Whereas Fed officials had perceived a hostile political climate with regard to Lehman's rescue, the political climate had quickly and significantly changed after Lehman's collapse, thereby allowing the Fed the maneuverability to intervene. Democratic Representative Barney Frank, chair of the powerful House Financial Services Committee, recalled the emerging political support for Fed's AIG intervention, especially among Republican members of Congress:

> When Hank Paulson and Ben Bernanke came to Congress in September 2008, representing President [George W.] Bush, the Republicans' instant reaction was supportive. . . . House Minority Leader John Boehner said that we would be crazy to let AIG fail. The Republican leadership, out of a sense of commitment to the country and out of the political need to work with President Bush, especially with an election pending, strongly supported the proposal. Senate Republicans were even more supportive.[47]

Similarly, Paulson recalled in his memoirs that, in meeting congressional leadership on the Hill on September 16, lawmakers were "stunned" by the news of the AIG rescue but were also "broadly supportive," although they fell short of publicly endorsing the Fed's and Treasury's intervention.[48] Furthermore, President Bush gave the green light, and the Fed received assurance through Paulson that the administration stood behind its assistance.[49] In short, the Fed's actions were now backed by political authorities, and such support was a key but often insufficiently recognized condition that helped the Fed overcome its reputational concerns, stretch the boundaries of monetary policy, and ultimately counter the deflationary forces that had been unleashed by financial instability.

Expanding the Boundaries of Monetary Policy

The Fed's embrace of quantitative easing (QE) has often been portrayed as an example of a central bank that has learned from past monetary policy mistakes, most notably from the Fed's inaction in the 1930s.[50] In the words of Bernanke, "Early in the Depression, policymakers' responses ran the gamut from passivity to timidity. They were insufficiently willing to challenge the orthodoxies of their day."[51] This "passivity" and "timidity" stand in stark contrast to the resolute measures that the Fed took to minimize the prospect of depression and deflation in the aftermath of the 2008 crisis as well as during the 2020 crisis. Nowhere is the Fed's resolve more visible than in the use of its balance sheet to purchase financial assets.

While it is certainly true that the Fed grew more resolute over time in the use of its balance sheet—so much so that in the aftermath of the COVID crisis, the Fed's purchases dwarfed those carried out over an entire previous decade—the step into QE terrain was far from straightforward. Focusing on the initial decision to venture into asset purchase programs thus helps reveal the problems the central bank confronted in deviating from orthodoxy as well as the factors that helped it overcome those problems. The first rounds of the Fed's large-scale asset purchase program that occurred between 2008 and 2010 are thus particularly important to understanding the process that led the Fed to venture into what was a largely untested policy tool at the time.[52]

Faced with the disruptions caused by Lehman's collapse, Fed policymakers focused on the possibility of using the Fed's balance sheet to counteract the recessionary and potentially dangerous deflationary scenario. In November 2008, the US central bank eventually decided to start the first round of what came to be called large-scale asset purchase programs (LSAP). Under this program, the Fed purchased $175 billion in agency debt, $1.25 trillion in agency mortgage-backed securities (MBS), and $300 billion in longer-term Treasury securities.[53] In November 2010, Fed policymakers agreed on a second round of LSAP, which entailed the purchases of an additional $600 billion in longer-term Treasury securities.

Although the Fed has resorted to asset purchases since then, including a third round of LSAP in 2012 and an extensive program in 2020, back in 2008, actively using the balance sheet to conduct monetary policy was still not a popular option.[54] One reason was the elevated uncertainty associated with what was then an unprecedented crisis and the limited data available to gauge the effectiveness of asset purchases aiming to stabilize the macroeconomic cycle. Indeed, when the Fed first started its QE programs, monetary authorities acknowledged that they were simply "flying blind" in the conduct of monetary policy at the zero lower bound.[55]

In addition to uncertainty, however, another motivation weighed against the adoption of QE among several FOMC members—namely, the recognition that QE posed a direct challenge to the Fed's anti-inflation reputation.[56] As the transcripts of the meetings of the FOMC reveal, one of the major concerns among monetary policymakers was the impact of large-scale asset purchases on future inflation. As then vice chair Donald Kohn explained, one important problem that Fed policymakers confronted was "the effects of the large volume of reserves created" by the Fed on purchasing assets.[57] In particular, according to standard monetarist theory, "extra reserves should induce banks to diversify into additional lending and purchases of securities, reducing the cost of borrowing for households and businesses, and so should spark an increase in the money supply and spending."[58] In other words, the introduction of QE entailed the risk of sparking inflationary pressures and thus questioning the Fed's organizational image as the guardian of price stability. That the reputational risk was real was made clear by several warnings directed at the Fed from its market and political audiences. For instance, in November 2010, the Republican leadership of the US Congress wrote to the Fed to express concerns about further asset purchases. In the letter, US policymakers wrote that "such a measure introduces significant uncertainty regarding the future strength of the dollar and could result both in hard-to-control long-term inflation."[59] In a subsequent letter published in the *Wall Steet Journal*, conservative economists and market participants reiterated the message by arguing that QE would lead to "currency debasement and inflation" and "distort financial markets and greatly complicate future Fed efforts to normalize monetary policy."[60]

Fed policymakers were aware of market and political audiences' concerns and the implication of these concerns for the Fed's reputation, as attested by an internal discussion in March 2010 when the Fed aimed to decide on additional asset purchases following the expiration of the 2008 LSAP. On that occasion, Jeffrey Lacker, president of the Federal Reserve Bank of Richmond, well captured the reasoning of the skeptics within the FOMC by arguing that additional asset purchases would jeopardize the Fed's reputation and thus its credibility for a "long, long time." In particular, he argued that a further round of asset purchases would appear more targeted at employment than the price stability mandate, thereby signaling a change in the Fed's reaction function to its audiences and thus a change in its reputation.[61] Thomas Hoenig, president of the Federal Reserve Bank of Kansas City and one of the most prominent critics of QE, succinctly stated the following: "I think adopting another LSAP program risks over time letting inflation expectations become unanchored, no matter our admonitions to the contrary, thereby undermining our credibility."[62]

In addition to the concerns related to inflation-averse reputation, in-house opposition and skepticism toward QE were largely motivated by concerns about the other tenet of the Fed's reputation—namely, the image of the Fed as a politically neutral institution. Indeed, Fed officials found themselves in the unusual circumstance for a technocratic body of having to operate absent well-established macroeconomic knowledge that could justify their policy choices. The Fed's vice president described the situation that monetary authorities confronted at the time as follows: "Currently, we are relying in large part on event studies analyzing how much interest rates declined when purchases were announced in the United States or abroad."[63] As an internal opponent of the Fed's bond-buying similarly argued, "My assessment is that we have little theory or evidence to guide us in constructing such a rule for these unconventional policies."[64]

Limited knowledge was not the only concern for monetary policymakers keen on protecting the Fed's apolitical reputation. Another major concern was the distributive implications of asset purchase programs. Indeed, by deciding which assets to purchase, the Fed would have inevitably benefited particular (as opposed to general) borrowers. Even supporters of asset purchases conceded that targeting specific assets conflicted with the alleged neutrality of central banks' interventions. According to Lacker of the Federal Reserve Bank of Richmond, "If we are going to expand our balance sheet . . . I believe we should do so in a way that is as neutral as possible across market segments."[65] Richard Fisher, president of the Federal Reserve Bank of Dallas, echoed this position by concluding that "the ultimate objective is to insulate ourselves as a central bank as much as possible from political pressures, so we can do what central bankers do."[66] Even Fed chair Bernanke expressed the importance of ensuring the neutrality of the Fed's intervention, noting that "to the extent that the Federal Reserve becomes involved in credit markets, we should try to do so in a broad way that addresses the macroeconomic situation as opposed to picking winners and losers within small categories of credit."[67]

Although the FOMC was ultimately able to overcome resistance to action, as attested by the limited number of dissenting votes on the adoption of the first rounds of LSAP,[68] both the decision-making process that led to the adoption of the early asset purchase programs and the numerous policy *fixes* that accompanied the adoption of the programs reveal the difficult balancing act that Fed policymakers performed to protect the Fed's reputation under changed economic conditions. For instance, economist Michael Woodford has forcefully noted that the Fed designed its early asset purchase programs by relying mostly on the purchases of extremely safe Treasury securities "in the hope that such purchases will improve general financial conditions without more direct involvement by the central bank in extending credit to particular sectors of the economy."[69] This policy design, however, might have undermined the potential anti-deflationary impact of balance sheet policies by letting the Fed shy away from more controversial yet empirically more effective types of asset purchases.[70]

The Fed's attempts at reputation protection can also be gleaned by the repeated emphasis that the Fed placed on the future exit (or "normalization") from its unconventional policies, alongside its implementation of LSAP. Although the Fed later recognized that a central bank has to "be careful not to exit too early" from loose monetary policies and "try to not talk about exit all the time" lest it weaken the reflationary impact—as Fed Chair Jay Powell declared in 2020—in the wake of the 2008 crisis, the potential threats to reputation led the central bank to instead repeatedly emphasize the exit strategies from the policy course that it had been taken.[71] For instance, this emphasis is nicely illustrated in the decision-making process that eventually led to the second round of large-scale asset purchase programs in November 2010. Between 2009 and 2010, Bernanke's economic preferences and ideas were clearly against tightening. As Bernanke himself explained in his memoirs, his preferences were largely shaped by the lessons drawn from two episodes in economic history: the US recession of 1937 and 1938, when excessive fears of future inflation led the Fed to premature monetary tightening, and Japan's experience in 2000 and 2007, when the Bank of Japan tightened its policy only to later reverse it in the face of continuing disinflationary pressure.[72] Despite the lessons learned from past deflationary episodes and the leadership position of Bernanke in the FOMC, the resolve to counteract recessionary and deflationary prospects was diluted by the concomitant signals of "normalization" and discussions of "exit strategies" from ongoing and future asset purchase programs that the Fed was sending to its market and political audiences. According to Bernanke, "It made sense for the FOMC to discuss and agree on the mechanics of normalizing policy. In addition, making clear that we had a workable strategy for tightening policy when time came might ease the concerns of both the hawks inside the Fed and our external critics."[73]

The adoption of a formal inflation-targeting regime in January 2012 can similarly be read as an attempt at reputation protection that Fed policymakers performed while at the same time continuing to adapt the central bank's policies to the recession and deflationary scenario. Before 2012, and unlike many central banks in high-income countries, the Fed was not a formal inflation-targeting central bank. That is, the Fed did not have an explicit numerical target for the inflation rate that the central bank communicated to the public to help guide interest rate decisions.[74]

The policy framework guiding the Fed's policymaking changed in January 2012 when the FOMC released a statement intended to clarify the FOMC's longer-term goals and policy strategy.[75] The statement clarified that an inflation rate of 2 percent is best aligned with the Fed's mandated goals of price stability and full employment. In line with established macroeconomic doctrine, the Fed also clarified that, unlike the inflation target, it was not appropriate to adopt an explicit employment target because the level of unemployment that can be achieved without sparking inflation is not largely determined by monetary factors.

Although the statement was released in January 2012, the issue of whether to adopt a formal inflation target had been on the FOMC tables at least since Bernanke took the helm of the Fed in 2006. Bernanke was a strong proponent of an inflation target as a way to improve transparency and policy effectiveness. However, Bernanke was also aware of the need to win congressional support for the adoption of the inflation target in order to dispel concerns about the Fed's crisis management activity.[76] For instance, in 2009, Bernanke approached the head of the House Banking Committee, Barney Frank, in an attempt to persuade him to provide congressional support to the introduction of a formal inflation target.[77] Interestingly, one of the key motivations that Bernanke put forward to justify this request was that the target "would permit [the Fed] to more aggressively loosen policy in support of job creation" because it would have helped to anchor the expectations of businesses and consumers "in the Fed's commitment to *low* inflation."[78] In other words, the adoption of an explicit inflation target was also meant to signal that the Fed was maintaining its anti-inflation image; this was a commitment that was perceived as necessary for the Fed to deviate from monetary orthodoxy and continue fighting deflationary forces.

High-Pressuring the Monetary Policy Strategy

The start of the global pandemic in 2020 was once again an important policy test for the US Fed. As noted earlier in this chapter (see also chapter 3), building on the post-2008 crisis policy script, the Fed responded quickly and intensively to the deterioration in economic conditions brought about by COVID-related restrictions. Specifically, the Fed scaled up some of the policy programs that had been tested during the preceding crisis of 2008. The expansion of its balance sheet programs is a telling example. Indeed, between March 2020 and May 2022, the Fed significantly expanded the size and speed of its asset purchase programs. In particular, the Fed's securities holdings more than doubled from approximately $3.9 trillion to $8.5 trillion. As a percent of the GDP, the holdings rose from 18 percent to 35 percent.[79] The US central bank also crossed new red lines in central banking practice by establishing new facilities through which the Fed went "direct" in providing support to US nonfinancial firms. In particular, the Fed started lending directly to corporations by buying new bond issues, providing loans, and purchasing existing corporate bonds in the secondary market.[80] The Fed even entered into the corporate "junk" market by adding junk bond exchange-traded funds to the list of assets it was willing to buy. Importantly, the Fed's continuing departure from orthodox monetary theory and practice was also made official with the announcement of a new monetary strategy in August 2020.

Speaking at the most important global economic meeting for central banks, the Economic Policy Symposium organized by the Federal Reserve Bank of Kansas City in Jackson Hole, Wyoming, Fed Chair Jerome Powell summarized the goal of the new strategy as follows: "Following periods when inflation has been running below 2 percent, appropriate monetary policy will likely aim to achieve inflation moderately *above* 2 percent for some time."[81] In other words, recognizing the deflationary problem that had bedeviled high-income countries since 2008, the Fed announced its commitment to overshoot the traditional inflation target by embracing a flexible form of average inflation targeting. In a rethinking of the Fed's view of the labor market, Powell also clarified that the Fed would from then on base its monetary decisions on "assessments of the shortfalls of employment from its maximum level" rather than "deviations from its maximum level."[82] What probably sounded as nothing more than an anodyne reading of labor markets data was in fact an important transformation in the Fed's interpretation of how monetary policy should balance the employment and price stability objectives. In particular, what the revised assessment entailed is the Fed's new view, which recognizes "the economy's ability to sustain a robust job market without causing an unwanted increase in inflation."[83]

Powell's announcement, which was formalized by a FOMC statement about its longer-run strategy and goals, marks an important policy shift in the Fed's approach to macroeconomic stabilization.[84] In particular, if in the decades preceding the 2008 crisis the Fed had tended to prioritize inflation over the employment objective, the decade-long crisis period brought about the recognition of a more balanced relationship between the two objectives. One could even conclude that the new strategy signals that the Fed has somehow accepted a (re)prioritization of the employment objective. Indeed, the new strategy suggests that the Fed is committed to tolerating inflation to sustain jobs and revive economic activity. The Fed has even reframed its views on maximum employment by stating that the goal that the Fed pursues is "broad-based and *inclusive*" employment. This more inclusive interpretation of the employment objective aims to increase the gains of low unemployment for minority groups and low-income communities—that is, the social groups that benefited less from the recovery of the US economy.[85]

How did the Fed get to this place? The standard answer is that the Fed's review of its policy strategy responded to structural changes in the economy, including the deflationary context and the flattening of the Phillips curve.[86]

Following the start of the global financial crisis in 2008, the Fed, like the other central banks in high-income countries, indeed struggled to revive inflation. This struggle became particularly intense for the Fed after the announcement of the official 2 percent target in 2012. Indeed, except briefly during 2018, inflation has eluded the target. Furthermore, the decade-long crisis showed that the relationship theorized in the Phillips curve, according to which low unemployment should lead to higher inflation, was simply no longer working, although economists still have not developed a consensus view on the underlying reasons why. At any rate, the breakup of the Phillips curve in the United States is certainly one important motivation that led monetary policymakers to look for new ways in which to achieve their legally mandated objectives.

While structural changes in the economy certainly weighed on the Fed's decision to launch a review of its monetary policy framework in 2019, economic conditions alone cannot satisfactorily account for the outcome of the review announced in 2020. In particular, a thorough explanation for why the Fed agreed to an important transformation of how it seeks to achieve its 2 percent inflation target and maximum employment needs to take into account the changed political context in which the Fed found itself operating after almost a decade of fighting deflation and recession. In particular, the politicization of the central bank cannot easily be dismissed to account for the Fed's new strategy, especially with regard to the rebalancing of the employment objective.

Public opinion surveys have revealed that a majority of US citizens think the Fed has poorly addressed the challenges of the economic downturn and its aftermath.[87] These views have coalesced in a growing negative assessment of the central bank by US citizens.[88] The changes in public attitudes toward the central bank are also reflected in the growing attacks of congressional policymakers from across the political spectrum. Indeed, since the start of the global financial crisis, the number of congressional proposals made that aim to curb the Fed's powers has increased markedly.[89] The Fed has also grown into an "easy" political target, as attested by former president Donald Trump's repeated accusations that the Fed is not sufficiently supportive of the US economy.[90] These views have been echoed in the US public. For instance, a poll conducted in spring 2020 showed that slightly more than half of Americans do not trust their central bank. In particular, citizens do not trust the Fed "to look out for the best interests of individual citizens and their family," as the poll question phrased it.[91]

The Fed's post-pandemic policy responses, particularly the outcome of the review to its monetary strategy, need to be understood against these broader sociopolitical conditions in which the Fed operates. As discussed in chapter 1, central banks require public support to withhold their institutional image and justify their power and independence. That support has been particularly strained after a decade of crisis fighting that has boosted the fortunes of Wall Street by way of the Fed's repeated monetary interventions while furthering social inequality.[92] The disconnect between the fortunes of Wall Street and those of Main Street, with the attendant politicization of the Fed's role among US citizens, stands in the background of the Fed's decision to revise its operational conduct. As one *Financial Times* market reporter perceptively stated, "The Fed's urgency to do more to aid the real economy is unsurprising, given that its policies have helped fuel one of the sharpest rebounds in the history of US markets. Meanwhile, so-called Main Street has languished, dogged by high unemployment and rising bankruptcies for small businesses. Narrowing Wall Street's lead, then, has become more than simply a matter of financial stability. It is also about the Fed's *reputation*."[93] From this perspective, the strategy review and its focus on employment can be read as the Fed's attempt to address the dissatisfaction with the central bank among the US public and to win back its support. As Fed Chair Powell stated, "This change [in the monetary policy framework] reflects our appreciation for the benefits of a strong labor market, particularly for many in low- and moderate-income communities."[94]

This "appreciation" for a strong labor market has been growing within the Fed since the aftermath of the global financial crisis. For instance, in a 2016 speech, Chair Janet Yellen argued that running the economy at "high pressure" could be a powerful tool to reverse the labor market hysteresis (i.e., a persistent surge in unemployment as the consequence of the erosion of skills among workers put temporarily out of work).[95] The Fed's new opening toward tight labor markets has also been informed by the exchanges between the Fed and the US public.[96] Indeed, the Fed solicited the views of invited members of the public as part of the review of its monetary policy framework through "Fed Listens" events held in 2019 and 2020. The total of nineteen events engaged many groups in society, such as "employee groups and union members, small business owners, residents of low- and moderate-income communities, workforce development organizations and community colleges, retirees, and others."[97] One of the Fed's regional banks summarized the main message coming out of these events: "One consistent takeaway was that minorities, including blacks and Hispanics who historically have suffered higher unemployment rates than whites, were finding more opportunities for employment and advancement as the recovery gained momentum."[98] That is, the Fed came to recognize that "while the [US] recovery [was] gathering strength, it has been slower for those in lower-paid jobs. Almost 20 percent of workers who were in the lowest earnings quartile in February of 2020 were not employed a year later, compared to 6 percent for workers in the highest quartile."[99]

In short, the recognition of social inequality and its link to the monetary policy that had been conducted for over a decade made its way into the US Fed and, in particular, into its 2020 strategy review. In particular, dwindling societal support have focused monetary policymakers' minds on "the potential benefits of running an economy 'hot,' that is, allowing employment to rise beyond current estimates of its long-run sustainable level."[100] Importantly, the new strategy is not just aimed at boosting potential growth. The Fed's new strategy also seeks to bring about benefits in terms of a more equitable income distribution, specifically by favoring the inclusion in the labor force of the most disadvantaged groups in society.[101] For an institution that considered the job of monetary policy almost exclusively in terms of keeping inflation in check and seeking to keep output stable during the precrisis period, the 2020 strategy review can be seen as the culmination of quite a journey.

THE EUROPEAN CENTRAL BANK

Created only at the end of the 1990s, the European Central Bank (ECB) quickly rose to become one of the major world's central banks. The ECB's status closely reflects the size of the economy it serves. Indeed, the ECB presides over the price stability of the world's third-largest economy—namely, the economic area made up of twenty European Union countries that have adopted the euro as their currency.[1]

Similar to its US counterpart, the ECB has confronted unprecedented policy challenges since the global and sovereign debt crisis of 2008 to 2010 and the 2020 COVID-19 crisis. These events unleashed potent recessionary forces that damaged the euro area's macroeconomic and financial stability. Faced with these new economic circumstances, the ECB broke with orthodoxy and adopted unconventional measures to support financial markets, boost economic recovery, and shield the euro area from a full-fledged deflationary spiral. Akin to what the US Federal Reserve did, the ECB reacted to both the 2008 and 2020 crises by increasing liquidity and loosening monetary policy, including through the adoption of controversial quantitative easing programs. Nevertheless, similar to the US Fed, the ECB expanded its remit to include social goals by elevating the fight against climate change and making it one of its policy priorities.

Despite the ECB's policy responses ultimately matching those of its US counterpart, the dominant view is that the ECB was a slower and more reluctant responder than the Fed.[2] This peculiar pattern is largely attributed to the technocratic character of the institution. That is, the ECB's behavior reflects the dominance of neoliberal and ordoliberal ideas among European monetary authorities and the attendant policy prescription that emphasizes price stability over growth and employment.[3] These ideas have been embedded in the legal design of the ECB. In particular, and in contrast to the Fed's dual mandate, the ECB has a clear single mandate: the achievement of price stability. Seen from this ideas-based perspective, the ECB ultimately moved away from monetary orthodoxy only when new ideas came to the fore. This is, for instance, what is deemed to have happened by approximately 2012, when new ideas stressing the systemic nature of the eurozone crisis gained the upper hand in the ECB's internal debate, which led the institution to scale up its unconventional policy toolkit.[4]

While technocratic ideas are certainly an important variable in explaining economic and monetary policy choices, the account that follows nuances these well-established views. In particular, based on a close examination of a set of decisive policies that the ECB undertook during the 2008–2010 crisis and the 2020 crisis, this chapter shows that the ECB departed from orthodoxy by venturing into unconventional policies in anticipation of the acceptance of new ideas among ECB officials. Further, the ECB was able to adapt its policy toolkit when a permissive political space emerged—that is, when political support materialized to protect the institution from the backlash deriving from actions that challenged its established reputation. This happened under conditions that were not significantly dissimilar from those identified in chapter 4 on the US Fed. Specifically, the ECB adopted some the most resolute actions to respond to recessionary and disinflationary forces when it secured political support from fiscal authorities or in an attempt to restore its public image before an increasingly discontent public opinion.

The analysis that follows provides empirical evidence to support these arguments. Similar to what was presented in chapter 4, this analysis combines both primary and secondary sources to ascertain the motivations that guided ECB policymakers. These sources include the public speeches issued by the European policymakers involved in decision making, press reports, analyses, and excellent secondary accounts of the eurozone crisis and eurozone politics and policymaking in the period under examination.

Before the Storm

Compared to most central banks in high-income economies, the ECB is a fairly young institution.[5] In particular, with the introduction of the euro on January 1, 1999, eurozone member states not only introduced a common currency but also created a new institution—the ECB—to administer the currency.

Similar to the US Fed, the ECB has a federal committee decision-making structure. The ECB's Governing Council functions as the ECB's interest rate-setting committee. It consists of the six members of the Executive Board and the twenty governors of the national central banks (NCBs) of the countries that have adopted the euro.[6] The six Executive Board members, including the ECB president and the vice president, are appointed by the European Council.[7] The Executive Board prepares the Governing Council's meetings, manages the day-to-day business of the ECB, and instructs the NCBs on the implementation of agreed monetary policy decisions. Each central bank's governor is appointed by the respective national government and regularly participates in all Governing Council meetings and votes on its decisions.[8]

All Governing Council members are expected to make decisions from a euro area perspective. In other words, when they sit on the Governing Council, European monetary policymakers are required not to act as national representatives or to take instruction from any member state or European Union (EU) body. They are instead required to act in a fully independent, personal capacity. This provision is meant to safeguard the institution's independence, which is further reinforced by the peculiar features of the EU political system. In particular, the ECB is one of the most independent central banks in the world because its mandate is enshrined in the founding Treaty of the European Union. This means that the ECB's independence enjoys quasi-constitutional status since revisions to it require the demanding agreement of all European member states.[9]

In contrast to the Fed's dual mandate, the ECB has a clear prioritization of the macroeconomic goals that it is expected to pursue. Indeed, the ECB's primary objective is to achieve price stability. Within this mandate, the ECB is also tasked to contribute to "the achievement of the objectives of the Union," which include "full employment" and "balanced economic growth."[10] The narrow and clearly hierarchical remit assigned to the ECB reflects the political origins of the institution and, in particular, the German influence on the design of the central bank.[11] A wider mandate for the ECB was initially among the proposals on the table during the negotiations that led to the creation of the European Monetary Union (EMU).[12] However, the ECB was eventually molded from the German Bundesbank and its inflation-focused mandate.[13] Not only the legal foundations but also the operational practice of the ECB have been based on the German example. The heritage of the Bundesbank's experience as "an anchor of stability" has played a special role in developing the ECB's policy framework and strategy.[14] As a result, the traditional German aversion to inflation, which was shaped by the hyperinflation experienced during the Weimar Republic and after the end of World War II, was transferred to the ECB and became one the most important legacies for the development of its institutional identity—akin to what Paul Volcker's fight against the Great Inflation meant for the development of the US Fed.

The construction of a reputation focused on the prioritization of low and stable inflation has also been closely associated with the distinct challenges that the ECB confronted as a newly created central bank. Indeed, as a new institution, one of the first challenges the ECB confronted was proving its ability to control inflation, thereby securing public and political support. Projecting a distinct organizational image as an anti-inflation institution was pivotal in helping the central bank steer markets toward its intended goal. For instance, as the official retrospective on the ECB for its twentieth anniversary reads, "At the start, the ECB had to establish its credibility from scratch as a new and untested central bank, in a field of policymaking which places a premium on track records."[15]

A key strategy that the ECB has pursued to establish its credibility and reputation has been the development of a monetary strategy aimed at signaling the central banks' policy priorities. As the influential first ECB chief economist Otmar Issing clarified, given "the special circumstances the new central bank would be confronted with," European monetary policymakers "came to the conclusion that the ECB should . . . adopt a strategy of monetary targeting." One of the major arguments used to justify this strategy was that, by adopting I, it would have been possible to transfer "credibility and *reputation* to the new institution which had to start without a track record of its own."[16] In particular, although the ECB did not opt for a formal inflation-targeting monetary strategy, it nonetheless adopted "a stability-oriented monetary policy framework." This policy framework was directed at the achievement of low and stable inflation.[17] In 2003, inflation was operationalized as an annual increase in the harmonized index of consumer prices (HICP) of *below* but close to 2 percent over the medium term.[18]

The ECB's monetary framework also helped the ECB to project an impartial, technocratic image as a guardian of price stability. By clarifying and communicating to the public the 2 percent target for monetary policy, the ECB—similar to other central banks—did not simply try to increase the predictability and thus the effectiveness of its policy decisions by shaping markets' and the public's expectations. The ECB's policy framework was also instrumental in signaling that its decisions are guided by a clearly predefined policy objective and justified through the best economic knowledge available. As the top ECB officials who presided over the central bank's creation stated, "The adoption of a monetary policy strategy is an attempt to characterize to the best possible extent, given the imperfect knowledge of the economy, the way in which the central bank will respond to the arrival of information."[19] That is, the monetary policy strategy reduces the "judgment" of central bankers by projecting an image of technocratic neutrality. This public image reinforced the legal provision that formally prohibits the ECB from financing the debts of EMU member states, thereby keeping the central bank away from decisions with clearly distributive implications across national lines. Indeed, according to the Treaty on the Functioning of the European Union, the ECB is prohibited from monetary financing. Specifically, it is not allowed to provide "overdrafts or any other type of credit facilities" to public entities, nor can the ECB purchase "debt instruments" directly from these public entities.[20]

Similar to how the Great Moderation cemented the US Fed's reputation, the first decade after the creation of the euro solidified the ECB's reputation. While in the decade before the ECB's creation, the average inflation rate for the euro area periphery (including Greece, Ireland, Italy, Portugal, and Spain) was approximately 12 percent, this rate was reduced to an average of 3 percent from 1999 to 2007. Perhaps more importantly, variation in inflation rates fell dramatically. As a former ECB vice president reflected in hindsight, "Although the ECB, as a newly created central bank, did not have a previous track record of successful policymaking, financial markets immediately understood the ECB's commitment to price stability as credible and factored it in their expectations."[21] In light of these developments, the euro experiment and its ECB guardian appeared to be highly successful. Most periphery countries saw substantial economic growth and stability, and several experienced consumption and investment booms encouraged by easy and cheap access to finance. These dynamics were largely viewed as positive, as the periphery was converging with the generally wealthier euro area core. However, the financial period of exuberance also created vulnerability. Eventually, the knots came to a head.

The ECB in a Changed Context

Although the 2008 crisis originated in the US market, it was quickly transmitted to the other side of the Atlantic through the financial sector channel. Similar to what happened in the United States, cheap and abundant liquidity led to significant risk taking in Europe. In particular, in the run-up to the global financial crisis, European banks increased their lending activities outside their home markets and increased their leverage to excessive levels, thus becoming overly dependent on wholesale short-term financing.[22] As a result, when the crisis in the United States started recording sizable losses on subprime-related securities, the capital and profitability of European financial institutions did not escape the hard hit. Uncertainty about exposures and counterparty risk further depleted confidence among major banks, which led to severe disruptions in the interbank market. Banks largely responded by deleveraging from their investments, including cutting credit to households and firms. The deleveraging process negatively affected credit conditions, mainly because in Europe, in contrast to the United States, bank credit is the dominant source of funding.[23] This tightening of credit conditions, in turn, damaged consumer and business confidence, which pushed several EU countries into recession.

It was against this backdrop that the financial crisis intersected with the peculiar characteristics of the eurozone, leading to the emergence of the sovereign debt crisis. Indeed, just one year after the collapse of Lehman Brothers in 2008, market confidence was shaken by the revelation that the Greek budget deficit amounted to 12.5 percent of gross domestic product (GDP), more than twice the amount previously reported. This announcement triggered markets' nervousness and set in motion the chain of events that led to a decade of sluggish growth and sustained disinflationary forces. Indeed, following the revelations of the true state of its public finances, Greece's credit rating was downgraded, and the spread on Greek bonds soared to pre-EMU levels. More tellingly, financial pressures did not remain confined to Greece. Instead, the situation in Greece was a wake-up call for market participants, leading them to reassess country-level risks throughout the eurozone, especially in its periphery.[24] Financial flows came to a "sudden stop," further weakening banks' financial stability throughout the region.[25] Absent a supranational backstop, eurozone governments stepped in to prop up their domestic banking system using national resources, furthering the pernicious sovereign-bank loop between financial institutions and governments' debt.[26] Fiscal interventions to support domestic banks further spooked markets' nervousness as investors started questioning crisis-hit countries' ability to manage increasing budget deficits and high public debt levels. Eventually, the same existence of the monetary union came into question; markets grew increasingly skeptical about peripheral countries' ability to remain in the euro area, thereby driving up their yield spreads and triggering a strong demand for safe-haven German bonds. By 2012, the risk of a eurozone break-up was clearly on the table.[27]

Despite the distinctive characteristics of the monetary union, the challenges that the ECB confronted in the wake of the crisis were not dissimilar to those that its US counterpart was confronted with. Indeed, the crisis set in motion serious deflationary and recessionary forces that took a huge toll on economic activity. Unlike in the United States, though, a double-dip recession ensued. In particular, after a temporary recovery in 2010–2011, the euro area plunged back into negative growth in 2012. Unemployment climbed to over 12 percent and only started decreasing in early 2013.[28] These effects have been particularly prolonged. The 2008–2020 period was characterized by a relatively muted recovery and a long stretch of modest growth and low inflation.[29] In particular, a decade after the onset of the sovereign debt crisis and immediately before the COVID-19

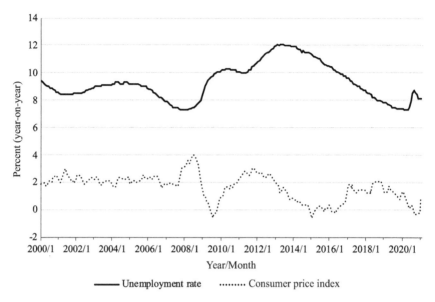

FIGURE 5.1.   Euro area unemployment rate and consumer price index, 2000–2020

Source: EUROSTAT

shock, the real GDP stagnated in the eurozone, especially in the eurozone periphery. The average annual growth in the 2010–2019 period was almost one percentage point below that the United States. Although in March 2020, the unemployment rate returned to that found in the precrisis period, the average unemployment rate from 2008 to 2020 hovered at approximately 10 percent. Furthermore, from January 2013 onward, inflation continued to be well below the ECB's target of 2 percent. In December 2014, the eurozone annual inflation rate fell into negative territory for the first time since the launch of the single currency. Deflationary pressures were not fully dispelled until the onset of post-COVID inflation (figure 5.1).

The COVID-19 crisis took place against this already weak macroeconomic scenario. On the backs of health-related restrictions and disruptions in supply chains and demand, eurozone economic activity contracted significantly. The real GDP fell by approximately 40 percent in the second quarter of 2020 (annualized quarter-over-quarter), while the annual contraction was approximately 6.5 percent, the largest decline since WWII.[30] As most members introduced strict lockdowns to slow down the spread of the virus, economies ground to a halt, and unemployment climbed back to over 8.5 percent.[31] Inflation remained subdued until 2021, before starting to rise again on the back of rising energy prices associated with Russia's war against Ukraine in 2022.

Similar to what happened in the United States, the ECB was naturally positioned to be a primary actor in managing the 2008–2010 and 2020 crises and their recessionary and deflationary aftermath. Similar to what the Fed did, the ECB reacted to the new economic challenges by adopting policies for repairing the financial sector and supporting economic activity. Without attempting to be exhaustive, the ECB's interventions focused on increasing liquidity for the European financial sector by lowering the funding costs for banks, extending maturities of the refinancing operations, and expanding the list of eligible collateral and counterparties in liquidity operations, among other measures.[32] Measures supporting the private sector largely concentrated on boosting bank lending because in Europe (as compared to the United States), debt financing is more dominant than equity.[33] Nevertheless, similar to what the Fed did, the ECB provided a backstop to specific market sectors to prevent these markets from seizing up with attendant recessionary and deflationary effects. For instance, the eligibility criteria of the Corporate Sector Purchase Program (CSPP), which was started as part of the 2016 round of quantitative easing (QE), were expanded as a pandemic response. The ECB also devised unprecedented policies to support economic activity and revive inflation. In particular, similar to what the Fed did, the ECB adopted a series of programs involving the purchase of private and public securities. Notably, in the wake of the COVID crisis, the ECB significantly expanded the financial envelope for the purchases of EMU countries' government debt.[34]

Similar to the unconventional policies that the US central bank adopted, the policies that the ECB designed have been carefully scrutinized, especially to ascertain their impact. While a definitive verdict remains out of reach, the general consensus view is that the ECB's break away from orthodoxy has been much bumpier and uncertain than the analogous trajectory in the United States. In what follows, I reconstruct such a trajectory by shedding light on the factors that constrained and enabled the central bank along its journey.

The ECB's Journey Away from Orthodoxy

Similar to what has already been noted regarding the US Fed, reconstructing a decade-long decision-making process inevitably entails a degree of subjective judgment of what policy decisions to focus on. This is especially the case because, over the time period under investigation, the ECB made a variety of policy decisions that targeted different problems and adjusted initial decisions to changed economic and financial circumstances. To avoid losing sight of the overall developmental dynamics that the ECB has gone through, the following section focuses on three sets of policy decisions that are representative of ECB's broad departure from monetary orthodoxy. These policies are the expansion of liquidity support, the provision of monetary accommodation through quantitative easing, and the revision of the monetary strategy.

Rescuing the Banking Sector

The ECB was the first of the world's major central banks to react to the signs of stress in the interbank market at the beginning of the crisis period analyzed herein. As early as August 2007, on the day that the French bank BNP Paribas suspended three of its funds because of exposure to the US subprime mortgage market, the ECB opened the tap on overnight lending. Since then, the ECB has repeatedly offered banks long-term funding at attractive conditions as a way to ease financing conditions for banks and stimulate lending to the real economy; this is what came to be known as longer-term refinancing operations (LTROs).[35]

The early and extended liquidity support that the ECB put in place both in 2008 and 2020 is usually regarded as the hallmark measure that the ECB took to stabilize the financial system and mitigate the impact of financial stress on economic activity. The ECB's focus on liquidity support, in turn, reflects the peculiar features of the European financial system compared to that of the United States. These features include the centrality of bank lending to the provision of credit to European households and firms, as well as the central role that banks play in the transmission of monetary policy in the euro area. In short, the ECB's attention to liquidity support throughout the crisis period largely reflects the structural features of the European financial system with its greater reliance on bank-based intermediation as compared to the financial system in the United States.[36]

Although liquidity operations have been the pillar of the ECB's responses to the crises and their aftermath, observers disagree on their effectiveness, especially in the early stages of the crisis period. For instance, while some scholars maintain that the ECB's nonstandard liquidity operations managed to interrupt disruptive deleveraging processes, others have noted that the positive impact of cheaper liquidity on demand and economic activity was very limited for euro members with more fragile banking systems. The latter finding is problematic, as it implies that the hardest hit (periphery) economies benefited the least.[37] The impact of liquidity measures on equity prices also appears to have been negligible.[38] Other scholars also have argued that, especially from 2008 to 2010, the ECB's liquidity encouraged European banks to engage in a perilous "carry trade," especially in the eurozone periphery. That is, banks used the ECB's liquidity mainly to buy their own government bonds, ultimately exposing themselves to increasing sovereign debt risks.[39] In a retrospective of the ECB's history, even internal officials acknowledged that the ECB's liquidity interventions did not sufficiently counteract the recessionary and deflationary forces that were unleashed by the market stresses in 2008 and 2010. In particular, the retrospective finds that the potency of longer-term refinancing operations to support economic activity and inflation might have been greater had the ECB designed its LTROs in a way that exploited the complementarity between the provision of liquidity and monetary policy—that is, by signaling the intention to maintain policy rates at very low levels for the entire life of the liquidity facilities.[40]

What explains the ECB's failure to take advantage of such complementarities and provide a more convincing response to recessionary and deflationary forces? A number of economic factors have certainly contributed to undermining the impact of the ECB's liquidity operations, including the weak demand throughout the eurozone.[41] However, a thorough explanation of the design of liquidity operations also needs to take into consideration the broader reputational constraints that the ECB had to navigate. Indeed, in designing its liquidity support, the ECB was extremely careful not to discard its organizational image as an anti-inflation and politically neutral institution. This is evident in the two key design features that marked the ECB's liquidity measures: the separation principle and the passive approach to liquidity.

The separation principle refers to the ECB's declared commitment not to mix the central bank's policies for repairing financial markets and ensuring liquidity with the policies aimed at influencing economic activity and inflation. That is, the ECB clearly established that it has a standard policy tool (i.e., the interest rate) that represents the ECB's monetary stance, and it has nonstandard policy tools that are strictly aimed at repairing the financial system and the monetary policy transmission mechanism. This principle was further reinforced by the passive approach to liquidity injections, which entails the central bank simply accommodating the increased liquidity demands of financial institutions and markets rather than actively easing financing conditions.

Both the separation and passive approach principles served an important political function from the ECB's perspective. Specifically, they helped preserve the central bank's reputation as an unrepentant inflation fighter. ECB insiders have explained the logic behind the design of the ECB liquidity programs as follows: "By separating rate policy from liquidity management, the message implicit in the 'separation' doctrine was that rates could always be raised *to tame inflation*, while extraordinary liquidity conditions could be maintained to safeguard financial stability."[42]

By reiterating the ECB's commitment to rein in inflation, even in the midst of strong deflationary pressures, the separation and the passive approach principles thus offered the ECB a policy fix for preserving its reputation as an institution primarily devoted to achieving low inflation. As a group of high-level officials have candidly explained, this operational design was instrumental in "deflecting insistent public criticism that the ECB's nonstandard measures would soon [have led] to runaway inflation."[43] In other words, the design QE the liquidity measures was instrumental in protecting the ECB's reputation from criticisms, including those leveled by ECB officials and those outside the central bank.[44]

In short, the reputation the ECB had invested in building since its creation interfered with the ECB's responses to financial market stress and attendant disinflationary forces. In particular, even if it were in a changed economic context, ECB officials were aware of the risks that massive liquidity operations posed to the ECB's organizational image as an inflation-averse, apolitical institution. Thus, in the attempt to protect its reputation, the ECB has often resorted to policy fixes when designing its unconventional liquidity policies, even if doing so means undermining the stimulative potential of the central bank's response in the midst of deflationary and recessionary forces.

Loosening the Purse Strings

Compared to the US Fed, the ECB was a latecomer in the purchases of public securities. The first ECB asset purchase program of this kind was the Securities Market Program (SMP). Introduced in 2010 following the growing tension in peripheral eurozone sovereign debt markets, the program consisted of targeted purchases of eurozone public and private bonds in the secondary markets. The SMP was replaced by the Outright Monetary Transactions (OMT) program in 2012, which developed from ECB President Mario Draghi's pledge to do "whatever it takes" to save the euro.[45] Building on these two initial programs, the ECB has since then designed new asset purchase programs to provide further accommodation to the euro area economy. They include the asset purchase program adopted in 2014, which had four parts, and by far the largest, the public-sector purchase program started in 2015.[46] In the wake of the COVID-19 crisis, the ECB also launched the Pandemic Emergency Purchase Program (PEPP), which, albeit temporary, took the ECB a further step away from monetary orthodoxy by increasing its flexibility to purchase government securities.[47] In particular, with the PEPP, the ECB expanded the scope of its monetary policy mandate by taking an overt responsibility to prevent market fragmentation in the euro area.

Similar to its US counterpart, the ECB adopted a QE program that was far from straightforward, as attested by the unusual and bitter political divisions present among European monetary policymakers. The decision making that led to the adoption of the first asset purchase program—the SMP—is emblematic of the tensions within the ECB's Governing Council. Indeed, the institution has frequently signaled that it makes decisions in a collegial manner and is keen on shedding internal disagreement to outside audiences.[48] Yet, in an unprecedented episode, several Governing Council members went public against the proposed asset purchase scheme. In particular, several Governing Council members, especially those from euro area creditor states, opposed the program because of its alleged implications for the ECB's reputation as an inflation-averse, technocratic institution. For instance, German monetary policymakers Axel Weber and Jürgen Stark opposed the SMP because the program was ultimately akin to "printing money" and would have thus stoked inflation throughout the eurozone.[49] This concern was shared among other ECB policymakers, and criticisms started to emerge from countries such as Austria and the Netherlands.[50] In addition to inflation concerns, opposition to the SMP also stemmed from concerns about the ECB's alleged political neutrality. Indeed, one of the major concerns of policymakers in Frankfurt was that the SMP risked blurring the responsibilities between fiscal and monetary policy.[51] That is, by lowering funding costs for domestic governments, especially for those under more intense market stress, the ECB risked making decisions that had redistributive implications along national lines. In short, the decision making surrounding the ECB's purchase programs was not just colored by technical considerations on how to provide monetary accommodation and for how long. From the ECB's perspective, what was at stake was basically "the core of the central bank's identity."[52]

The importance that the ECB attached to institutional reputation was translated into the great care that ECB officials devoted to distancing European quantitative easing from the type of QE conducted by other major central banks. As Jean-Claude Trichet, the former ECB president, repeatedly emphasized, for instance, the SMP "should not be confused with quantitative easing. In simple words, we are not printing money. This confirms and underpins our commitment to price stability."[53] To further stress the ECB's continuing adherence to its past reputation, the ECB also took great care in designing its QE programs to minimize the deviation from well-established monetary practices. For instance, both the SMP and the OMT program limit the scope of the ECB's interventions in terms of the market in which the central bank intervenes (i.e., the secondary market) and the types of assets that the central bank can purchase (i.e., short-term government bond yields with a maturity between one and three years for the OMT program).[54] In doing so, the central bank meant signaling its political neutrality by steering away from financing governments' needs in primary markets.

Although designed with "caveats" meant to signal the ECB's continued adherence to its past reputation, the adoption of asset purchase programs is still a puzzle in its own right. In particular, given the technical uncertainties surrounding the consequences of these programs and the extent of the internal opposition, a different outcome was to be expected. That is, the ECB might have well decided not to start asset purchase programs or to not expand them over time. The adoption of the SMP and OMT thus requires further attention. In particular, attention is needed regarding the conditions that allowed the ECB to act and thus overcome the reputational limits on monetary accommodation.

In general, explanations for the ECB's adoption of asset purchase programs emphasize the ideational changes and learning dynamics that have taken place among ECB officials since the start of the global financial crisis.[55] The argument here is that the ECB gradually moved away from an interpretation of the crisis that emphasized member states' budgetary laxity (and thus prescribed fiscal austerity as an effective policy strategy to cope with the crisis) to an interpretation that stressed the systemic nature of the crisis (and thus justified the ECB's intervention in sovereign bond markets as the most appropriate measures by which to address financial fragility in the euro area).[56] The ideational changes that supported the ECB's step into quantitative easing were also facilitated by leadership changes within the institution.[57] At the end of October 2011, Jean-Claude Trichet handed over the ECB's presidency to Mario Draghi. At around the same time, the composition of the ECB's Executive Board changed; Peter Praet took over the key role of chief economist following Jürgen Stark's resignation, and, as of March 1, 2012, Benoit Coeuré became the Executive Board member in charge of the market operations department.

Although ideational and leadership changes are certainly important factors when accounting for the evolution of the ECB's policy stance over time and especially from 2012 onward, the same explanation sits much more uncomfortably in explaining why the ECB started its balance sheet policy already in 2010—that is, at a time when policy ideas against this measure prevailed. Explaining the ECB's monetary accommodation thereby requires identifying the factors that allowed the ECB to overcome its ideational limits and thus to act, even before ideational innovation or learning materialized. These factors are to be found in the political context in which the ECB operated. In particular, excellent analyses on eurozone crisis policymaking, as well as the timing of policy adoption, suggest that the ECB's monetary accommodation was conditional on the actions taken by eurozone fiscal policymakers.[58] Specifically, the creation of the European Financial Stability Facility (EFSF), which was the temporary stabilization fund that eurozone governments agreed to on May 9, 2010, was a precondition for the ECB's decision to venture into QE terrain because it offered the central bank a political cover with which to protect its past reputation.[59]

From the ECB's perspective, the EFSF was indeed instrumental in minimizing the risk of reputation tarnishing that would have emerged following the launch of the SMP in at least two major respects. First, since the EFSF was assigned the responsibility of providing financial assistance to eurozone states through the issuance of bonds and other debt instruments, the ECB's interventions in sovereign debt markets could be presented as limited in scope and time. In other words, with the EFSF in place, "an eventual commitment of the ECB to buy bonds would not be bottomless and with time was likely to be superseded by the stabilization mechanism itself."[60] Second, the EFSF provided the ECB with the opportunity to downplay the distributive implications of its interventions in government bond markets. Indeed, the financial support provided through the EFSF was conditional on the adoption of a macroeconomic adjustment program that would have dealt with potential fiscal problems in the recipient state. In other words, the EFSF offered the ECB a political cover with which to frame its bond-buying interventions as temporary and limited in their fiscal consequences, thereby protecting the inflation-averse, politically neutral image of the ECB. Given the importance of euro area government interventions to the ECB, it is probably not surprising that the ECB was particularly active in pushing governments to act. For instance, it is a well-established fact that ECB President Jean-Claude Trichet forcefully asked euro area governments to step up their efforts to develop a stabilization fund to support crisis-stricken member countries as the precondition for the ECB to intervene in the sovereign debt markets. The ECB even waited for the agreement about the ESFS to be made among euro area countries before it publicly announced the SMP.[61]

The importance of euro area governments' policy actions for ECB bond purchases can also be ascertained in the decision-making process that led the ECB to resume SMP purchases in 2011. For instance, the ECB president stressed that a "fundamental" factor leading to the new purchases was that eurozone "governments [stood] ready to activate the European Financial Stability Facility" and had expanded the facility's ability to allow it "to purchase in the secondary market."[62] Governments' fiscal actions were equally important to the ECB's bond-buying decisions. For instance, the September 2011 *Monthly Bulletin* explained the rationale that led the ECB to further intervene in sovereign debt markets in order to counter both financial distress and its adverse disinflationary consequences: "In taking the decision to resume its interventions under the SMP, the Governing Council took note—among other things—of Italy's and Spain's announcements concerning measures and reforms to be adopted in the areas of fiscal and structural policies, as well as euro-area governments' commitment to meeting their fiscal targets."[63] In short, "SMP purchases were . . . premised on collective action on the part of eurozone governments."[64]

It is important to stress that eurozone government decisions—both in terms of fixing the institutional architecture of the EMU and adopting fiscal discipline—were also profoundly shaped by interactions with the ECB. Indeed, and controversially, the ECB repeatedly asked member states to reaffirm their commitment to fiscal discipline and structural reforms as the strategy with which to respond to the crisis, implicitly subordinating the ECB's monetary support to such commitments. One of the most well-known and debatable attempts the ECB made to solicit government actions was the confidential correspondence the ECB sent to the Italian and Spanish prime ministers, whose countries where experiencing rising bond yields in 2011.[65] The pressures that the ECB exerted on member governments have been rightly criticized. In particular, serious questions have been raised about the bases on which an independent central bank can impose its will on elected governments and about whether the ECB's power has grown unchecked.[66] In addition to these important democratic considerations, what these episodes reveal is the connection between the ECB's monetary accommodation and euro area government decisions. That is, the expansion of monetary accommodation through bond purchases was ultimately conditional on the institutional and economic policy decisions agreed on by euro area governments. These decisions were critical for the ECB to mitigate the reputational risks that bond purchases entailed for the central banks and were thus a necessary factor for the ECB to provide such accommodation.

The importance of political support from eurozone governments for the ECB to adopt further monetary accommodation is also evident in the adoption of the OMT in 2012.[67] In particular, the actions taken by eurozone countries were pivotal for the ECB to accept the potential risks to its inflation-averse, technocratic reputation that would have stemmed from its new bond purchases. Similar to what had happened with the adoption of the SMP following the creation of the EFSF, the creation of the European Stability Mechanism (ESM) by eurozone governments in 2012 provided the ECB with the precondition to adopt the OMT. Specifically, the ESM offered the ECB political *cover* with which to justify the adoption of a policy that openly clashed with the institutional image that the ECB had been projecting. Indeed, the ESM was created to serve as the euro area's permanent stabilization fund and thus tasked with the responsibility of providing financial assistance to member states under strict macroeconomic conditionality.[68] The ESM institutional features were particularly important for the ECB's decision to provide further accommodation. In particular, by working alongside the ESM, the ECB could present its balance sheet interventions as both temporary (as the ESM would have ultimately taken the lead in supporting crisis-stricken countries) and politically neutral (as the distributional implications of ECB purchases would have been neutralized by the governments' fiscal commitments under the ESM conditionality framework). Indeed, OMT interventions were subordinated to the activation of an ESM program through which member countries would have committed to profound fiscal and structural reforms. As a group of ECB officials acknowledged regarding the relationship between the OMT and eurozone governments' decision to create the ESM, "the OMTs could not have happened, however, without . . . the possibility, created by the prior efforts of President Trichet, to foster the birth of the ESM and develop it into an institution that could partner the central bank in an extreme emergency."[69]

Rebalancing and Greening the Monetary Strategy

By the time the COVID-19 crisis started in early 2020, the ECB had certainly come a long way from the institution that confronted the global and sovereign debt crisis in 2008 and 2010. In particular, the actions that the ECB had taken to respond to the crises and the deflationary aftermath had led the ECB away from monetary orthodoxy. Indeed, despite the ECB's attempts to defend its past reputation and thus its past policy practices, the central bank had ultimately diluted its overarching low inflation objective by accepting responsibility for financial stability and even for the survival of the euro area. Furthermore, similar to other central banks in the group of high-income countries, the ECB had de facto accepted to expand the tools of monetary policy well beyond the use of interest rates. Interestingly, however, similar to the US Fed (chapter 4), the ECB's institutional transformation was made official (and one might add even enhanced) by the announcement of a new monetary policy strategy in July 2021. Indeed, the new policy strategy brought about three major transformations in the developmental trajectory of the ECB: it reinterpreted the ECB's low inflation objective in a more symmetrical manner, it ratified the expansion of the ECB's monetary policy toolkit, and it further expanded the remit of monetary policy to include the fight to climate change.[70]

First, the new strategy review revised the previous policy target of inflation "below but close to two percent" over the medium term.[71] As the 2021 policy statement reads, "The Governing Council considers that price stability is best maintained by aiming for two percent inflation over the medium term."[72] That is, the ECB came to endorse the view that both overshoots and *undershoots* of the inflation target are equally undesirable outcomes, thereby rebalancing the price stability objective. In other words, whereas before 2021, the ECB monetary policy playbook had basically emphasized the risks of deviations above the 2 percent target, the price stability objective in 2021 was meant to restore symmetry in the way in which the ECB should respond to both upward and downward price risks. Similar to what had been noted for the Fed's 2020 monetary strategy (chapter 4), a key implication of the new ECB policy strategy rested on the acceptance of a sort of "high pressure" economy—that is, the explicit acceptance that combating deflationary forces might "imply a transitory period in which inflation is moderately above target."[73] Similar to the US Fed, this conclusion suggests the presence of a growing weight attached to employment and growth compared to the inflation objective. Indeed, although price stability remained the major objective pursued by the ECB, as mandated by the EU Treaty, the ECB's new strategy signaled growing concerns about the risks of premature tightening, especially in the presence of supply disturbances, which may dampen employment and growth. As the ECB itself explains regarding the logic of the new policy strategy: "In the presence of an adverse supply shock, the Governing Council may decide to lengthen the horizon over which inflation returns to the target level in order to avoid pronounced falls in economic activity and employment, which, if persistent, could themselves jeopardise medium-term price stability."[74]

Second, the new monetary strategy "normalized" the expanded policy toolkit that had emerged from a decade of fighting financial crisis and deflation. In particular, the strategy review reiterated that interest rate policy should still be considered the primary monetary policy with which the central bank should respond to economic challenges. However, the new policy statement also concluded that "in recognition of the effective lower bound on policy rates, the Governing Council will also employ in particular forward guidance, asset purchases and longer-term refinancing operations, as appropriate."[75] In other words, the review made it official that the ECB can use a number of policy tools, including asset purchases, to supplement the interest rate policy. The 2021 strategy also left the door open to new policy tools in the future by invoking the use of 'flexibility' to respond to new economic challenges.

Finally, the new policy strategy marked a significant expansion in the scope of monetary policy, especially for an institution such as the ECB that had long conceived of monetary policy strictly in terms of price stability. In particular, the 2021 policy statement expanded the ECB's monetary policy responsibility to include the fight against climate change.[76] As the new policy statement reads, "Within its mandate, the Governing Council is committed to ensuring that the Eurosystem fully takes into account, in line with the EU's climate goals and objectives, the implications of climate change and the carbon transition for monetary policy and central banking."[77] This statement has not been confined to a declaration of principles. Concomitant with the adoption of the 2021 new policy strategy, the ECB's Governing Council has also committed to an ambitious climate-related action plan accompanied by the publication of a roadmap of climate-related actions.[78] These actions range from the incorporation of climate factors in the ECB's formal monetary policy assessments to the introduction of disclosure requirements for private-sector assets as a requirement for eligibility as collateral and asset purchases.

In short, the 2021 strategy review did not simply ratify the changes that had taken place in the operational conduct of monetary policy. Rather, it also deepened the institutional transformation of the ECB by reconsidering its price stability objective and expanding this objective to include climate considerations. How can we make sense of this further step away from the precrisis period monetary orthodoxy?

Similar to the US Fed, an immediate—but partial answer—to this question can be found in the economic conditions that the ECB, similar to other central banks, had been confronted with. That is, the ECB started its strategy review process to tackle the problems posed by the post-2010 deflationary context, including the inability of the ECB to bring inflation back to target.[79] Indeed, inflation had been persistently low—and below the ECB's inflation 2 percent target—since 2013.

Although the economic conditions that the ECB had been confronting are certainly important in explaining the decision to start the strategy review, the political and social conditions that the ECB had been confronted with are also particularly relevant in explaining its outcome. In particular, the strategy review can also be read in light of the politicization of the ECB and thus as a way for it to win back popular support and even legitimacy.[80] Indeed, since the start of the crisis period, the ECB has been the target of intense contestation, especially from the northern euro area countries. A striking example of the new (hostile) political context in which the ECB must operate is its legal battle with the German constitutional court in a case brought by the German economists and supported by the Bundesbank. German public and political elites had traditionally supported the independence of the ECB since its creation.[81] However, the constitutional court ruled in May 2020 that the ECB had acted beyond its competences with respect to the bond-buying program. Although the court in Karlsruhe ultimately backtracked, this episode speaks to the weakening of political and social support for the ECB.[82] Importantly, contestation of the ECB did not remain confined to political elites but spilled over to civil society, too. The ECB had been the main target of mass protests in Frankfurt that largely overlap with those promoted against the embrace of fiscal austerity in the EU as a remedy to the crisis.[83] The ECB has also been the target of green group activists, who shed light on how monetary policy helps fund fossil fuel companies.[84] Furthermore, public attitudes toward the ECB changed dramatically. As figure 5.2 shows, between 2008 and 2014, EU citizens' trust in the ECB plummeted. This result is particularly stunning, especially compared to EU citizens' steadier trust in the euro, of which the ECB is the guardian.[85]

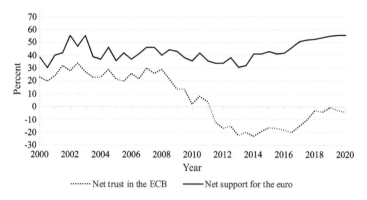

FIGURE 5.2. Public trust in the ECB and support for the euro, 2000–2020

Source: Eurobarometer. Net support for the euro is calculated as the share answering "for" minus the share answering "against" to the question: "Please tell me whether you are for or against it: A European economic and monetary union with one single currency, the euro."

The change in public support has been a crucial concern for ECB officials. For instance, the results of a 2020 survey of former members of the Governing Council showed that ECB officials regard "trust" as the most important objective of central bank communication, along with "credibility." Importantly, the responses pointed to the need to improve communication with and thus trust by the general public.[86] Furthermore, the ECB has dedicated an increased amount of attention to issues related to trust in its internal publication series.[87] An analysis of the content of these publications suggests that the ECB acknowledges the challenges posed by the rising level of public distrust to the effectiveness of both monetary and institutional independence.[88] As extensively discussed in chapter 1, maintaining public trust is important to all central banks. This is particularly true for a central bank in a multinational polity made up of different publics like the ECB is. It is therefore not surprising that the increased contestation of the ECB has been accompanied by a number of transformations in the communicative practices through which the ECB engages with the public and provides information about its activities and decisions. For instance, in January 2015, the ECB started publishing accounts of its internal deliberations, which was a notable shift for an institution that has consistently justified its accountability through the achievement of the price stability objective rather than through disclosure to the public.[89] The ECB has also started the practice of appearing before a number of national parliaments to engage in communication about the concerns of elected policymakers, to increase the frequency and scope of communication with the European Parliament, and to engage with European citizens through a social media presence and listening events.[90]

The influence of public contestation on ECB activities can be similarly extended to explain the 2021 strategy review. Indeed, a key declared objective of the new policy strategy was to increase the level of public *trust* in the central bank. As the ECB chief economist explained regarding the dual objectives of the ECB's revised strategy, "First, it provides policymakers with a coherent analytical framework that maps actual or expected economic developments into policy decisions; and, second, it serves as a tool for communicating with the public."[91] In particular, the ECB aimed at making "it easier for the ECB to be held accountable and for it to build trust among the general public."[92] In other words, building (or recovering) public trust came to be regarded as important to the ECB as clarifying the objectives, tools, and analytical framework of its policy decisions. The official policy statement on the new monetary strategy spells out this logic clearly: communicating about the new policy strategy is "essential for ensuring public understanding of and trust in the actions of the ECB."[93]

That the ECB felt compelled to respond to the changes in its political and social environment to build back public support can further be gleaned in the policy process that led to the 2021 strategy announcement. Similar to that of the US Fed, the review period of the ECB was characterized by a series of public events through which the central bank reached out to EU citizens and civil society organizations to collect their views on the priorities that it should pursue.[94] Interestingly, the necessity for the ECB to become involved in climate change emerged from these meetings, despite disagreement among ECB officials about the central banks' involvement in greening the economy.[95] As the ECB summarized the findings of its outreach events, "the costs of climate change and possible future economic and financial crises were mentioned prominently across all listening channels," along with concerns about the long-term impact of the coronavirus pandemic on the economy and the effects of digitalization on employment.[96] The ECB further noted that "nongovernmental organizations, climate change organizations, consumer protection groups, youth representatives, think tanks and members of the public called on the ECB to better address wider societal and economic issues, such as promoting economic growth and employment and protecting the environment."[97]

In short, the 2021 strategy review marked the culmination of a long process of policy and institutional transformations for the ECB. At the beginning of the process, the ECB resisted some of the most transformative policies, mostly because of adherence to its past reputation as a conservative and politically neutral institution. Such resistance could be overcome either by hiding behind policy "caveats" or by relying on the political cover offered by government actions to stabilize the eurozone. Even if cautious and cloaked behind the veil of its reputational mantle, the actions taken to respond to the crises and their aftermath did not prevent the ECB from becoming a target of political and public criticism. Faced with such a pressing threat from its political and social environment, the ECB felt compelled to build back political support by signaling that more attention would be given to growth and employment and even to social goals such as the protection of the environment.

THE LONG JOURNEY OF CENTRAL BANKS

I began this lecture by referring to the victory over inflation under Fed chairs Volcker and Greenspan, an experience that promoted the view among central bankers that lower inflation is always better. We have come almost full circle: in a world in which low nominal neutral rates threaten the capacity of central banks to respond to recessions, too-low inflation can be dangerous. Consistent with their declared "symmetric" inflation targets, the Federal Reserve and other central banks should defend against inflation that is too low as least as vigorously as they resist inflation that is too high.

—Bernanke 2020, 47

We have come full circle indeed. For over four decades, domestic societies, especially in high-income countries, have been mostly preoccupied with inflation. The Great Inflation that started in the 1960s and deepened in the 1970s caused significant and long-lasting damage in many countries. As inflation rose, economic growth stagnated, and unemployment soared across the board. The process of taming inflation was not straightforward and often marked by renewed inflationary virulence. The experience of fighting inflation has been so central to economic theory and policy that it is widely recognized as "the defining macroeconomic event of the second half of the twentieth century."[1] In particular, the success in controlling inflation, heralded by the Volcker Fed in the early 1980s, marked the rise of a distinct monetary—and broadly macroeconomic—regime. Under the new regime, low inflation was elevated as the primary macroeconomic goal for domestic societies to pursue, and independent central banks were empowered to achieve that goal via the use of interest rate technology. A narrow mandate centered on price stability and a strict separation of responsibilities between monetary and fiscal policy, became the orthodox way to think of central banks in domestic societies.

Then, the world simply changed. Akin to the momentous shift that ended the Great Inflation, the aftermath of the 2008 and 2020 crises ushered in the Great Recession and the Great Lockdown, respectively. Deflation thus supplanted inflation as the major economic problem that domestic societies had to confront.

By the end of 2020, for instance, inflation was well below the widely used 2 percent target in all high-income countries, and even in emerging market economies, inflation expectations were at a relatively low level compared with historical averages.[2]

Not only did external circumstances change. The guardians of the old macroeconomic regime changed as well. Central banks moved away from orthodoxy by expanding both the goals and tools of monetary policy. To fight recessionary and deflationary forces, central banks have indeed stepped into policy terrain—including financial stability, social inequality, and even climate change—that would have been simply an anathema to any casual central banking observers well into the beginning of the 2000s. The transformation of monetary policy has also brought about a profound change in the relationship with domestic governments. The large-scale purchase of government bonds under the various quantitative easing programs has indeed challenged the central banks' mantra against any form of fiscal dominance.[3] For institutions that like to think of themselves as "boring" and predictable,[4] the first two decades of the twenty-first century have been quite an adventurous journey.

This book offers a closer look at this journey. In particular, the book aimed at explaining the puzzling evolution of some of the most powerful institutions in domestic societies and of the macroeconomic regime built upon them. Although it might be tempting to read the transformation in central banking as almost inevitable in hindsight, given the extent of the economic and social challenges that policymakers confronted in the wake of the 2008 and 2020 crises, it is worth reminding that the same transformation was hardly predictable when the crises started, especially in light of the uncertainty and informational problems that bedeviled monetary policymaking at the zero lower bound. In other words, there was nothing automatic in the evolutionary trajectory of central banks analyzed herein or in the cross-country embrace of unconventional policies and social goals ranging from inequality to climate change. The book thus started off with the assumption that a different trajectory might have been possible; it also showed that, at different points in time, central banks had a choice in deciding the direction to go. The key issue is thus to shed light on the question of what drove their decisions and ultimately the transformation in central banking and in the macroeconomic regime it had underpinned for a long time.

To answer this question, this book advances a distinct interpretation that challenges the conventional view of central banks as technocratic actors. The conventional view looks at central banks as instances of independent and expert-based institutions. Independence from political pressures, as enshrined in legal provisions, and expertise, as ensured by the professionalization of central banks' staff, are indeed usually regarded as the most important resources that central banks command and use to legitimize their power over domestic economies. Building on this view, the scholarship that has examined central banks' evolution has come to interpret change as a basically technocratic affair. As extensively discussed in previous chapters, the standard narrative is basically as follows: central banks have adapted to changed economic circumstances because their independence provided them with the institutional capacity to act (as the "only game in town" narrative has it) or because the embrace of new economic ideas and learning among monetary experts motivated the adoption of unconventional policies (as the "ideational" narrative posits).

This book has challenged this technocratic argument. In particular, the book has suggested an alternative way of thinking about central banks. That is, central banks are ultimately instances of public institutions, and like all institutions in domestic societies, they need political support to justify their powers and secure their same existence—independence and expertise, notwithstanding. From this perspective, one of the most important resources that central banks command is their reputation. It is through their reputation that central banks reach out to their heterogeneous audiences, which span from financial markets to governments, and try to shore up and maintain political support for their role and activities. Maintaining reputation and thus political support, however, is far from being straightforward. It requires active management, especially in the face of changed external circumstances. In particular, it requires two simultaneous actions: sticking to the script that established reputation prescribes, on the one hand, and responding to present circumstances, on the other. While these two actions can be compatible, they can also conflict when present circumstances require policy responses that are not aligned with past reputation. This is what happened to central banks as their reputation was challenged by the emergence of a deflationary context. From this perspective, the transformation in central banking has been less technocratic than standard accounts concede. Central banks deviated from orthodox monetary theory and practice as a strategic attempt to protect reputation under changed circumstances. Reputation protection led them to move away from well-established monetary practices only when political support for deviations was in place (i.e., when governments supported the central banks' unconventional actions) or when support was waning (as evidenced in public backlash), thereby requiring new policies to win back that support.

The book, however, does not solely look at the past. Instead, the legacy of central banks' past policy records is crucial to understanding how they will respond to future challenges. Among these challenges, the return of inflationary pressures in the wake of the post-COVID recovery in 2021 and the war of Russia against Ukraine in 2022 stand out. Specifically, after having struggled with policies aimed at sustaining prices and economic activity for over a decade, central banks have found themselves to grapple with the old challenge of pushing prices down and of avoiding a recession at the same time. Indeed, with inflation reaching levels not seen since the 1970s, the ghost of the Great Inflation has reappeared, and historical comparisons with the stagflation era have abounded. The threat that post-2021's central banks confront might be far from a repeat of the 1970s, given the factors that are driving inflation—namely, a supply-side shock associated with high energy prices and disrupted global supply chains after the pandemic.[5] Today's political context is also profoundly different from that of the 1970s, following decades of labor market reforms that have weakened trade unions and the prospect of an across-the-board wage-price spiral.[6] Despite these differences, central banks have firmly risen to the front seat of economic policymaking and cannot escape the blame or praise for how inflation will evolve, similar to what happened in the 1970s and 1980s. Hence, a serious analysis of the response to the post-2021 inflationary problem must start with an analysis of the recent past and the journey that led central banks here.

Before discussing the future of central banks and of the macroeconomic regime at large, this concluding chapter starts with the findings of the empirical analysis developed in the preceding chapters and connects them to policy and scholarly debate on the role of central banks in domestic societies. In particular, two major findings emerged from the preceding empirical analysis.

First, the book shows the limits that central banks confronted in fighting deflationary forces throughout the crisis period—notwithstanding Bernanke's quote, as stated at the beginning of this chapter, according to which central banks can fight inflation that is too low "as vigorously as they resist inflation that is too high" (Bernanke 2020, 47). As shown in preceding chapters, central banks' fight against deflation was often hindered by their need to preserve their past reputation and not elicit a political backlash that might have endandered support for their power and independence in domestic societies. Shedding light on the limitations that central banks have been confronted with since 2008 calls for reflecting on the institutional setup of contemporary macroeconomic policymaking and, in particular, on the allocation of responsibility among economic decision makers. Specifically, recognizing the limitations that central banks are confronted with invites one to think about greater cooperation between monetary and fiscal authorities. This cooperation is needed not only to confront future deflation but also to address other policy challenges, including challenges related to inflation management and the green transition.

Second, the book's findings speak to a central debate in political economy, especially in critical political economy, regarding which political actors lend their support and legitimize central banks and the neoliberal macroeconomic regime centered around price stability.[7] In particular, the findings of the book highlight that central banks do not care solely about the support provided by financial markets. They also care deeply about their relationship with political principals and the public at large and thus adapt their behavior to retain their support. The importance that central banks devote to different audiences varies over time, though. In particular, when the distributive effects of monetary policy become more visible, political audiences (including citizens and their representatives) become much more influential on central banks' policy than at other times. Shedding light on the changing relationship between central banks and political audiences thereby also speaks to the debate on the democratic oversight of independent agencies and the importance of a more sustained interaction with domestic governments and the societies they represent.

The remainder of this concluding chapter is organized around these two major contributions. In particular, in what follows, I connect the findings presented in the preceding chapters to the debates on the alleged symmetry of the inflation mandate and on the coordination between monetary and fiscal authorities. Then, I turn to the debate on the political and social forces that sustain and legitimize central bank independence and policies. Before doing so, however, I return to the reputational argument to assess how it fares compared to alternative explanations.

Revisiting the Technocratic View of Central Banks

History usually offers important episodes against which to make sense of contemporary events. After 2008, the key episode that served as the benchmark for the type of economic and societal challenges that lied ahead was the Great Depression of the 1930s. The Wall Street crash of October 1929 triggered what was then an unprecedented financial and economic crisis that, in turn, affected societal alignments and political stability. In particular, the 1929 stock market crash initiated a broader collapse in asset prices, widespread bank panic, massive economic contraction and unemployment, and severe price deflation in many countries. Among these countries, the United States is the most emblematic case of the economic and social disruptions that deflation can bring about. As a Bank for International Settlements study illustrates, between 1929 and 1933, real output in the United States dropped by almost one-third, and consumer prices dropped by almost a quarter. At the same time, nominal wages fell by approximately one-fifth, while the unemployment rate rose from 3 percent to an astonishing 25 percent.[8] In Europe, the deflationary context also provided a fertile context for social discontent that helped facilitate the rise of fascisms of different types.[9]

Back in the 1930s, central banks were the villains because they failed to counteract the recessionary and deflationary forces at play. Again, the United States offers one of the clearest examples of central banks' inability to stand up to the deflationary challenge. Indeed, it is widely recognized that the US Fed did not sufficiently accommodate the liquidity needs of the domestic banking sector and even made the economic contraction worse and longer by prematurely withdrawing its monetary support.[10] Similar mistakes are attributed to the Bank of Japan's handling of the post–market crash in the 1990s (see chapter 2). Indeed, the Japanese central bank has often been criticized for its "exceptionally poor monetary policymaking" because of its failure to ease policy adequately during the 1991–1994 period, as asset prices, the banking system, and the economy declined.[11]

Fast-forward to the 2000s and a different story emerged: central banks were now "the heroes" that "helped the world pull back from the precipice of another Great Depression."[12] This does not mean that mistakes were not made. However, the conventional argument is that this time, central banks were able to rise to the challenge and adapt to changed circumstances, despite the uncertainty associated with the use of largely untested unconventional policies.

What explains central banks' willingness and ability to step into action? Two major explanations have thus far offered the standard accounts to explain the behavior of central banks in the deflationary context of the post-2008 and post-2020 crises. Importantly, both explanations emphasize the importance of technocratic features, albeit of different kinds.[13]

The first explanation emphasizes the importance of the key feature of modern central banks—namely, their independence from political pressures. From this perspective, central banks were able to respond to the unusual deflationary challenge because they were not embroiled in politics as fiscal policymakers were. That is, central banks were not constrained by polarized political systems or ideological divisions similar to the constraints that made fiscal policymakers unable or unwilling to act. Central banks thus rose up as the "only game in town." The second explanation emphasizes another key feature of modern central banks—namely, their expertise and epistemic community character. From this perspective, the policy behavior of the central banks has largely been explained as a reflection of distinct economic ideas among central bank officials on how to deal with the crises at hand. Ideas helped frame the problem at play and favored learning processes, thereby leading central banks to avoid the mistakes made during the Great Depression.

Both explanations certainly have merit in shedding light on important drivers of the central banks' policy choices. However, as the empirical evidence assembled in the preceding chapters shows, these explanations do not provide a complete and entirely persuasive account of central banks' responses to the new deflationary context. Starting with the "only game in town" narrative, for instance, the evidence provided in the preceding chapters clearly indicates that independence was not the permissive factor that this narrative implies it to be. That is, in responding to the crises and their aftermath, a key concern for the two central banks analyzed here was that of damaging their independence. In other words, central banks were aware that the use of unconventional policies and the expansion of mandates to new policy areas would have meant undermining their independence from politics. It is thus difficult to accept the logic according to which central banks acted *because* of their independence. Rather, central banks acted *despite* their independence.

As for the ideational explanation, the analysis carried out in the preceding chapters offers only mixed support. In particular, the acceptance of new ideas among central bank officials was often insufficient to push central banks to respond to deflationary and recessionary forces. For instance, despite a broad consensus among the Fed's top policymakers about the potent disinflationary forces that the collapse of Lehman Brothers would have unleashed, the ideas of monetary policymakers were not enough to lead the Fed to act (chapter 4). Furthermore, central banks repeatedly acted in the middle of ideational battles; that is, when no consensus had yet been reached within the epistemic communities of central banks. For instance, the European Central Bank (ECB) adopted asset purchase programs early on, before the ideational repositioning of the central bank, which is often dated to have taken place only after 2012 (chapter 5). In short, central banks' technocratic features cannot fully account for the central banks' responses to the recessionary and deflationary challenges they were confronting.

The limits of technocratic explanations lead to the importance of the political explanation advanced herein. In particular, this book has argued and illustrated that central banks' decisions and evolutionary trajectories cannot be thoroughly explained without taking into account the politics of central banking—namely, the importance of political support for their activities. In particular, the preceding empirical analysis shows that central banks often adopted policies that led them away from the preexisting monetary orthodoxy in an attempt to protect their reputation under changed external conditions. Reputation, which is herein conceived as the institutions' public image before its heterogeneous audiences, is indeed a key (but underappreciated) resource that helps central banks sustain political support behind their activities, thereby leading central banks to act in a way that is meant to protect this critical resource.

This reputation protection behavior is clearly visible throughout the period investigated herein. For instance, at the beginning of the crisis period in 2008, the Fed and the ECB often acted to *preempt* future damage to their reputation as conservative and politically neutral institutions. This dynamic is evident in the specific operational features of the early unconventional monetary policies. These policies included a number of policy caveats expressly designed to circumscribe the scope of the policies adopted and so signal compatibility with the past reputation of the central banks. In addition to policy caveats, government interventions were also particularly important to preempt the reputational risks stemming from the deviation from orthodoxy. Some of the most unorthodox decisions were made exactly when governments offered central banks political cover for monetary decisions that openly challenged the conservative and apolitical reputation that central banks had carefully built since the 1980s. For instance, the US Fed's decision to rescue big financial firms could have hardly taken place without the support of the US administration, as the nondecision in the Lehman case also attests (chapter 4). That is, the fact that the US Fed let Lehman fail is also associated with the fact that, in that episode, government support and the attendant political cover were not offered. A similar dynamic was at play in Europe. Some of the ECB's most unorthodox decisions, including the early asset purchase programs with their distributive implications across national lines, were subordinated to the interventions of the euro area governments. In short, rather than being "the only game in town," as the argument has it, the performance of the Fed and the ECB during the crisis instead indicates that policy coordination was often a precondition for central banks' actions.

Central banks did not only act when they could signal their new policies as being aligned with their past reputation or when they could hide behind the political cover offered by government interventions. Central banks also acted in an attempt to *manage* the criticisms and win back political support. In particular, the analysis conducted in the preceding chapters shows that the politicization of central banking in the United States and in the euro area, meaning the increased salience and contestation of monetary policy among citizens, led the Fed and the ECB to further deviate from past monetary orthodoxy as a way in which to signal the institutions' willingness to meet the demands and expectations articulated by the domestic public. Specifically, the Fed and the ECB revised their monetary strategies also as a way to signal increased attention to employment considerations, as well as to attain social goals, including the pursuit of inclusive growth (in the United States) and climate change (in Europe).

In short, central banks are simply more than technocratic actors whose behavior is driven by the independence granted to them or by the ideas that monetary experts develop and come to accept. Central banks are also political actors, and as such, they need to tailor their behavior to ensure political support. Reputation is a key tool through which technocratic institutions seek to achieve such a necessary support. That is, projecting a distinct institutional image and following through the policy script that this image entails is the way that central banks use to build support for their policies and their role in domestic societies across multiple audiences. Maintaining political support requires active management, especially when external circumstances change and threaten existing reputation. The institutional evolution of central banks reflects such an imperative. That is, central banks deviated from orthodoxy in an attempt to preempt reputational threats (by using strategies to secure political support, like government involvement and framing tactics) and manage the same threats (by signaling actions that are meant to assuage criticisms and win back support).

Central Banks Cannot Have It Both Ways

As already noted, central banks' actions during the recent crisis period have often been compared with the actions that central banks—and, in particular, the US Fed—failed to take during the Great Depression in the 1930s. While central banks actively contributed to the crisis in the 1930s and the attendant deflationary malaise by letting financial institutions collapse and contracting the money supply, central banks in 2008 and 2020 expanded the remit and tools of monetary policy to provide broad-based support and massive liquidity to financial markets and economic actors.

Seen from the prism of the 1930s, the evolutionary trajectory of central banking can thus be read as evidence that central banks did not just learn the lessons of the Great Depression but also possessed the institutional capacity to address deflationary pressures—and not just the inflationary pressures that have been so key to the birth of central banks as we know them today (as discussed in chapter 2). In other words, as former Fed chair Ben Bernanke's quote at the beginning of this chapter states, the historical record analyzed herein seems to lend support to the view that despite the technical limitations posed by the zero lower bound, independent central banks can in fact "defend against inflation that is too low as least as vigorously as they resist inflation that is too high."[14]

The findings of this book nuance this conclusion. In particular, the findings indicate that the alleged symmetry of the price stability mandate, according to which central banks are supposed to react equally to inflationary and deflationary forces, is not as symmetrical as it might appear at first glance. Rather, central banks often resisted growing into the role of deflation fighter and did not "do it alone" but in coordination with fiscal authorities.

We saw such resistance at play at several crucial points in time, especially in the early stages of the crisis period, as chapters 4 and 5 have shown. In particular, the legacy of the central bank's reputation as an inflation-averse, technocratic institution systematically influenced the Fed's and ECB's policies aiming to support economic activity and counter disinflationary forces. This influence translated into the operational design of liquidity and balance sheet policies, which were often intended to signal the central banks' continuing adherence to an organizational image as an apolitical inflation fighter, even under changed economic circumstances. This is, for instance, clearly visible in the way in which the ECB designed its early liquidity operations to support markets and economic activity. Indeed, the ECB designed those policies by self-committing to the separation principle— that is, committing not to mix policies to repair financial markets and ensure liquidity with the policies aimed at influencing economic activity and inflation. By separating liquidity from formal monetary policy, "the message implicit in the 'separation' doctrine was that rates could always be raised *to tame inflation*," as a group of ECB officials later acknowledged.[15] Similar design constraints can be found in the design of the ECB's early asset purchase programs; both the Securities Market Program (SMP) and Outright Monetary Transactions (OMT) were designed to absorb the liquidity injected by the central bank's purchases (the so-called sterilization) to control potential inflation and allow the ECB to continue projecting an image as a conservative institution (chapter 5). That the design of unconventional policies was geared at not compromising past reputation is also visible in the Fed case. For instance, as detailed in chapter 4, the Fed designed its early asset purchase programs by relying mostly on the purchases of extremely safe Treasury securities, intending to affect general financial conditions and mitigate the risk to its apolitical reputation that would stem from extending credit to particular sectors of the economy. The Fed's repeated calls for policy "normalization" and "exit strategies," along with the implementation of its unconventional policies, are further examples of the "caveats" that the central bank used to signal a return to monetary policy as usual and so protect its reputation.

Although an effectiveness analysis of central banks' responses is outside the scope of this book, there are strong indications that the policy design used by central banks in order to not compromise their reputation might have had serious consequences for central banks' success in counteracting recessionary and deflationary forces. For instance, it has been suggested that the caution with which both the Fed and the ECB designed their asset purchase programs may have undermined the stimulative effects of their actions.[16] As a consequence, their action translated into a "failure" to revive inflation.[17] In other words, central banks were not as prompt in fighting inflation that was too low as they had been in fighting inflation that was too high in the past.

The asymmetry of central banks' price stability mandate can also be glimpsed in the active search for cooperation with governments. In particular, as already discussed in the previous section, both the Fed and the ECB did not step into action alone. Instead, the adoption of reflationary policies often required government support and coordination between monetary and fiscal policy.

Different types of policy coordination mattered for central banks' policy responses to deflationary forces. In particular, in the United States, policy coordination broadly took the form of shared responsibility, whereas in Europe, a division of responsibility framework prevailed. That is, in the US, coordination between monetary and fiscal authorities came in the form of open Treasury support of the Fed's controversial liquidity support for financial firms, as was the case with the Bear Stearns rescue, as well as credit protection in the event of losses, as was the case with the Fed's interventions in asset-backed securities markets since 2008 (chapter 4). In Europe, coordination took the form of a sequenced division of responsibilities among the eurozone governments and the ECB. Specifically, eurozone governments developed new policy instruments to lower pressures in sovereign debt markets (such as the European Stability Mechanism) and committed to fiscal austerity, which, in turn, created the conditions for the ECB to adopt policies that could more decidedly counteract recessionary and deflationary forces, at least in the aftermath of the 2010 crisis (chapter 5). Irrespective of the form, however, coordination has been critical for central banks to respond to deflationary forces, especially for the adoption of policies with high visibility and distributive effects, as in the case of policies that supported financial markets and specific financial firms or in the case of asset purchase programs.

In short, the process through which the Fed and the ECB have adapted to the deflationary challenges in the wake of the 2008 and 2020 crises shows the difficulties that independent central banks confronted when economic conditions made deflationary forces the main problem to be addressed. Importantly, these difficulties did not solely stem from the limits posed to interest rate policy by the zero lower bound. A crucial hindrance that central banks had to overcome stemmed from past historical developments. Specifically, past experience led these institutions either to choose those policies that could be made compatible with their preexisting reputation or to venture into controversial policies when the conditions for protecting their institutional image were in place.

Recognizing the difficulties that even powerful institutions such as central banks confront to achieve economic stability calls for reflecting on the importance of coordination among economic policy authorities and, in particular, between monetary and fiscal authorities. Specifically, the findings call for reconsidering the precrisis economic gospel staked on the stark separation between monetary and fiscal policy, with the former expected to be conducted at arm's length from the latter to avoid fiscal dominance.[18] Indeed, as I have just discussed, what the findings summarized herein show is that coordination with fiscal authorities was an important condition for central banks to overcome their reputational concerns and provide the necessary accommodation in a downturn. Extending this insight to a different context, the case for cooperation can also be made in an inflationary context, such as the one that materialized after 2021. As central banks ponder how much monetary tightening is needed to tame the inflationary pressures driven by higher energy prices and supply chain disruptions, greater coordination with fiscal authorities could help in the task to bring inflation under control without crashing economic growth and employment. Specifically, fiscal policy can help address the sources of the distributional conflict between firms and workers that often fuel inflationary dynamics, with the former raising prices of goods and services and the latter asking for higher wages. Although the debate is open as to the type of interventions that fiscal authorities can put in place to support the monetary policy lever, fiscal policy can, for example, subsidize the cost of energy for workers and so limit the pressure on nominal wages to rise. Still, fiscal can introduce taxes and price controls to limit the price rise of specific goods by specific firms.[19]

A similar case for cooperation can be made with regard to the crucial challenge of the green transition. Turning capitalist economies into low-carbon economies requires redirecting capital to finance structural transformations. Central banks can play a powerful role in this necessary endeavor by supporting public green investments and credit allocation among sectors of the economy. However, how central banks will implement their environmental role can bring about very different results. For instance, as Daniela Gabor captures the state of play of ongoing green monetary policy experiments, noting that there is the risk that central banks prioritize "the appearance of independence against . . . charges that greening monetary/regulatory policies means green interventionist credit policies."[20] This decision comes at the cost of undermining the decarbonization pathway, though. Therefore, different proposals have been advanced to rethink the role of central banks in the macroeconomic regime, with the most ambitious of them arguing for monetary policy to be reoriented more explicitly toward credit allocation in coordination with state-led green industrial policies.[21]

The policy debate about the specific operational modalities of monetary–fiscal coordination is extremely important. However, it should not distract from the overall message provided herein: the post-2008 historical record clearly shows that central banks have difficulties switching from fighting one policy challenge to fighting another, and that adapting to new challenges often required cooperation with other economic policymakers. The challenges ahead, including those related to energy-driven inflation and the green transition, are not going to be different. The gains from cooperation are much larger than those made by adhering to macroeconomic mantras whose time has passed.

Who Do Central Banks Listen To?

The shift from an inflationary to a deflationary regime was not the only challenge that central banks faced when the crisis period analyzed herein started back in 2008. Central banks also confronted the challenge of navigating a significantly different political context than the one that had marked the rise of the monetary regime centered on independent central banks and inflation control in the 1990s. Since the 1990s, central banks have enjoyed what has been termed a "cosmic coincidence": politicians and the public have come to endorse or benevolently neglect central banks' activities (see chapter 3). However, in the post-2008 environment, that cosmic coincidence has come to an end. The enormous influence that central banks exerted during crisis management and their aftermath has not gone unnoticed, reigniting concerns that their powers have grown excessive and unchecked.[22] That is, monetary policy and its guardians have become increasingly visible and contested. In a nutshell, central banking has become politicized.

The politicization of central banks could be read in light of broader political developments across Western economies, with central banks embodying a technocratic mode of governance that has been increasingly questioned, especially following the wave of populist voting since the 2008 crisis.[23] However, accusations have not remained confined to populist politicians and voters. After a decade of unconventional policy, central banks have indeed become a target of criticism from virtually all corners of the political spectrum. At one end of the spectrum, the reflationary policies of the central banks have been blamed for having stoked alleged inflationary risks and threatened currency debasement. At the other end, central bank policies have been blamed for rising social inequality, as visibly attested to by the decoupling of fortunes between financial markets and the real economy. Politicization has thus become a new phenomenon in the usually insulated, technocratic central bank community.[24]

The changed relationship between central banks and political audiences is clearly visible in the two central banks analyzed herein: the Fed and the ECB. As discussed in chapters 4 and 5, the level of public trust in the Fed and ECB has plummeted over the past decade, and the two central banks have become the target of an unusual string of mass protests.

The politicization of monetary policy is particularly relevant—but usually an underappreciated variable—for the transformation of central banks. Indeed, independent central banks are not customarily expected to listen to public concerns and certainly not to adjust policy to respond to public contestation. Rather, the principle of independence is actually expected to give rise to the opposite behavior. Nevertheless, even for those scholars who have long warned of the fallacies of independence, public audiences do not usually figure among the constituencies that are able to influence the policy and behavior of central banks. If there is a constituency that central banks respond to, it is the constituency made up of financial markets, not the public.

The analysis carried out in the preceding section indicates otherwise: central banks did not ignore public contestation but rather acted on it to protect their reputation. For instance, the analysis indicates that public contestation has been extremely important in shaping strategy reviews in both the United States and Europe since the 2020 crisis. In particular, both the Fed and the ECB felt compelled to build back public support by signaling more attention to growth and employment and by expanding the remit of monetary policy to include social goals such as inequality and the protection of the environment.[25] The differences in social goals that the two central banks came to prioritize further speak to the importance of societal pressures on central banks' behavior. That is, the fact that the Fed prioritized inequality while the ECB prioritized climate change can be read as a reflection of the different expectations placed by citizens on the two sides of the Atlantic. In other words, the evolution of monetary policy can be traced to societal expectations and demands.

In short, the analysis carried out in the preceding chapters provides empirical support for a key insight in the critical political economy literature—namely, the observation that central bank independence does not depoliticize monetary policymaking.[26] That is, even if conducted by independent authorities, monetary policy always makes "winners and losers" and thus reflects the power of those advantaged by monetary decisions. In contrast to critical IPE explanations, which usually see central banks as reflecting the power of financial interest groups especially by virtue of a shared economic ideology, this book shows that central banks are permeable to the expectations and demands of different audiences based on the challenges these audiences raise to central banks' reputation. In other words, reputation (and reputation protection) is a key channel through which politics makes its way into technocratic, independent institutions, shaping their behavior and their evolutionary trajectory.

Stressing the importance of political and public audiences in shaping the behavior of central banks is not meant to suggest that central banks have become immune to the expectations of other audiences—first and foremost, the expectation for low inflation as articulated by financial markets. What the book's findings suggest is that central banks have to navigate a complex political environment characterized by heterogeneous audiences whose influence may vary over time. The key question is how to establish when one audience becomes more powerful than others, such that it can exert the greatest threat to central banks' reputation and trigger a response. While more empirical evidence is needed, the evidence collected in this work suggests that the influence of public audiences over monetary policy increases in prolonged crisis times that bring to the fore the distributive effects of central banks' policy decisions. That is, while "quiet" times play more in the hands of financial market actors, crisis times open up more space for the public at large to orient the choices of central banks.[27] In particular, lengthy crisis periods expose the distributive nature of monetary policy as well as its actual impact across different constituencies. The increased visibility of the distributive effects of monetary policy puts pressures on central banks to legitimize their decisions before public audiences and thus defuse political backlash that may impair their independence in the future.

That central banks "listen to" society is a welcome reminder that monetary policy is not a technical affair that is distant from citizens' everyday life. However, the fact that central banks listen to and engage with societal demands only at specific times and under specific conditions also indicates the problems of democratic oversight over independent monetary institutions.[28] These problems are of particular concern after a decade that has witnessed to the expansion of the powers assigned to central banks and at a time where several countries are considering further expansion by assigning central banks responsibility for issues ranging from the fight against climate change to the regulation of digital currencies, among others. While the debate is still open on whether central banks should ultimately assume these new policy responsibilities, this debate should not merely take into consideration whether monetary policy can be tailored to suit new policy goals from a mere technical perspective. Rather, any serious debate also has to consider the value and principles that citizens care about in different societies and how governments can translate them as part of the polity's economic goals.

Back to the Future?

Central banks have always been central to political economy scholarship. Among others, scholarship on central banks has helped shed light on important debates about globalization, international economic cooperation, policy and regulatory diffusion, and power and legitimacy in global economic governance.[29] This book has built on this scholarship tradition to show that the historical evolution of central banks can yield important insights into the broader transformations in the macroeconomic regime that had, until recently, been dominant in most capitalist economies.

Indeed, the period that started with the 2008 global financial crisis and continued with the 2020 COVID-19 crisis is likely to be remembered as one of the most momentous times in economic history. Central banks in high-income countries have been at the center of these momentous transformations. By preventing a full-fledged collapse of highly integrated financial systems and by shielding governments and households from the effects of the pandemic, central banks have shaped the trajectory of capitalist systems by altering the distribution of wealth in domestic societies and the institutional configuration that has dominated macroeconomic policymaking since the 1980s. Indeed, in little more than a decade, central banks have basically called into question a key pillar of the neoliberal macroeconomic regime that was dominant for over three decades: the precrisis regime centered on the well-circumscribed pursuit of low inflation through the allegedly distributive-neutral tool of interest rate policy under the purview of independent monetary authorities.[30]

The transformation in central banking has proceeded hand-in-hand with at least two other major developments that call into question the neoliberal macroeconomic regime. First, the crisis period questioned the benefits of globalization. The disruptions brought about by an overly integrated financial system (in 2008) and by an integrated global economic system, in which supply chains proved suddenly fragile and harmful to economic activity (in 2020), have indeed highlighted the risks and constraints that domestic economies confront in tapping global financial and good markets.[31] This, in turn, have contributed to the growing political backlash against globalization.[32] This backlash has been visible in the voting behavior of citizens in high-income countries, including increased electoral volatility and the systematic defeat of mainstream political parties.[33] Second, the period between 2008 and 2020 has also visibly exposed the increased inequality that exists within capitalist economies and, in particular, the inequality in the distribution of wealth and the attendant unequal distribution of benefits favoring finance over labor.[34] Inequality exposes the limits of the neoliberal economic regime and its promise of widespread well-being, thus increasing the pressure for regime change.

While the concomitant transformations in central banking, in the attitudes toward globalization, and in the distribution of income and wealth have the potential to alter the macroeconomic regime that has been in place since the 1980s, the return of inflationary forces in late 2021 may also push the regime in the opposite direction and toward a return to the precrisis regime. Again, the historical experience of the Great Inflation is telling. As discussed extensively in chapter 2, inflation is probably the single most important determinant of the changes in central banking since the 1980s and of the shift away from the post-WWII macroeconomic regime that prioritized full employment and a wage-led growth model for the organization of domestic capitalist economies.[35] Extending these historical lessons to the present situation, one might argue that the post-2020 inflation has the potential to undermine and even undo the transformations that took place from 2008 onwards. In particular, the return of inflation might spell a return to "normal" monetary policy, with central banks abandoning their renewed focus on growth, employment, and social objectives to help reestablish the neoliberal regime that we have become acquainted with.

At the time of writing, for instance, most central banks seem keen on restoring the precrisis monetary regime by prioritizing the fight to inflationary forces regardless of the economic and social costs that tighter monetary policy implies. Indeed, by the end of 2023, basically all central banks in high-income countries had rolled back the monetary accommodation and set the stage for repeated interest rate rises.

While this evidence seems to point to a return to the old macroeconomic regime, the institutional transformations that have taken place in central banking are too profound to be dismissed without consequences. In other words, the transformation in central banking that I have analyzed in this book makes a return to "normal" less likely than it might appear at first glance. For instance, it is difficult to think that central banks' expanded mandate in the area of financial stability or climate change could be unraveled in the face of renewed inflationary pressures. Furthermore, the increased politicization of central banking and the impact on central banks' behavior, which has been analyzed in the preceding chapters, has raised the stakes for monetary tightening. That is, the open question is whether central banks can afford to cause a painful recession or even a fiscal crisis in a context where politicization prevails and where central banks can become an easy target for public and political criticisms.

While the return of inflation has injected significant uncertainty into the institutional evolution of central banks and the macroeconomic regime in which they have been the guardians, it is nonetheless important not to lose sight of the lessons that emerged in the years from 2008 to 2020 and that have been forgotten for quite some time. In particular, the recent historical record clearly shows that inflation is not the only danger that domestic societies confront: deflation can be as much as threatening for economic and societal well-being and some the underlying forces driving secular stagnation, including automation and demographics, still loom in the background. Furthermore, inflation is not the only problem domestic societies are likely to confront in the future. Just as deflation appeared unannounced, other challenges might soon lie ahead for central banks and other economic authorities to confront. The transition toward a green economy is but the most glaring example of the enormous challenges that monetary authorities are likely to confront soon.

What we know at the end of this journey is that central banks today are different institutions than they used to be a little more than a decade ago. We were used to thinking of central banks as the "masters of the economic universe"— that is, political actors who could steer domestic societies out of the woods of an economic and financial crisis. This flattering image largely stemmed from the success that central banks had reaped in fighting inflation for over three decades. Fighting deflation, however, has fully exposed the limitations that central banks are confronted with as political institutions, which calls for greater cooperation with fiscal authorities. Independent central banks are poorly equipped to fight deflationary forces because the policies needed to counteract deflation call into question their institutional identity, which is staked on their reputation as conservative, technocratic institutions. Central banks are also poorly equipped to sustain reflationary policies over time because doing so invites social and political backlash with regard to their independence. Central banks have long aspired to be "boring," as the Governor of the Bank of England once quipped.[36] However, their wish might need more than just time to come true.

Notes

INTRODUCTION

1. The literature on the delegation of monetary policy responsibility to independent central banks is sizable in both the political science and economics scholarships. For some of the most insightful analyses in political science, see, among the others, Johnson 2016 and McNamara 2002.

2. A core aspect of the neoliberal macroeconomic regime is the prioritization of low inflation over the pursuit of growth and employment. On the process that helped cement this economic consensus and the role of central banks in it, see, in particular, McNamara 1998.

3. Borio 2011, 1.

4. Woodford 2012, 1.

5. Throughout 2022, central banks of Australia, Canada, the euro area, New Zealand, Norway, Sweden, Switzerland, the United Kingdom, and the United States, which together account for around half of global gross domestic product, have raised their policy rates by around 200 to 300 basis points.

6. El-Erian 2016.

7. For a seminal work on the relationship between the Great Depression and monetary policy mistakes in the United States, see Friedman and Schwartz 1963.

8. On the learning and technocratic evolution in central banks postcrisis, see Ban and Patenaude 2019; Ferrara 2019; Johnson, Arel-Bundock, and Portniaguine 2019; Matthijs and Blyth 2017.

9. Gourevitch 1986, 19.

10. As will be discussed in chapter 1, in developing the notion of reputation, I build on the work of Carpenter 2010a and 2010b.

11. See also Tucker 2018, chap. 18.

12. I thank Elliott Posner for having suggested this terminology to capture the temporal tension discussed in the book.

13. Here, I borrow the notion of "irresponsibility" from Krugman 1998.

14. IMF, *World Economic Outlook*, April 2022.

15. Among the several studies that have stressed the difference in monetary policy on both sides of the Atlantic during the crisis period here analyzed, see Braun 2017; Lombardi and Moschella 2016; Reisenbichler 2020.

16. On the myth of depoliticization of money and monetary policy run by independent central banks, see Grabel 2003; Kirshner 2000, 2003; McNamara 2002. For a political theory perspective, see also Eich 2022. See also chapter 2 in this book and the references therein.

17. See Berman and McNamara 1999.

18. Cipolla 1989, vii.

19. Goodhart 2010. On the historical evolution of central banks and central banking features, see, among the others, Bordo 2007; Bordo and Siklos 2017; Siklos 2002; Ugolini 2017.

20. Chapter 2 provides a full-fledged historical reconstruction of the rise of modern central banking since the Great Inflation.

21. Woodford 2012, 1.

22. Orphanides 2003, 102.

23. See Bernanke 2003; Bernanke, Reinhart, and Sack 2004; Bordo et al. 2005; IMF 2003. For a thorough analysis of the evolution of Japanese monetary policy see Park et al. 2018.

24. IMF 2003. Throughout the book, I am referring to disinflation and deflationary dynamics that are not benign—that is, those that are associated with weak demand instead of positive supply shocks, such as technological innovations and productivity increase or gains from trade liberalization.

25. Issing 2000, 180.

26. Viñals 2000, 50.

27. See IMF 2018.

28. Summers 2014.

29. Inflation started to pick up around mid-2021, in the wake of the COVID-19 shock (March to April 2021 in the United States and July to August in the euro area).

30. Gopinath 2020.

31. Svensson 2003, 147.

32. The type of unconventional policies adopted since the crisis period is broader, including changes in communication policy (i.e., forward guidance) and negative interest rates. An overview of the larger sets of unconventional policies and their distributive consequences is provided in chapter 3.

33. On the evolution of central banks' embrace of financial stability objective, see Thiemann 2022.

34. See chapters 4 and 5.

35. Borio 2020, 2.

36. Borio 2020, 2.

37. As already hinted at, by modern central banks, I mean the institutional and operational setup that has guided the activity of central banks since the 1980s.

38. The historical origins of credibility are examined in chapter 2. On the hidden, ideological foundations of credibility, see, in particular, Grabel 2000, 2003.

39. There is a large stream of literature focused on monetary economics related to time inconsistency. For canonical papers, see Barro and Gordon 1983; Calvo 1978; Kydland and Prescott 1977.

40. McNamara 2002.

41. On the importance to central banks' credibility to rely on legitimacy see especially Best 2019. The lessons that the international monetary community extrapolated from its experiences in the 1970s and the 1980s are discussed in detail in chapter 2.

42. The diffusion and acceptance of reputation is also regarded as one of the clearest indicators of the cohesiveness of the transnational central banking community. See Johnson 2016.

43. For an analysis on the limits of the notion of neutrality, see Van 't Klooster and Fontan 2019.

44. Paul Krugman (1998) used the notion of "irresponsibility" to itemize the problems that the Bank of Japan faced in a deflationary context.

45. As will be discussed extensively in chapter 1, the argument advanced here builds on the reputation-based accounts of the behavior of public administrations, starting with the works of Daniel Carpenter (in particular, Carpenter 2001, 2010a, 2010b.

46. For a review of these arguments, see Lombardi and Moschella 2016.

47. On the politicization of central banking and the implications for the behavior of central banks, see McPhilemy and Moschella 2019; Moschella, Pinto, and Martocchia Diodati 2020.

48. As will be discussed in chapters 4 and 5, the new emphasis on running a high-pressure economy culminated in revisions being made to the internal monetary policy strategy of both central banks (i.e., in 2020 for the Fed and in 2021 for the ECB).

49. See, for instance, *The Economist* 2022; and *Bloomberg* 2021

50. See, for instance, Braun 2017; Ferrara et al. 2022; Jones and Matthijs 2019; Mc-Philemy and Moschella 2019; Tucker 2018.

51. Bateman and van 't Klooster 2023.

52. Some of the original contributions to the economics literature on the positive relationship between central bank independence and low inflation are Cukierman, Webb, and Neyapti 1992; Grilli et al. 1991. For works in the field of political science that have built and expanded on this relationship, see, among others, Bodea and Hicks 2015; Keefer and Stasavage 2003; and Broz 2002. For an understanding of the relationship between independence and low inflation from a critical political economy perspective, see Kirshner 2001.

53. See Park et al. 2018 for a notable exception.

54. On the relationship between the exigencies of the global economy and democratic policymaking see Barta and Johnston 2022.

55. On the postcrisis changes in electoral politics, see Bellucci, Costa Lobo, and Lewis-Beck 2012; Hernàndez and Kriesi 2016; Hopkin 2020.

1. CENTRAL BANKS AS POLITICAL INSTITUTIONS

1. On some of the seminal contributions in political science, see Pierson 2004; Skocpol 1992; Steinmo, Thelen, and Longstreth 1992; Streeck and Thelen 2005; Thelen 2004.

2. Goodhart 2010.

3. Bordo 2007; Eichengreen 1992.

4. Dietsch, Claveau, and Fontan 2018; Jacobs and King 2016; Tucker 2018.

5. For the debate on whether central bank independence has been weakened because of central banks' responses to the 2008 and 2020 crises, see Goodhart 2010; Issing 2017; Orphanides 2013. On the changing relationship between independence and accountability, see Ferrara et al. 2022; Jones and Matthijs 2019; McPhilemy and Moschella 2019.

6. Gabor 2021.

7. The notion of the "only game in town" was popularized by Mohamed El-Erian (2016), but its use is widespread.

8. See also Mandelkern 2016; Matthijs and Blyth 2017.

9. For one of the most thorough accounts on the lessons learned from the experience of the 1930s for managing the 2008 crisis and its aftermath, see Eichengreen 2015.

10. This is, for instance, the common narrative among central bankers themselves. See, among the others, Bernanke 2010; Fischer 2011; Wessel 2014.

11. Ferrara 2019. For the interpretation of central banks as an instance of epistemic and policy communities where ideas and expertise are the main drivers of organizational behavior, see Johnson 2016; Marcussen 2006; McNamara 1998; Park et al. 2018; Thiemann, Melches, and Ibrocevic 2021; Tsingou 2014; Verdun 1999.

12. Schmidt 2016, 2020.

13. Johnson, Arel-Bundock, and Portniaguine 2019.

14. Hall 1986, 229.

15. Kirshner 2001, 42. See also the contributions in Kirshner 2003.

16. Feygin 2021.

17. Grabel 2003; see also McNamara 2002.

18. Grabel 2003, 41.

19. See also Adam Posen (1995, 254), according to whom low inflation and central bank independence could not have been sustained without the "protection of [central

banks] counterinflationary activities" by the financial sector. Echoes of this thinking can also be found in analyses of central banks' responses to the crisis period that started in 2008, according to which central banks have ultimately served financial interests rather than general societal interests. For instance, see Dietsch, Claveau, and Fontan 2018; Jacobs and King 2016.

20. Grabel 2003; see also Kirshner 2000, 422.

21. Carpenter 2010b, 45.

22. Busuioc 2016, 43. For an application of the concept of bureaucratic reputation to central banks, see McPhilemy and Moschella 2019; Moschella and Pinto 2019.

23. Carpenter and Krause 2012, 26.

24. Moschella and Pinto, 2019; Gilad 2015.

25. Maor, Gilad, and Bloom 2013, 585.

26. Ban 2015.

27. Ben Clift (2018) applies a similar logic to explain the policy evolution of an international bureaucracy (i.e., the International Monetary Fund).

28. Carpenter 2010b, 45.

29. Carpenter and Krause 2012, 27.

30. Carpenter 2010b, 10. The importance of reputation to win autonomy and deference from an institution's principals is similarly acknowledged in the literature on international organizations. See, for instance, Broome 2010.

31. Hood 2011; Baker 2013; Ban, Seabrooke, and Freitas 2016.

32. Bach et al. 2022, 1043. See also Wæraas and Maor 2015.

33. On the development of central banks' reputation in the aftermath of the Great Inflation, see the historical reconstruction discussion in chapter 2 and the references therein.

34. Blinder 1999, 64–65.

35. A detailed historical reconstruction of central banks reputation and its consolidation is provided in chapter 2.

36. Bryan 2013.

37. Goodfriend 2005, 250, emphasis added.

38. See, among the others, Mishkin 2007, 5–6.

39. Masciandaro and Romelli 2015, 263. For the standard argument on the social benefits of a conservative central banker, see Rogoff 1985.

40. Rostagno et al. 2019, 39.

41. Hayo and Hefeker 2010, 185.

42. Steelman 2011. See also chapter 2.

43. On the diffusion of inflation targeting as one of the key "practices" of the transnational community of central banks, see Johnson 2016. For a central banker's perspective, see Blinder 2004.

44. Blinder 2004, 15.

45. The institutional trajectory of the US Fed and the ECB is extensively examined in chapter 4 and chapter 5, respectively.

46. Mishkin 2007, 2.

47. In the words of a well-known study, "monetary policy decisions tend to be based on systematic analysis of alternative policy choices and their associated macroeconomic impacts: this is science"; a title-provoking article by Eric Leeper (2010) thus described monetary policy to clearly distinguish it from "fiscal alchemy."

48. Van 't Klooster and Fontan 2019, 869.

49. Bateman and van 't Klooster 2023; Diessner and Lisi 2020.

50. Agur et al. 2022b.

51. Irwin 2013, 106. See also Johnson 2016; Marcussen 2009; Tsingou 2014.

52. Bernanke 2007.

53. Conti-Brown 2016, 148.

54. Johnson 2016, 9.

55. Buiter 2014, 36. On the importance of political and societal support to central bank independence, see also Goodman 1991.

56. Krugman 1998, emphasis in original.

57. Rostagno et al. 2019, 10.

58. Wall Street Journal 2010.

59. Committee on the Global Financial System 2019.

60. Copelovitch and Singer 2008.

61. The distributive effects of unconventional policies have been extensively investigated, including within central banks. Some of the examples of these important analyses carried out in the central banks of high-income countries include Domanski, Scatigna, and Zabai 2016; Dossche, Slačálek, and Wolswijk 2021; Inui, Sudo, and Yamada 2017; Joyce, Tong, and Woods 2011. See also chapter 3 and the discussion therein.

62. See Kirshner 2003 and the contributions therein.

63. Similar distributional consequences stem from other unconventional policies, including liquidity and credit support.

64. For a detailed discussion of the transmission channels of quantitative easing see, for instance, Bowdler and Radia 2012.

65. See Committee on the Global Financial System 2019, especially concerning the 2008 financial crisis.

66. Carpenter 2010b, 18.

67. Carpenter 2002, 2004; Gilad, Maor, and Bloom 2015; Hood 2011; Maor 2011; Maor, Gilad, and Bloom 2013; Moschella and Pinto 2019.

68. Van der Veer 2020. In the case of central banks, see, in particular, Jacqueline Best's argument according to whom the credibility of monetary policy ultimately depends on its legitimacy (Best 2019).

69. Carpenter 2010a, 832

70. Carpenter and Krause 2012.

71. Given audience heterogeneity, it is not unusual for reputational scholarship to treat the identification of the agency's key audiences as the research question itself. That is, this scholarship aims at mapping an agency's key audiences using a variety of methods ranging from historical analysis and interviews with officials to quantitative methods (Bellodi 2023; Busuioc 2016).

72. Carpenter 2002; Maor, Gilad, and Bloom 2013; Van der Veer 2020.

73. See, in particular, Braun 2020 on the deep entanglements between central banks and financial actors for the implementation of monetary policy.

74. Grabel 2003; see also Baker 2010.

75. See, in particular, Ban and Patenaude 2019; Thiemann, Melches, and Ibrocevic 2021.

76. Baker 2013; Ban, Seabrooke, and Freitas 2016.

77. In his last press conference as chair of the US Fed, Ben Bernanke captured the fragility of the Fed's independence by offering a single piece of advice to his successor at the Fed's helm: "Congress is our boss." See Federal Reserve 2013.

78. Goodman 1991, 335. On central banks' maneuvering in relation to political principals, also as a function of societal support, see also Lohmann 1998.

79. See, for instance, Maor, Gilad, and Bloom 2013.

80. Maor, Gilad, and Bloom 2013; Moschella and Pinto 2019.

81. For a review of the criticisms of the ECB's responses to crises as compared with the US Fed, see Lombardi and Moschella 2016.

82. See, for example, Woodford 2012. For a full discussion of the Fed's journey away from orthodoxy, see chapter 4.

83. This definition draws from the scholarship in public policy. See, in particular, Peters 2018. Policy coordination may result from legal changes or emerge voluntarily, including through informal contacts among public officials.

84. See, for instance, Hinterleitner and Sager 2017, 598.

85. Mabbett and Schelkle 2019, 440.

2. CONSTRUCTING REPUTATION AND MONETARY ORTHODOXY

1. The diffusion and acceptance of such a reputation across central banks around the world is also regarded as one of the clearest indicators of the cohesiveness of the transnational central banking community. See Johnson 2016.

2. See, in particular, Grabel 2000, 2003.

3. Bordo and Orphanides 2013, 2.

4. Although inflation dynamics were similar in all advanced economies, some important differences are worth mentioning. In particular, while inflation exceeded 20 percent in the United Kingdom and Japan and well above 10 percent in France and the United States, it never exceeded single digits in Germany.

5. Blinder 1982.

6. See, for instance, the contributions in Bordo and Orphanides 2013 and in Hall 1982.

7. For instance, DeLong 1997. On the implications of the end of the Bretton Woods system not only for inflation but also for the rise of a new macroeconomic and financial regime, see Helleiner 1994, esp. chap. 6.

8. Hetzel 2013, 98.

9. On the evolution of monetary and fiscal policymakers' economic ideas in the United States since the 1960s, see Blyth 2002. In regard to economics, see Romer and Romer 2002.

10. See, in particular, Hetzel 2008, esp. chap. 7.

11. Goodfriend 2005, 244.

12. Meltzer 2009, 824.

13. Bryan 2013.

14. Burns 1987.

15. Burns 1987, 688.

16. Burns 1987, 688–689.

17. Volcker and Feldstein 2013; Taylor 2005, 269–270.

18. Lindsey, Orphanides, and Rasche 2005, 196.

19. Volcker and Feldstein 2013, 108.

20. Orphanides and Thornton 2005, 141.

21. Volcker and Feldstein 2013.

22. For instance, even during the period of monetary targeting, as chair of the Fed, Volcker maintained a skeptical opinion of monetarism (Lindsey, Orphanides, and Rasche 2005).

23. See Volcker and Feldstein 2013. According to historic data from FRED, in January 1981, the average monthly effective federal funds rate was 19.08 (FRED, Federal Reserve Economic Data, Federal Reserve Bank of St. Louis, https://fred.stlouisfed.org/series/FEDFUNDS).

24. See Best 2022, 569.

25. See, for instance, Beyer et al. 2008.

26. Goodhart 2005, 299.

27. According to the IMF's World Economic Outlook database, the Democratic Republic of Congo and Angola were the only countries with inflation over 100% in 2000.

28. On the importance of the theory of credibility for the depoliticization of monetary policy, see, in particular, Grabel 2000, 2003. On credibility as one of the major legacies from the Volcker era, see also Bernanke 2005.

29. Volcker and Feldstein 2013, 108.

30. Lucas 1976.

31. This conclusion stands in contrast to an idea made popular after WWII, according to which government policy is systematically able to influence individual economic decisions.

32. This interpretation contrasts to the neo-Keynesian interpretation, according to which disinflation costs can be traced back to staggered wage and price adjustments. For a peek into the debate between neo-Keynesian and neoclassical economists, see Ball 1991.

33. Bernanke 2005, 281.

34. McNamara 2002, 51.

35. On the political drivers behind the diffusion of the governance model centered on independent central banks outside high-income countries, see, in particular, Johnson 2016; Maxfield 1997.

36. Arnone et al. 2007; Crowe and Meade 2008; De Haan et al. 2018; Masciandaro and Romelli 2015.

37. Kenneth Rogoff (1985) offers one of the original formulations behind this intuition; he suggests choosing a conservative central banker—someone who places a greater importance on achieving low inflation—and then giving that individual the independence to conduct monetary policy.

38. Bernanke 2020, 47, emphasis is mine.

39. Goodhart and Lastra 2018, 51.

40. Goodfriend 2007, 55.

41. On the limits of the notion of depoliticization and monetary neutrality, see Kirshner 2003 and Kirshner 2001 and, more recently, Van 't Klooster and Fontan 2019.

42. Bernanke 2005, 281.

43. Bernanke 2004.

44. Cecchetti and Debelle 2004. The importance of monetary policy to explain the success of the Great Moderation is also stressed in Bernanke 2004; Blanchard and Simon 2001; Stock and Watson 2002.

45. The real GDP contracted by 0.91 percent in the fourth quarter of 1990 and by 0.32 percent in the first quarter of 2001 (U.S. Bureau of Economic Analysis, Real Gross Domestic Product [GDPC1], FRED, Federal Reserve Bank of St. Louis, accessed July 3, 2022, https://fred.stlouisfed.org/series/GDPC1).

46. See the contributions in the retrospective on the Greenspan era in Hoenig 2005 and, in particular, the summary of the findings of the symposium provided in Kahn 2005. In particular, George Kahn summarizes the agreement among participants in the symposium, in spite of the variety of views expressed: "One key principle that everyone agreed guided monetary policy in the Greenspan era . . . was the idea that achieving and maintain prices stability was central to attaining maximum sustainable growth" (Kahn 2005, xxiv).

47. Blinder and Reis 2005, 77, emphasis is in the original.

48. Blinder and Reis 2005, 77.

49. On the diffusion of inflation targeting, see, for instance, Mukherjee and Singer 2008; Wasserfallen 2019.

50. On monetary policy governance in developing and emerging market countries, see Maxfield 1997.

51. Bernanke 2011.

52. Greenspan 2002.

53. As Alan Blinder and Ricardo Reis note (2005, 67), "For example, the Fed more or less announced that it stood ready to supply as much liquidity as necessary to keep markets functioning after the stock market crash of 1987, during the international financial crisis of 1998, and after the 9/11 attacks."

54. Gandrud 2012; Masciandaro 2007.

55. Borio 2011, 2.

56. On the rationale for inflation targeting, see, among the others, Svensson 1999a, 1999b.

57. Issing et al. 2001, 38.

58. Issing et al. 2001, 38.

59. For a trenchant critique of the notion of neutrality, see Kirshner 2001.

60. Also Fernández-Albertos 2015, 226–227.

61. Agur et al. 2022b.

62. Baker 2006; Johnson 2016.

63. See, for instance, Howarth and Rommerskirchen 2016; Hayo 1998; Tognato 2012.

64. Irwin 2013, 110.

65. King 2000b.

66. Liaquat 2009; Johnson 2016; Irwin 2013.

67. Woodward 2000.

68. These views are well exemplified by Ben Bernanke's analysis of the Japanese economy. In his words, the problems that Japan confronted in the 1990s can largely be ascribed to a "paralyzed" monetary policy, which is a "paralysis that is largely self-induced" (Bernanke 2000). See also Bernanke 2003; Ito and Mishkin 2004; Kuttner and Posen 2004.

69. Cargill, Hutchison, and Ito 2000.

70. Nikkei Industry Research Institute, "Nikkei Stock Average, Nikkei 225 (NIKKEI225)," FRED, Federal Reserve Bank of St. Louis, accessed July 3, 2022, https:// fred.stlouisfed.org/series/NIKKEI225.

71. Cargill, Hutchison, and Ito 2000, 2.

72. For the Japanese view on the problems that BoJ confronted at a time, see Ueda 2001.

73. As discussed in this book's introduction, a liquidity trap refers to a situation where deflationary forces and entrenched expectations risk nullifying the effect of monetary policy in stimulating aggregate demand. The original formulation of the "liquidity trap" is associated with the work of John Maynard Keynes. However, it is important to note that Keynes "dismissed the notion that monetary policy would become ineffective during a slump—provided policymakers were willing to take deliberate and vigorous action toward restoring prosperity" (Orphanides 2003, 1).

74. As will be discussed below, the BoJ has been criticized for its policy stance in the run-up to the crisis. In particular, the critics argue that the BoJ's "accommodative monetary policy, attempting to limit yen appreciation against a background of low consumer price inflation, inadvertently provided liquidity that accommodated asset inflation" (Cargill, Hutchison, and Ito 2000, 4).

75. Ito 2006, 106.

76. See also Park et al. 2018, chap. 5.

77. For a thorough reconstruction of the actions taken by the BoJ from the Japanese perspective, see Baba et al. 2005; Ueda 2001.

78. Kumar et al. 2003, 22.

79. Ito and Mishkin 2004, 2.

80. Bernanke 2000. See also Bernanke 2003.

81. Ito and Mishkin 2004, 31.

82. Krugman 1998.

83. Ito and Mishkin 2004, 31.

84. See the discussion in Baba et al. 2005. For a thorough analysis of the evolution of the Japanese monetary policy from the 1990s, see Park et al. 2018.

85. For a detailed analysis of the BoJ Policy Board's discussion on inflation targeting and the theoretical debate on the benefits of its adoption to fight deflation, see Ito 2004.

86. This is, for instance, one of the criticisms raised at the BoJ under the leadership of Governor Hayami (Ito and Mishkin 2004, 10).

87. Cargill, Hutchison, and Ito 2000, esp. 172–173.

88. Ito and Mishkin 2004, 31.

89. Krugman 1998.

90. Park et al. 2018.

91. Bordo and Filardo 2005, 1, emphasis added.

3. CHALLENGING MONETARY ORTHODOXY IN A NEW CONTEXT

1. Davies and Green 2010, 1.

2. For the notion of politicization as "the process of making an issue political, that is debating it in the public sphere as an issue of public contestation," see De Vries, Hobolt, and Walter 2021, 308.

3. The literature on the origins of the global financial crisis and the attendant Great Recession is huge and interdisciplinary. For some of the most detailed and engaging historical and political reconstruction, see Helleiner 2011; Eichengreen 2015; Tooze 2018.

4. For instance, IMF 2010; Khaler and Lake 2013; Temin 2010.

5. Kar-Gupta and Le Guernigou 2007.

6. Shin 2009.

7. See, for instance, Bernanke 2013b.

8. Stempel and Comlay 2008.

9. Chen, Mrkaic, and Nabar 2019, 6.

10. Data taken from IMF 2010.

11. Baldacci, Gupta, and Mulas-Granados 2014.

12. See Blyth 2013; Farrell and Quiggin 2017; Mandelkern 2016; Matthijs and McNamara 2015. For highlights of how external demand shocks "enable" the ideational austerity bias, see Polyak 2022a and 2022b.

13. See, among many others, Bernanke and Reinhart 2004; Borio and Disyatat 2010; IMF 2013. Among other important policy measures that are not properly discussed herein, central banks provided further monetary accommodation by revising their communication policy. In particular, several central banks resorted to forward guidance (i.e., using public statements to communicate the likely future trajectory of monetary policy). As nominal interest rates approached the zero lower bound and could not sufficiently stimulate demand, central banks sought to push long yields down by verbally signaling that they would tolerate higher inflation in the future.

14. For cross-country reviews of unconventional monetary policies adopted in the ten years between 2008 and 2018, see Potter and Smets 2019.

15. This is one example where the dividing line between liquidity measures and balance sheet policies can be extremely blurred. Paul Tucker (2009) and Paul Fisher (2010), for example, likened the Bank of England's purchases of private-sector securities to a function of market maker of last resort.

16. Summers later formalized his thinking in a speech to the National Association for Business Economics (see Summers 2014).

17. Teulings and Baldwin 2014.

18. Chen, Mrkaic, and Nabar 2019, 8.

19. Chen, Mrkaic, and Nabar 2019, 7.

20. Lagarde 2014.

21. Chen, Mrkaic, and Nabar 2019, 5.

22. Summers and Stansbury 2019.

23. Buiter 2019.

24. Bernanke 2020.

25. World Bank 2020.

26. Bank for International Settlements 2012, 34; 2016, 63; 2019, 26.

27. Data on the evolution of the COVID-19 health emergency are drawn from "A Timeline of the Coronavirus Pandemic." *New York Times*, April 21, 2020, https://www.nytimes.com/article/coronavirus-timeline.html

28. IMF 2020b.

29. This risk was, and still is, especially elevated in those countries that started from weaker fiscal positions, such as some southern eurozone countries. The pattern of growing public debt after the crisis period is analyzed in more detail in the section that follows.

30. Bank for International Settlements 2020, 1.

31. Again, this overview is not meant to provide an exhaustive list of all the policies that central banks have adopted in the wake of the 2020 crisis. The purpose is to exemplify the major set of policies. For a detailed overview of central bank crisis responses in advanced economies, see Cavallino and Fiore 2020.

32. Lagarde 2013.

33. As happens quite often, a cover of *The Economist* captured the mood around central banks amid desperate calls for crisis leadership. An August 2011 issue on "Reviving the world economy" featured a modified version of the famous Rembrandt painting with a group of doctors studying a corpse. The titular Dr. Nicolaes Tulp is holding a defibrillator and above his head is a caption reading, "Stand back, I'm a central banker." In its briefing, the newspaper stressed how "central banks have shown themselves ready and able to act" while elected politicians "seem inadequate for the task." See The Economist 2011.

34. For some of the most trenchant criticisms, see Dietsch, Claveau, and Fontan 2018; Jacobs and King 2021; Jones and Matthijs 2019; Van 't Klooster and Fontan 2019. For the political consequences of the perception of central banks as overstepping their mandate and favoring some interests over others, see Tucker 2018.

35. On the importance of recognizing the distributive effects of the low inflation objective pursued by central banks in the precrisis period, see, for instance, Kirshner 2001.

36. Over the past decade, central banks have devoted an increasing amount of research attention to the distributive effects of unconventional policies. Examples of these important analyses carried out in the major central banks in high-income countries include Domanski, Scatigna, and Zabai 2016; Dossche, Slačálek, and Wolswijk 2021; Inui, Sudo, and Yamada 2017; Joyce, Tong, and Woods 2011.

37. While the effect of central banks' asset purchases on wealth inequality is widely recognized, there is more debate on their impact on income inequality. Indeed, central banks' purchases also support employment and so ultimately help reduce income inequality. See Silva et al. 2022 for a review of the theoretical arguments and empirical evidence.

38. Data is from Bank for International Settlements. The group of advanced countries include Australia, Canada, Denmark, the euro area, Japan, New Zealand, Norway, Sweden, Switzerland, the United Kingdom, and the United States. The group of emerging market economies include Argentina, Brazil, Chile, China, Colombia, the Czech Republic, Hong Kong Special Administrative Region, Hungary, India, Indonesia, Israel, Korea, Malaysia, Mexico, Poland, Russia, Saudi Arabia, Singapore, South Africa, Thailand, and Turkey. "Total nonfinancial sector" covers the government, nonfinancial corporations, and households.

39. As reported in Jeffery 2020.

40. Data is from IMF World Economic Outlook database.

41. Jones and Matthijs 2019, 138.

42. The term "permissive consensus" borrows from Hooghe and Marks 2009 on the European Union (EU). In the early stages of the EU integration process, European public opinion was largely quiescent and even implicitly supportive of the EU political project. A similar reasoning can be extended to central banks in the precrisis period analyzed herein.

43. A manifesto of these criticisms is provided in "Open Letter to Ben Bernanke" (Wall Street Journal 2010).

44. For instance, Dietsch, Claveau, and Fontan 2018; Jacobs and King 2021; Tucker 2018.

45. Hopkin 2020.

46. Trump blasted the Fed on Twitter for "putting [the US] at a decided economic & physiological [sic] disadvantage" (March 13, 2020), called the Federal Reserve Board, among others, "pathetic, slow moving" (March 10, 2020), "derelict in its duties if it doesn't lower the Rate and even, ideally, stimulate" (October 29, 2019), and insulted them multiple times, calling them the "No Clue Fed" (September 29 and August 28, 2019) or "Boneheads" (September 11, 2019). See Quealy 2021.

47. Rajan 2017.

48. Buiter 2016; Goodhart and Lastra 2018; Masciandaro and Passarelli 2018; Rajan 2017.

49. Ferrara et al. 2022.

50. See also Ehrmann, Soudan, and Stracca 2013; Jones 2009; Roth, Gros, and Nowak-Lehmann 2014.

51. Financial Times 2015a, 2015b.

52. Pew Research Center 2020; Rabouin 2021.

53. See Binder and Spindel 2017.

54. Blinder et al. 2008, 941. See also Moschella, Pinto, and Martocchia Diodati 2020.

55. Lohmann 2003, 105.

56. Jones 2009, 1093.

57. Wessel 2017.

58. Fraccaroli, Giovannini, and Jamet 2018; Moschella, Pinto, and Martocchia Diodati 2020; Schmidt 2020.

59. Analysis by the Bank for International Settlements finds that in a sample of advanced economies, the share of central banker speeches mentioning these terms has grown from approximately 2 percent in 2007 to approximately 10 percent in 2020. See Bank for International Settlements 2021, 40.

4. THE US FEDERAL RESERVE

1. Siklos 2002, 91.

2. Eichengreen 2015.

3. Tooze 2021.

4. For one of the most trenchant criticisms of the influence of financial markets over the Fed's monetary policy decisions, see Jacobs and King 2016.

5. Woodford 2012.

6. For some of the classical accounts of the Fed history, see Friedman and Schwartz 1963; Meltzer 2009. For some of the contributions in political science, see Binder and Spindel 2017; Broz 1997; Lavelle 2013.

7. The Fed's mandate was specified in the Federal Reserve Reform Act of 1977. The mandate actually comprises three elements: price stability, full employment, and moderate long-term interest rates. However, the focus on the "dual" mandate refers to the

understanding according to which the interest rate goal is viewed as a by-product of the other two goals. See Board of Governors of the Federal Reserve System, "Monetary Policy: What Are Its Goals? How Does It Work?" accessed May 24, 2023, https://www.federalreserve.gov/monetarypolicy/monetary-policy-what-are-its-goals-how-does-it-work.htm.

8. Axilrod 2011, 89.

9. Bernanke 2013a. See also Lindsey, Orphanides, and Rasche 2005.

10. Lindsey, Orphanides, and Rasche 2005, 231.

11. Bernanke 2013a.

12. The Yellen quote is as reported in Giles 2013.

13. Although the trigger of the crisis can be found in the developments in the US mortgage market, the crisis reflected a much larger credit boom and encompassed regulatory failures. In other words, the causes of the crisis have profound roots in the workings of financial markets and their political regulation, with the housing boom reflecting these deeper forces at play. On the political origins of the US financial crisis, see Helleiner 2014; Schwartz 2009; Thompson 2009; Tooze 2018.

14. Ben Bernanke, among others, used the analogy of the "bank run" to account for the financial panic dynamic in the broad US financial sector. See, for instance, Bernanke 2009a.

15. U.S. Bureau of Economic Analysis, Real Gross Domestic Product (GDPC1), *FRED, Federal Reserve Bank of St. Louis*, https://fred.stlouisfed.org/series/GDPC1, July 16, 2022; U.S. Bureau of Labor Statistics, All Employees, Total Nonfarm (PAYEMS), *FRED, Federal Reserve Bank of St. Louis*, https://fred.stlouisfed.org/series/PAYEMS, July 16, 2022.

16. For the details of individual monetary policy decisions and their chronology, see Board of Governors of the Federal Reserve System 2023.

17. For the debate on the societal and inequality implications of monetary policy during the crisis period, see Dietsch, Claveau, and Fontan 2018.

18. The creation of the Term Auction Facility (TAF) in the fall of 2007 is a case in point; through this facility, banks could continue to acquire short-term funds after the collapse of the ABCP market. For more on this topic, see Tooze 2018, 207–208.

19. El-Erian 2016, 14.

20. The policy preferences of Fed Chair Ben Bernanke are extrapolated from both his public pronouncements and his memoirs published in 2015.

21. Bernanke 2015, 219.

22. Nelson 2014, 79.

23. Kohn 2010, 6.

24. Bernanke 2015, xiii.

25. Bernanke 2015, 216.

26. Paulson 2011, 101.

27. Bernanke 2015, 220.

28. The letter from Paulson reads: "I [Secretary Paulson] support this action as appropriate and in the government's interest, and acknowledge that if any loss arises out of the special facility extended by the [New York Fed] to [JPMorgan], the loss will be treated by the [New York Fed] as an expense that may reduce the net earnings transferred by the [New York Fed] to the Treasury general fund." See Paulson 2009.

29. In particular, the Fed created a special-purpose vehicle, Maiden Lane LLC, to purchase approximately $30 billion of real estate assets that JPMorgan did not want as part of the deal to acquire Bear Stearns. Maiden Lane was financed with a $29 billion loan from the New York Federal Reserve Bank, which was collateralized by the $30 billion in assets and a $1 billion subordinated loan from JPMorgan.

30. Bernanke 2015, 216.

31. See also Paulson 2011, 149.

32. Kohn 2010, 6.

33. Geithner 2014, 156, emphasis added.

34. Ball 2016, 184.

35. Ball 2018; Blinder 2013; Cline and Gagnon 2013; Ferguson and Johnson 2009; Sorkin 2010; Tooze 2018, 176–177.

36. See, for instance, Ball 2016. See also Financial Times 2018.

37. Bernanke 2015, 262.

38. Ball 2016, 2.

39. Geithner 2014, 154.

40. Bernanke 2015, 261.

41. Bernanke 2015, 290.

42. Bernanke 2015, 290.

43. Nocera 2009.

44. Bernanke 2015, 291.

45. Bernanke 2009b, 76.

46. As reported in Ball 2016, 208.

47. Frank 2011, xlviii.

48. Paulson 2011, 240; Bernanke 2015, xii.

49. Paulson 2011, 229.

50. On the comparison with the 1930s, see Eichengreen 2015.

51. Bernanke 2010.

52. It is also important to note that subsequent rounds of asset purchases were shaped by the legacy of the previous rounds, both in terms of policy success and learning. Focusing on the Fed's early decisions to use its balance sheet thereby allows minimizing the confounding factors that might have contributed to later rounds.

53. Following completion of the program, the Fed rolled over maturing Treasury securities and started reinvesting principal payments from agency debt and agency MBS (initially, in longer-term Treasury securities) in order to keep the size of securities holdings roughly constant.

54. The September 2012, LSAP included monthly purchases of $40 billion in agency MBS; starting in January 2013, it also included monthly purchases of $45 billion in longer-term Treasury securities. The Fed started "normalizing" its monetary policy stance in January 2014 before resuming the purchase of massive amounts of securities following the start of the COVID-induced crisis in 2020.

55. Giles 2013.

56. In contrast to the liquidity assistance measures discussed in the preceding section, where the main policymaking actor was the Board of Governors of the Federal Reserve System, quantitative easing decisions fell within the remit of the FOMC.

57. The Federal Reserve funded its securities purchases by crediting the accounts that banks hold with the Fed.

58. Kohn 2010, 14.

59. "Dear Mr. Bernanke: No Pressure, but . . . ," *The Caucus* (blog), *New York Times*, November 17, 2010, https://archive.nytimes.com/thecaucus.blogs.nytimes.com/2010/11/17/dear-mr-bernanke-no-pressure-but/

60. For the "Open Letter to Ben Bernanke," see Wall Street Journal 2010.

61. Jeffrey M. Lacker, President of the Federal Reserve Bank of Richmond. Federal Reserve 2010, 137–138.

62. Thomas Hoenig, president of the Federal Reserve Bank of Kansas City. Federal Reserve 2010, 159.

63. Kohn 2010, 12–13.

64. Charles I. Plosser, president of the Federal Reserve Bank of Philadelphia. Federal Reserve 2010, 143.

65. Jeffrey M. Lacker, president of the Federal Reserve Bank of Richmond. Federal Reserve 2009a, 42.

66. Richard W. Fisher, president of the Federal Reserve Bank of Dallas. Federal Reserve 2009a, 47.

67. Ben S. Bernanke, chair. Federal Reserve 2009b, 54.

68. Only one FOMC participant cast a dissenting vote from September 2008 to December 2009. In particular, Jeffrey Lacker, the president of the Richmond Fed, dissented in January 2009 based on his preference to expand the monetary base through the purchase of US Treasury securities rather than through targeted credit programs. As for QE2, only Thomas Hoenig, the Kansas City Fed president and well-known hawk, cast a dissenting vote in November 2010 on the grounds that additional purchases would risk further misallocation of resources and cause long-term inflation expectations to rise.

69. Woodford 2012, 86.

70. Woodford 2012, 3.

71. As reported in Politi 2021.

72. Bernanke 2015, 469–470.

73. Bernanke 2015, 270.

74. It is worth stressing that, even before 2012, the Fed already adhered to the basic principles of inflation targeting, including transparency about its outlook, objectives, and policy strategy.

75. Board of Governors of the Federal Reserve System 2012.

76. See also Binder and Spindel 2017, especially chap. 7, 201–231.

77. Among the tasks it performs, the House Banking Committee oversees the workings of the Federal Reserve.

78. Bernanke 2015, 527, emphasis added.

79. See Ihrig and Wolla 2022.

80. It is important to stress that all major emergency lending facilities set up by the Federal Reserve at the start of the COVID crisis, including the programs to lend to small businesses and to state and local governments, were adopted with the approval of the Treasury secretary (on the Fed's COVID facilities see Milstein and Wessel 2021). That is, similar to what happened during the 2008 crisis, government support was crucial for the Fed to deviate from orthodox monetary policies. Government support can also be seen in the expansion of fiscal support during the crisis. In particular, the US fiscal stimulus in 2020 was sizable and far exceeded the one provided in the wake of the 2008 crisis. For instance, by June 2020, the US overall fiscal stimulus amounted to approximately 12 percent of the national GDP compared to the almost 5 percent present in the period from 2008 to 2010. See McKinsey & Company 2020.

81. The speech in which the Fed chair announced the new strategy is found in Powell 2020. Emphasis has been added.

82. Federal Reserve 2020.

83. Powell 2021b.

84. Federal Reserve 2020.

85. The increased attention the US Fed devoted to social inequalities was evident in a conference it organized on disparities in labor market outcomes; see Board of Governors of the Federal Reserve System 2017.

86. For some of the research on the flattening of the Phillips curve, see Galí and Gambetti 2019; Hooper, Mishkin and Sufi 2020; Ratner and Sim 2022.

87. Harris Interactive 2009.

88. For instance, a 2014 Pew Research Study found that 37 percent of American citizens have an unfavorable view of their central bank. The survey also found that negative attitudes toward the Fed are significantly affected by political orientation, with Republican voters being more likely to declare a negative opinion about the Fed. See Pew Research Center 2015.

89. For a systematic analysis of congressional politics and the Fed, see Binder and Spindel 2017.

90. Between 2019 and 2020, Trump repeatedly demanded that the Fed take a series of actions such as decisive interest rate reductions and the restart of crisis-era policies in order to stimulate economic growth.

91. Ipsos/Axios 2020.

92. On the dynamics driving inequality in the United States and at the global level, see Card and DiNardo 2002; Dabla Norris et al. 2015; Jacobs and Myers 2014; Saez and Zucman 2019.

93. Smith 2020, emphasis added.

94. Powell 2020.

95. Yellen 2016.

96. It is important to note that by accepting the principle of tighter labor markets, the Fed's strategy review downplays the concept of the "natural" rate of unemployment (i.e., the level above which the labor market is overheated and inflation should increase). See Bank for International Settlements 2021, chap. 2.

97. Federal Reserve 2022.

98. Sablik 2021.

99. Powell 2021a.

100. Sablik 2021.

101. See Brainard 2017; Daly 2020.

5. THE EUROPEAN CENTRAL BANK

1. The euro area represents the world's third-largest economy after the US and China in terms of global GDP share See European Central Bank, "Structure of the Euro Area Economy," https://www.ecb.europa.eu/mopo/eaec/html/index.en.html. Accessed June 25, 2023.

2. This criticism mostly applies to the ECB's management of the 2008 and 2010 crisis and its aftermath. However, even at the beginning of the 2020 crisis, the ECB initially appeared slower and more hesitant than the Fed in reacting to the slowdown in economic activity and its financial consequences. For instance, at the beginning of March 2020, when the European economic outlook was quickly worsening with the rapid rise of COVID-19 infections, ECB President Christine Lagarde went public in announcing that "we [the ECB] are not here to close spreads," in a reference to the crisis-induced growing gap between Italian and German bond yields (see Lagarde 2020). The comment triggered one of the worst market routs in historical records.

3. McNamara 1998. Several studies have also focused on the influence of neoliberal and ordoliberal ideas on the European crisis response at large. See, for instance, Blyth 2013; Dellepiane-Avellaneda 2015; Helgadóttir 2016; Matthijs and McNamara 2015.

4. On the evolution of the ideas among ECB officials since the start of the crisis period, see, in particular, Ban and Patenaude 2019; Ferrara 2019.

5. On the political process that led to the creation of the ECB, see Howarth and Loedel 2003, McNamara 1998; Verdun 1999.

6. The European countries that have adopted the euro as their single currency are Austria, Belgium, Cyprus, Estonia, Finland, France, Germany, Greece, Ireland, Italy,

Latvia, Lithuania, Luxembourg, Malta, the Netherlands, Portugal, Slovakia, Slovenia, and Spain.

7. In appointing members, the European Council acts by a qualified majority based on a recommendation from the Council of the European Union and after having consulted the European Parliament and the Governing Council.

8. According to the European System of Central Banks Statute, the number of NCBs with the right to vote in the Governing Council cannot exceed fifteen. Hence, a system of rotation was established once the upper limit was reached in 2008, and it came into effect in 2015.

9. As discussed in chapter 4, the independence of the US Fed can be revised by congressional majorities.

10. Article 127(1) of the Treaty of the Functioning of the European Union.

11. Howarth and Loedel 2003, 52.

12. James 2012, 290–292.

13. Also McNamara 1998.

14. Issing et al. 2001, 102.

15. Rostagno et al. 2019, 6.

16. Issing 2003, emphasis added.

17. Issing 2004.

18. As will be discussed below, the ECB revised its monetary strategy in 2021. In particular, the new policy target is now 2 percent over the medium term, which is a reflection of the ECB's decision to increase the symmetry of the target, which had been tilted toward upward deviations from the target in the 2021 period.

19. Issing et al. 2001, 38.

20. Article 123 of the Treaty on the Functioning of the European Union.

21. Papademos 2007.

22. On the buildup of financial risks in the Eurozone and the impact on financial stability in the early stages of the crisis, see Feyen and Mazo 2013; and IMF 2008.

23. On the differential impact of the global financial crisis on national banking systems, see Hardie and Howarth 2013.

24. De Grauwe and Ji 2012.

25. The literature on the causes of the Eurozone crisis is extensive. For a collection of studies in political science that examined the origins of the crisis from different theoretical perspectives, see Copelovitch, Frieden, and Walter 2016, Matthijs and Blyth 2015, Howarth and Quaglia 2016.

26. Howarth and Quaglia 2016.

27. On the existential threat to the euro area and the role of the ECB in diffusing the threat, see Schelkle 2017, which discusses, among other topics, the massive extension of monetary solidarity signified by ECB President Mario Draghi's "whatever it takes" statement and the ensuing OMT program.

28. Eurostat data on real gross domestic product (Euro/ECU series) for euro area (nineteen countries).

29. European Central Bank 2012.

30. IMF 2020a.

31. However, the generous furlough schemes that were widely introduced to safeguard jobs contributed to mitigating the impact of the crisis on the duration of high unemployment levels (OECD 2020).

32. For a chronology and details of all the policy measures adopted since the start of the COVID-19 crisis, see European Central Bank 2021f.

33. See, for instance, Massoc 2021.

34. Similar to the Fed and other central banks in advanced economies, the ECB provided further monetary accommodation by way of revising its communication policy. In particular, the ECB used forward guidance to provide information on the expected future path of its monetary policy stance. In June 2014, the ECB also tweaked its convention interest rate tool to become the first major central bank to lower one of its key interest rates into negative territory.

35. Initially designed to provide financing to credit institutions at attractive conditions to support lending to the real economy, long-term refinancing operations evolved into *targeted* long-term refinancing operations in 2014. In particular, under the LTRO framework, the amount that banks can borrow from the ECB is conditional on their loans to nonfinancial corporations and households.

36. Borio and Disyatat 2010, 68.

37. Cahn, Matheron, and Sahuc 2017 has a positive assessment, finding that the ECB's LTROs played a key role in averting a major credit crunch. However, focusing on a later period, Boeckxa, Dosscheb, and Peersmanc 2017 and Burriel and Galesi 2018 add that these liquidity injections have heterogenous effects and are less effective in members with more fragile banking systems. See also Potter and Smets 2019 for a comparative overview of the impact of lending operations and other unconventional monetary instruments.

38. Mody and Nedeljkovic 2018.

39. See Acharya and Steffen 2015; Drechsler et al. 2016; Mody and Nedeljkovic 2018.

40. Rostagno et al. 2019, 13–14.

41. On the Eurozone's weak domestic demand problem and overreliance on external demand, see Polyak 2022a, 2022b.

42. Rostagno et al. 2019, 13, emphasis added.

43. Rostagno et al. 2019, 13.

44. As will be discussed at greater length below, throughout the crisis period, the ECB monetary policies were not only criticized by outsiders. The decisions undertaken to respond to the crises and their aftermath also brought to the surface important divisions within the ECB, in particular, among members of the ECB's Governing Council. On the cleavages among ECB officials, see Moschella and Diodati 2020.

45. See Draghi 2012 for the verbatim remarks of the "whatever it takes" speech.

46. Three smaller programs are the Corporate Sector Purchase Program (from 2016), the Asset-Backed Securities Purchase Program (from 2014), and the third Covered Bond Purchase Program (from 2014). For the rationale behind the programs adopted since 2014, see European Central Bank 2014.

47. For the greater flexibility of the PEPP as compared to the other asset purchase programs, see Quaglia and Verdun 2023.

48. Moschella and Diodati 2020.

49. It also likely that both Weber and Stark voted against the first asset purchase program because they both resigned shortly after its announcement in 2010, perhaps out of disagreement or protest against the program's distributional implications.

50. See Reuters 2011, 2012, 2016. On the difficulties of overcoming internal opposition, see also the interview by former ECB President Mario Draghi with the *Financial Times* (Barber and Jones 2019).

51. This concern, and the attendant "moral hazard," was most forcefully articulated by the German Governing Council member Axel Weber. See, for instance, Weber 2010.

52. Bastasin 2012, 200.

53. Trichet 2010.

54. Another limitation of the SMP is the preset amount of purchases that the ECB announced. In contrast, OMT purchases are unlimited. Furthermore, as I am going to

discuss at greater length below, another key design feature of the OMT concerns the terms of the conditions that determine activation (i.e., activation of the OMT is not automatic but rather dependent on member states' activation of an official adjustment program).

55. For instance, Ban and Patenaude 2019; Ferrara 2019; Johnson, Arel-Bundock, and Portniaguine 2019.

56. For one of the most compelling studies showing the ideational evolution that has taken place within the ECB since the start of the 2008–2010 crisis, see Ferrara 2019.

57. On the importance of political leadership, see Verdun 2017.

58. For some of the most comprehensive analyses of the politics of the eurozone crisis management, see Bastasin 2012, 2015; Brunnermeier, James and Landau 2017; Matthijs and Blyth 2015; Mody 2018; Pisani-Ferry 2014; Sandbu 2015. For eyewitness accounts, see Djankov 2014; Papadia and Välimäki 2018.

59. Council of the European Union 2010.

60. Bastasin 2012, 200. On the political negotiations that led to the creation of the EFSF, including the ECB policy preferences, see also Gocaj and Meunier 2013; Moschella 2016.

61. On the standoff between the ECB and euro area governments in the early stages of the crisis period, see, in particular, Henning 2016.

62. The full statement is as follows: "[The ECB] equally considers fundamental that governments stand ready to activate the European Financial Stability Facility (EFSF) in the secondary market" (European Central Bank 2011b).

63. European Central Bank 2011a, 53.

64. Henning 2016, 183.

65. Sacchi 2015; Ban 2016, chap. 8.

66. For a comprehensive analysis of the ECB democratic legitimacy in the wake of the 2008–2010 crisis, see Braun 2017.

67. However, it should be noted that, compared to the other ECB bond purchase programs, the OMT was not designed only to provide monetary accommodation but also to dispel concerns of a eurozone breakup in the face of growing financial fragmentation and rising bond yields across EMU countries, especially in the eurozone periphery. Although the ECB made no interventions under the OMT program, the announcement proved to be quite effective at decreasing financial volatility and depressing sovereign bond yields.

68. Following the agreement reached at the European Council on January 30, 2012, the ESM Treaty stipulates that the granting of financial assistance is conditional on the ratification of the Treaty on Stability, Coordination, and Governance in the Economic and Monetary Union (the "Fiscal Compact") by the borrowing country. In other words, financial assistance is reserved for those members that commit to the principle of fiscal discipline by including balanced budget rules in national constitutions (or equivalent legislation).

69. Rostagno et al. 2019, 15.

70. The new policy strategy also revised the former two-pillar approach informing the ECB's Governing Council's decision making, an approach based on economic and financial stability analysis. In particular, the ECB had now moved into using an integrated assessment to guide its policy decisions—that is, a framework in which the Governing Council relies on, as President Christine Lagarde explained, "a careful evaluation of the effectiveness, efficiency and proportionality of its actions, including their potential side effects" (Lagarde 2022). The proportionality assessment is quite crucial, given that this was the explicit requirement of the German Constitutional Court in its May 2020 verdict (Bundesverfassungsgericht 2020).

71. The target of inflation below but close to 2 percent had been agreed upon by the Governing Council in 2003.

72. European Central Bank 2021e.

73. European Central Bank 2021e. See also Lane 2020.

74. European Central Bank 2021e.

75. European Central Bank 2021e.

76. See also Deyris 2023. On how the 2021 review of the monetary policy strategy constitutes an important break with the ECB hierarchical conception of its mandate, see Van 't Klooster and Boer 2023.

77. European Central Bank 2021e.

78. European Central Bank 2021d, 2021a.

79. The 2021 review was carried out between 2020 and 2021.

80. On the changing sources of the ECB legitimacy since the crisis period started, see Schmidt 2020.

81. Brunnermeier, James, and Landau 2017; Hayo 1998; Howarth and Rommerskirchen 2013.

82. One of the most criticized elements of the May 2020 decision was that the German Federal Constitutional Court (GFCC) contradicted a decision made by the European Court of Justice, which ruled in December 2018 that the ECB acted within its mandate with regard to asset purchases. This questioning of the primacy of EU law even prompted an infringement procedure by the European Commission. The May 2020 decision called on the ECB to justify the proportionality of its actions. One year later, in May 2021, the GFCC ultimately ruled in favor of the bond-buying scheme, arguing that the ECB already addressed the concerns raised in the May 2020 ruling. See Deutsche Welle 2021.

83. Della Porta 2020.

84. Treeck 2021.

85. For some of the studies that have investigated the drivers of the shift in public opinion in the EU, see Bergbauer et al. 2020; Dotti and Magistro 2016; Foster and Frieden 2017; Roth, Gros, and Nowak-Lehmann 2014.

86. Ehrmann et al. 2021.

87. For instance, by using the keyword "trust" in the ECB Working Papers repositories, it appears that this topic was basically nonexistent in ECB research before the crisis period started.

88. Angino and Secola 2022; Christelis et al. 2021; Ioannou, Jamet, and Kleibl 2015.

89. See Jabko 2003.

90. Fraccaroli, Giovannini, and Jamet 2018; Moschella, Pinto, and Martocchia Diodati 2020; Tesche 2018; Moschella and Romelli 2022.

91. Lane 2022.

92. Lane 2022. The dual purpose of the strategy is also spelled out in European Central Bank 2021e.

93. European Central Bank 2021e.

94. During the strategy review period, the ECB listened to the views of EU citizens and social organizations through ad hoc listening events and a web survey conducted from February to October 2020. According to the ECB, approximately 4,000 respondents answered questions on four topics relevant to the monetary policy strategy review: (1) price stability, (2) economic issues, (3) global challenges, and (4) central bank communication. See European Central Bank 2021b, 2021c.

95. European Central Bank 2021b.

96. European Central Bank 2021b.

97. European Central Bank 2021b.

CONCLUSION

1. Bryan 2013. See also Bordo and Orphanides 2013.

2. IMF 2020b.

3. On the postcrises debate about central banks and monetary financing, see Agur et al. 2022a; Gabor 2021.

4. The former governor of the Bank of England, Mervyn King, used the adjective "boring" to describe the purpose of central banking as a metaphor to indicate the central banks' ambition of limiting economic volatility (King 2000a).

5. For the historical account of the Great Inflation, see chapter 3 and the references therein.

6. On the impact of labor market organizations on the monetary policy of independent central banks, see Hall and Franzese 1998; Iversen 1998.

7. On the politics of apparently "depoliticized" monetary policy conducted by independent central banks, see Grabel 2003; Kirshner 2000, 2003; McNamara 2002. On the issue from a political theory perspective, see Eich 2022. See also chapter 1 in this book and the references therein.

8. Borio et al. 2015, 38. Some of the most influential economic studies on the Great Depression include Bernanke 1995; Eichengreen 1992; Friedman and Schwartz 1963; Temin 1989.

9. The seminal work of Karl Polanyi (1944) is relevant here. On the political consequences of the 1930s economic crisis, and later WWII, one the standard references in political economy is Gourevitch 1986. See also Berman 1998.

10. The seminal contribution here is the history of American monetary policy by Milton Friedman and Anna Schwartz (1963).

11. Bernanke, 2000. For an analysis of the Japanese monetary policy after the 1990s, see, in particular, Park et al. 2018. See also chapter 3 and the references therein.

12. Lagarde 2013.

13. The two "technocratic" explanations are discussed in detail in chapter 1. References to specific scholarly works can be found therein.

14. Bernanke 2020, 47.

15. Rostagno et al. 2019, 13, emphasis added.

16. On the US Fed, see Woodford 2012; on the ECB, see Grauwe 2012. For instance, commenting on the Securities Market Programme (SMP) design, Paul De Grauwe (2012) notes that the ECB "structured this program in the worst possible way. . . . By announcing the program would be limited in size and time, the ECB mimicked the fatal problem of an institution that has limited resources," thus hopelessly impairing its success.

17. Krugman 2014, 66–67.

18. Even long-term central banks practitioners and observers have started exploring the possibility of monetary authorities working *with* fiscal authorities to stabilize economic activity based on the experience of the past decade. For some of the unexpected supporters of monetary–fiscal cooperation, see, for instance, Bartsch, Fischer, and Hildebrand 2019.

19. See, for instance, Jacobs and Weber 2022; Weber 2021.

20. Gabor 2022, 41.

21. See, for instance, Braun and Gabor 2022.

22. See, for instance, Braun 2017; Jacobs and King 2016; Jones and Matthijs 2019; McPhilemy and Moschella 2019; Tucker 2018.

23. Hopkin 2020.

24. Braun 2016; McPhilemy and Moschella 2019; Moschella, Pinto, and Martocchia Diodati 2020.

25. These findings are in line with those of a number of analyses that show changes in the Fed's and ECB's communication as a response to public and political contestation— for instance, Fraccaroli, Giovannini, and Jamet 2018; Moschella and Pinto 2019; Moschella, Pinto, and Martocchia Diodati 2020; Tesche 2018.

26. On the myth of depoliticization of money and monetary policy run by independent central banks, see Grabel 2003; Kirshner 2000, 2003; McNamara 2002. For a political theory perspective on this issue, see Eich 2022. See also chapter 2 in this book and the references therein.

27. This finding is compatible with Pepper Culpepper's analysis of the power of business in democratic societies (Culpepper 2012). Indeed, Culpepper's work clearly shows that in "quiet" times, the public rarely pays attention to issues of corporate control. As a result, political parties and legislatures also ignore the issue. In this context, the power of business is magnified.

28. Berman and McNamara 1999.

29. On globalization, see Helleiner 1994. On economic cooperation globally, see McNamara 1998. On policy and regulatory diffusion, see Ban 2016; Johnson 2016. On power and legitimacy in global governance, see Hall 2008.

30. Blyth and Matthijs 2017.

31. For a recent and thorough analysis of the constraints that even high-income countries confront under conditions of financial globalization see Barta and Johnston 2022.

32. For a thorough review of the scholarship that has examined the backlash against globalization, see Walter 2021.

33. Hopkin 2020.

34. For a long-term overview of wealth inequality in democratic countries, see Scheve and Stasavage 2017.

35. See also Baccaro, Blyth, and Pontusson 2022.

36. King 2000a.

References

Acharya, Viral V., and Sascha Steffen. 2015. "The "Greatest" Carry Trade Ever? Understanding Eurozone Bank Risks." *Journal of Financial Economics* 115 (2): 215–236.

Agur, Itai, Damien Capelle, Giovanni Dell'Ariccia, and Damiano Sandri. 2022a. "Monetary Finance: Do Not Touch, or Handle with Care?" IMF Departmental Paper DP/2022/001, January 2022.

Agur, Itai, Damien Capelle, Giovanni Dell'Ariccia, and Damiano Sandri. 2022b. "Should Monetary Finance Remain Taboo?" *IMF Blog*, February 22, 2022.

Angino, Siria, and Stefania Secola. 2022. "Instinctive versus Reflective Trust in the European Central Bank." ECB Working Paper Series 2660, May 2022.

Arnone, Marco, Bernard J. Laurens, Jean-François Segalotto, and Martin Sommer. 2007. "Central Bank Autonomy: Lessons from Global Trends." IMF Working Papers 2007/088, April 2007.

Axilrod, Stephen H. 2011. *Inside the Fed: Monetary Policy and Its Management, Martin through Greenspan to Bernanke*. Cambridge, MA: MIT Press.

Axios/Ipsos. 2020. "Americans Do Not Trust the Federal Reserve to Look out for Them," May 20, 2020.

Baba, Naohiko, Shinichi Nishioka, Nobuyuki Oda, Masaaki Shirakawa, Kazuo Ueda, and Hiroshi Ugai. 2005. "Japan's Deflation, Problems in the Financial System and Monetary Policy." BIS Working Papers 188, November 2005.

Baccaro, Lucio, Mark Blyth, and Jonas Pontusson, eds. 2022. *Diminishing Returns*. New York: Oxford University Press.

Bach, Tobias, Marlene Jugl, Dustin Kohler, and Kai Wegrich. 2022. "Regulatory Agencies, Reputational Threats, and Communicative Responses." *Regulation & Governance* 16 (4): 1042–1057.

Baker, Andrew. 2006. *The Group of Seven: Finance Ministries, Central Banks and Global Financial Governance*. London: Routledge.

Baker, Andrew. 2010. "Restraining Regulatory Capture? Anglo-America, Crisis Politics and Trajectories of Change in Global Financial Governance." *International Affairs* 86 (3): 647–663.

Baker, Andrew. 2013. "The New Political Economy of the Macroprudential Ideational Shift." *New Political Economy* 18 (1): 112–139.

Baldacci, Emanuele, Sanjeev Gupta, and Carlos Mulas-Granados. 2014. "How Effective Is Fiscal Policy Response in Financial Crises?" In *Financial Crises: Causes, Consequences, and Policy Responses*, edited by Stijn Claessens, Ayhan Kose, Luc Laeven, and Fabian Valencia, 421–457. Washington DC: International Monetary Fund.

Ball, Laurence. 1991. "The Genesis of Inflation and the Costs of Disinflation." *Journal of Money, Credit and Banking* 23 (3): 439–452.

Ball, Laurence. 2016. "The Fed and Lehman Brothers." Paper prepared for a meeting of the NBER Monetary Economics Program, July 14, 2016. https://data.nber.org/data-appendix/w22410/The%20Fed%20and%20Lehman%20Brothers.pdf.

Ball, Laurence M. 2018. *The Fed and Lehman Brothers: Setting the Record Straight on a Financial Disaster.* Cambridge: Cambridge University Press.

Ban, Cornel. 2015. "Austerity versus Stimulus? Understanding Fiscal Policy Change at the International Monetary Fund Since the Great Recession." *Governance* 28 (2): 167–183.

Ban, Cornel. 2016. *Ruling Ideas: How Global Neoliberalism Goes Local.* Oxford: Oxford University Press.

Ban, Cornel, and Bryan Patenaubade. 2019. "The Professional Politics of the Austerity Debate: A Comparative Field Analysis of the European Central Bank and the International Monetary Fund." *Public Administration* 97 (3): 530–545.

Ban, Cornel, Leonard Seabrooke, and Sarah Freitas. 2016. "Grey Matter in Shadow Banking: International Organizations and Expert Strategies in Global Financial Governance." *Review of International Political Economy* 23 (6): 1001–1033.

Bank for International Settlements. 2012. *Annual Economic Report.* Basel: Bank for International Settlements.

Bank for International Settlements. 2016. *Annual Economic Report.* Basel: Bank for International Settlements.

Bank for International Settlements. 2019. *Annual Economic report.* Basel.

Bank for International Settlements. 2020. *Annual Economic Report.* Basel: Bank for International Settlements.

Bank for International Settlements. 2021. *Annual Economic Report.* Basel: Bank for International Settlements.

Barber, Lionel, and Claire Jones. 2019. "Mario Draghi: Interview in the Financial Times," September 30, 2019. https://www.bis.org/review/r191001a.pdf.

Barro, Robert J., and David B. Gordon. 1983. "Rules, Discretion and Reputation in a Model of Monetary Policy." *Journal of Monetary Economics* 12 (1): 101–121.

Barta, Zsófia, and Alison Johnston. 2023. *Rating Politics.* Oxford: Oxford University Press.

Bartsch, Elga, Jean Boivin, Stanley Fischer, and Philipp Hildebrand. 2019. "Dealing with the Next Downturn: From Unconventional Monetary Policy to Unprecedented Policy Coordination." Macro and Market Perspectives, BlackRock Investment Institute, August 15, 2019.

Bastasin, Carlo. 2012. *Saving Europe: How National Politics Nearly Destroyed the Euro.* Washington, DC: Brookings Institution Press.

Bastasin, Carlo. 2015. *Saving Europe: Anatomy of a Dream.* Washington, DC: Brookings Institution Press.

Bateman, Will, and Jens van 't Klooster. 2023. "The dysfunctional taboo: monetary financing at the Bank of England, the Federal Reserve, and the European Central Bank." *Review of International Political Economy* 1–25.

Bellodi, Luca. 2021. "A Dynamic Measure of Bureaucratic Reputation: New Data for New Theory." *American Journal of Political Science.*

Bellucci, Paolo, Marina Costa Lobo, and Michael S. Lewis-Beck. 2012. "Economic Crisis and Elections: The European Periphery." *Electoral Studies* 31 (3): 469–471.

Bergbauer, Stephanie, Nils Hernborg, Jean-Francois Jamet, and Eric Persson. 2020. "The Reputation of the Euro and the European Central Bank: Interlinked or Disconnected?" *Journal of European Public Policy* 27 (8): 1178–1194.

Berman, Sheri. 1998. *The Social Democratic Moment: Ideas and Politics in the Making of Interwar Europe.* Cambridge, MA: Harvard University Press.

Berman, Sheri, and Kathleen R. McNamara. 1999. "Bank on Democracy: Why Central Banks Need Public Oversight." *Foreign Affairs* 78 (2): 2–8.

Bernanke, Ben. 2000. "Japanese Monetary Policy: A Case of Self-Induced Paralysis?" Presentation for the Allied Social Sciences Association (ASSA) meetings, Boston, January 9, 2000.

Bernanke, Ben, and Vincent R. Reinhart. 2004. "Conducting Monetary Policy at Very Low Short-Term Interest Rates." *American Economic Review* 94 (2): 85–90.

Bernanke, Ben S. 1995. "The Macroeconomics of the Great Depression." *Journal of Money, Credit and Banking* 27 (1): 1–28.

Bernanke, Ben S. 2003. "Some Thoughts on Monetary Policy in Japan." Speech delivered at the Japan Society of Monetary Economics, Tokyo, May 31, 2003.

Bernanke, Ben S. 2004. "The Great Moderation." Remarks at the meetings of the Eastern Economic Association, Washington, DC, February 20, 2004.

Bernanke, Ben S. 2005. "What Have We Learned since October 1979? Panel Discussion." *Federal Reserve Bank of St. Louis Review* 87 (March/April, part 2). 277–292.

Bernanke, Ben S. 2007. "Monetary Policy under Uncertainty." Speech delivered at the Thirty-Second Annual Economic Policy Conference, Federal Reserve Bank of St. Louis, October 19, 2007.

Bernanke, Ben S. 2009a. "Reflections on a Year of Crisis." Speech delivered at the Federal Reserve Bank of Kansas City Economic Symposium, Jackson Hole, Wyoming, August 21, 2009.

Bernanke, Ben S. 2009b. "Transcript of Testimony before the Financial Crisis Inquiry Commission, Closed Session," November 17, 2009. http://fcic-static.law.stanford .edu/cdn_media/fcic-docs/FCIC%20Interview%20with%20Ben%20Bernanke,%20 Federal%20Reserve.pdf.

Bernanke, Ben S. 2010. "Economic Policy: Lessons from History." Speech delivered at the Forty-Third Annual Alexander Hamilton Awards Dinner, Center for the Study of the Presidency and Congress, Washington, DC, April 8, 2010.

Bernanke, Ben S. 2011. "The Effects of the Great Recession on Central Bank Doctrine and Practice." Speech delivered at the Federal Reserve Bank of Boston Fifty-Sixth Economic Conference, Boston, October 18, 2011.

Bernanke, Ben S. 2013a. "A Century of US Central Banking: Goals, Frameworks, Accountability." *Journal of Economic Perspectives* 27 (4): 3–16.

Bernanke, Ben S. 2013b. "The Crisis as a Classic Financial Panic." Speech delivered at the Fourteenth Jacques Polak Annual Research Conference, Washington, DC, November 8, 2013.

Bernanke, Ben S. 2015. *The Courage to Act: A Memoir of a Crisis and Its Aftermath.* New York: W. W. Norton.

Bernanke, Ben S. 2020. "The New Tools of Monetary Policy." Presidential address at the American Economic Association, January 4, 2020.

Bernanke, Ben S., Vincent R. Reinhart, and Brian P. Sack. 2004. "Monetary Policy Alternatives at the Zero Bound: An Empirical Assessment." *Brookings Papers on Economic Activity* 2:21–78.

Best, Jacqueline. 2019. "The Inflation Game: Targets, Practices and the Social Production of Monetary Credibility." *New Political Economy* 24 (5): 623–640.

Best, Jacqueline. 2022. "Uncomfortable knowledge in central banking: Economic expertise confronts the visibility dilemma." *Economy and Society* 51(4):559–83.

Beyer, Andreas, Vítor Gaspar, Christina Gerberding, and Otmar Issing. 2008. *Opting Out of the Great Inflation: German Monetary Policy after the Break Down of Bretton Woods.* Cambridge, MA: National Bureau of Economic Research.

Binder, Sarah, and Mark Spindel. 2017. *The Myth of Independence: How Congress Governs the Federal Reserve.* Princeton, NJ: Princeton University Press.

Blanchard, Olivier J., and John Simon. 2001. "The Long and Large Decline in US Output Volatility." *Brookings Papers on Economic Activity* 1:135–164.

Blinder, Alan S. 1982. "The Anatomy of Double-Digit Inflation in the 1970s." In *Inflation: Causes and Effects*, edited by Robert E. Hall, 261–282: NBER Books from National Bureau of Economic Research.

Blinder, Alan S. 1999. *Central Banking in Theory and Practice.* Cambridge, MA: MIT Press.

Blinder, Alan S. 2004. *The Quiet Revolution: Central Banking Goes Modern.* New Haven, CT: Yale University Press.

Blinder, Alan S. 2013. *After the Music Stopped: The Financial Crisis, the Response, and the Work Ahead.* New York: Penguin Press.

Blinder, Alan S., Michael Ehrmann, Marcel Fratzscher, Jakob De Haan, and David-Jan Jansen. 2008. "Central Bank Communication and Monetary Policy: A Survey of Theory and Evidence." *Journal of Economic Literature* 46 (4): 910–945.

Blinder, Alan S., and Ricardo Reis. 2005. "Understanding the Greenspan Standard." *Proceedings of the Jackson Hole Economic Policy Symposium*, 11–96. Kansas City: Federal Reserve Bank of Kansas City.

Blyth, Mark. 2002. *Great Transformations. Economic Ideas and Institutional Change in the Twentieth Century.* New York: Cambridge University Press.

Blyth, Mark. 2013. *Austerity: The History of a Dangerous Idea.* New York: Oxford University Press.

Blyth, Mark, and Matthias Matthijs. 2017. "Black Swans, Lame Ducks." *Review of International Political Economy* 24 (2): 203–231.

Bloomberg. 2021. "Summers Slams Woke Fed for Risking Losing Control of Inflation," October 14, 2021, https://www.bloomberg.com/news/articles/2021-10-13/summers -slams-woke-fed-for-risking-losing-control-of-inflation

Board of Governors of the Federal Reserve System. 2012. "Federal Reserve Issues FOMC Statement of Longer-Run Goals and Policy Strategy." Press release, January 25, 2012.

Board of Governors of the Federal Reserve System. 2017. "Disparities in the Labor Market: What Are We Missing?" Conference agenda, September 26–27, 2017. https://www .federalreserve.gov/conferences/disparities-in-the-labor-market-about-2017.htm.

Board of Governors of the Federal Reserve System. 2020. "Statement on Longer-Run Goals and Monetary Policy Strategy," August 27, 2020. https://www.federalreserve.gov /monetarypolicy/review-of-monetary-policy-strategy-tools-and-communications -statement-on-longer-run-goals-monetary-policy-strategy.htm.

Board of Governors of the Federal Reserve System. n.d. "Monetary Policy." Accessed May 24, 2023. https://www.federalreserve.gov/monetarypolicy.htm.

Board of Governors of the Federal Reserve System. n.d. "Monetary Policy: What Are Its Goals? How Does It Work?" Accessed May 24, 2023. https://www.federalreserve .gov/monetarypolicy/monetary-policy-what-are-its-goals-how-does-it-work.htm.

Bodea, Christina, and Raymond Hicks. 2015. "Price Stability and Central Bank Independence: Discipline, Credibility, and Democratic Institutions." *International Organization* 69 (01): 35–61.

Boeckxa, Jef, Maarten Dosscheb, and Gert Peersmanc. 2017. "Effectiveness and Transmission of the ECB's Balance Sheet Policies." *International Journal of Central Banking* 13 (1): 297–333.

Bordo, Michael, and Andrew Filardo. 2005. "Deflation in a Historical Perspective." BIS Working Papers 186, November 2005.

Bordo, Michael, Andrew Filardo, Andrés Velasco, and Carlo A. Favero. 2005. "Deflation and Monetary Policy in a Historical Perspective: Remembering the Past or Being Condemned to Repeat It?" *Economic Policy* 20 (44): 801–844.

Bordo, Michael D. 2007. "A Brief History of Central Banks." *Federal Reserve Bank of Cleveland, Economic Commentary*, December 2007.

Bordo, Michael D., and Athanasios Orphanides, eds. 2013. *The Great Inflation: The Rebirth of Modern Central Banking*. Chicago: University of Chicago Press.

Bordo, Michael D., and Pierre L. Siklos. 2017. "Central Banks: Evolution and Innovation in Historical Perspective." NBER Working Paper Series 23847, September 2017.

Borio, Claudio. 2011. "Central Banking Post-Crisis: What Compass for Uncharted Waters?" BIS Working Papers 353, September 2011.

Borio, Claudio. 2020. "When the Unconventional Becomes Conventional." Speech delivered at the ECB and the Watchers XXI Conference, Frankfurt, September 30, 2020.

Borio, Claudio, and Piti Disyatat. 2010. "Unconventional Monetary Policies: An Appraisal." *The Manchester School* 78 (1): 53–89.

Borio, Claudio, Magdalena Erdem, Andrew Filardo, and Boris Hofmann. 2015. "The costs of deflations: a historical perspective." In *Quarterly Review, March*, edited by Bank for International Settlements. Basel.

Bowdler, Christopher and Radia, Amar (2012) 'Unconventional monetary policy: the assessment'. *Oxford Review of Economic Policy* 28(4):603–21.

Brainard, Lael. 2017. "Why Persistent Employment Disparities Matter for the Economy's Health." Speech delivered at Board of Governors of the Federal Reserve System Conference, Washington, DC, September 26, 2017.

Braun, Benjamin. 2016. "Speaking to the People? Money, Trust, and Central Bank Legitimacy in the Age of Quantitative Easing." *Review of International Political Economy* 23 (6): 1064–1092.

Braun, Benjamin. 2017. *Two Sides of the Same Coin? Independence and Accountability of the ECB*. Brussels: Transparency International EU.

Braun, Benjamin. 2020. "Central Banking and the Infrastructural Power of Finance: The Case of ECB Support for Repo and Securitization Markets." *Socio-Economic Review* 18 (2): 395–418.

Braun, Benjamin, and Daniela Gabor. 2022. "Green Macrofinancial Regimes." Mimeo.

Broome, André. 2010. *The Currency of Power: The IMF and Monetary Reform in Central Asia*. Basingstoke: Palgrave Macmillan.

Broz, Lawrence J. 1997. *The International Origins of the Federal Reserve System*. Ithaca, NY: Cornell University Press.

Broz, Lawrence J. 2002. "Political System Transparency and Monetary Commitment Regimes." *International Organization* 56 (4): 861–887.

Brunnermeier, Markus K., Harold James, and Jean-Pierre Landau. 2017. *The Euro and the Battle of Ideas*. Princeton, NJ: Princeton University Press.

Bryan, Michael. 2013. "The Great Inflation: 1965–1982." *Federal Reserve History*, November 22, 2013. https://www.federalreservehistory.org/essays/great-inflation.

Buiter, Willem. 2016. "Dysfunctional Central Banking: The End of Independent Central Banks or a Return to 'Narrow Central Banking'—or Both?" *Citi Research*, December 21, 2016.

Buiter, William. 2019. "The Federal Reserve Will Have to Be Creative in the Next Recession." *Financial Times*, December 8, 2019.

Buiter, William H. 2014. "Central Banks: Powerful, Political and Unaccountable?" CEPR Discussion Paper 10223, October 2014.

Bundesverfassungsgericht. 2020. "ECB Decisions on the Public Sector Purchase Programme Exceed EU Competences." Press release, May 5, 2020.

Burns, Arthur F. 1987. "The Anguish of Central Banking." Per Jacobsson Lecture, Belgrade, Yugoslavia, September 30, 1979.

Burriel, Pablo, and Alessandro Galesi. 2018. "Uncovering the Heterogeneous Effects of ECB Unconventional Monetary Policies across Euro Area Countries." *European Economic Review* 101:210–229.

Busuioc, E. Madalina. 2016. "Friend of Foe? Inter-Agency Cooperation, Organizational Reputation, and Turf." *Public Administration* 94 (1): 40–56.

Cahn, Christophe, Julien Matheron, and Jean-Guillaume Sahuc. 2017. "Assessing the Macroeconomic Effects of LTROs during the Great Recession." *Journal of Money, Credit and Banking* 49 (7): 1443–1482.

Calvo, Guillermo A. 1978. "On the Time Consistency of Optimal Policy in Monetary Economy." *Econometrica* 46 (6): 1411–1428.

Card, David, and John DiNardo. 2002. "Skill-Biased Technological Change and Rising Wage Inequality: Some Problems and Puzzles." *Journal of Labor Economics* 20 (4): 733–783.

Cargill, Thomas F., Michael M. Hutchison, and Takatoshi Ito. 2000. *Financial Policy and Central Banking in Japan.* Cambridge, MA: MIT Press.

Carpenter, Daniel P. 2001. *The Forging of Bureaucratic Autonomy: Reputations, Networks and Policy Innovation in Executive Agencies, 1862–1928.* Princeton, NJ: Princeton University Press.

Carpenter, Daniel P. 2002. "Groups, the Media, Agency Waiting Costs, and FDA Drug Approval." *American Journal of Political Science* 46 (3): 490–505.

Carpenter, Daniel P. 2004. "Protection without Capture: Product Approval by a Politically Responsive, Learning Regulator." *American Political Science Review* 98 (4): 613–631.

Carpenter, Daniel P. 2010a. "Institutional Strangulation: Bureaucratic Politics and Financial Reform in the Obama Administration." *Perspectives on Politics* 8 (3): 825–846.

Carpenter, Daniel P. 2010b. *Reputation and Power: Organizational Image and Pharmaceutical Regulation at the FDA.* Princeton, NJ: Princeton University Press.

Carpenter, Daniel P., and George A. Krause. 2012. "Reputation and Public Administration." *Public Administration Review* 72 (1): 26–32.

Cavallino, Paolo, and Fiorella De Fiore. 2020. "Central Banks' Response to Covid-19 in Advanced Economies." *BIS Bulletin* 21 (June).

Cecchetti, Stephen, and Guy Debelle. 2004. "Has the Inflation Process Changed?" Paper prepared for the Third BIS Annual Conference: Understanding Low Inflation and Deflation, Brunnen, Switzerland, June 18–19, 2004.

Chen, Wenjie, Mico Mrkaic, and Malhar Nabar. 2019. "The Global Economic Recovery 10 Years after the 2008 Financial Crisis." IMF Working Papers WP/19/83, March 2019.

Christelis, Dimitris, Dimitris Georgarakos, Tullio Jappelli, and Maarten van Rooij. 2021. "Trust in the Central Bank and Inflation Expectation." ECB Working Paper Series 2375, February 2021.

Cipolla, Carlo M. 1989. Preface to *Giolitti e la nascita della Banca di Italia nel 1893*, by Guglielmo Negri, ed, vii–xi. Collana Storica della Banca di Italia: Laterza.

Clift, Ben. 2018. *The IMF and the Politics of Austerity in the Wake of the Global Financial Crisis.* Oxford: Oxford University Press.

Cline, William R., and Joseph E. Gagnon. 2013. "Lehman Died, Bagehot Lives: Why Did the Fed and Treasury Let a Major Wall Street Bank Fail?" *Peterson Institute for International Economics Policy Briefs* 13–21 (September).

Committee on the Global Financial System. 2019. "Unconventional Monetary Policy Tools: A Cross-Country Analysis." *CGFS Papers* 63 (October).

Conti-Brown, Peter. 2016. *The Power and Independence of the Federal Reserve.* Princeton, NJ: Princeton University Press.

Copelovitch, Mark, Jeffry Frieden, and Stefanie Walter. 2016. "The Political Economy of the Euro Crisis." *Comparative Political Studies* 49 (7): 811–840.

Copelovitch, Mark S., and David Andrew Singer. 2008. "Financial Regulation, Monetary Policy, and Inflation in the Industrialized World." *Journal of Politics* 70 (3): 663–680.

Crowe, Christopher, and Ellen E. Meade. 2008. "Central Bank Independence and Transparency: Evolution and Effectiveness." *European Journal of Political Economy* 24 (4): 763–777.

Cukierman, Alex, Steven B. Webb, and Bilin Neyapti. 1992. "Measuring the Independence of Central Banks and Its Effect on Policy Outcomes." *World Bank Economic Review* 6 (3): 353–398.

Culpepper, Pepper. 2012. *Quiet Politics and Business Power: Corporate Control in Europe and Japan.* Cambridge: Cambridge University Press.

Dabla-Norris, Era, Kalpana Kochhar, Nujin Suphaphiphat, Franto Ricka, and Evridiki Tsounta. 2015. "Causes and Consequences of Income Inequality: A Global Perspective." IMF Staff Discussion Note 13, June 2015.

Daly, Mary C. 2020. "Is the Federal Reserve Contributing to Economic Inequality?" Remarks delivered by the president and CEO of the Federal Reserve Bank of San Francisco, virtual presentation, University of California, Irvine, October 13, 2020.

Davies, Howard, and David Green. 2010. *Banking On the Future: The Fall and Rise of Central Banking.* Princeton, NJ: Princeton University Press.

De Grauwe, Paul. 2012. "The ECB Can Save the Euro—but It Has to Change Its Business Model." *INET Blog*, July 30, 2012.

De Grauwe, Paul, and Yuemei Ji. 2012. "Mispricing of Sovereign Risk and Macroeconomic Stability in the Eurozone." *JCMS: Journal of Common Market Studies* 50 (6): 866–880.

De Haan, Jakob, Christina Bodea, Raymond Hicks, and Sylvester C. W. Eijffinger. 2018. "Central Bank Independence before and after the Crisis." *Comparative Economic Studies* 60 (2): 183–202.

De Vries, Catherine, Sarah Hobolt, and Stefanie Walter. 2021. "Politicizing International Cooperation: The Mass Public, Political Entrepreneurs and Political Opportunity Structures." *International Organizations* 75 (2): 306–332.

Della Porta, Donatella. 2020. "A Europe of Struggles: Blockupy as a Political Moment." *European Journal of Cultural and Political Sociology* 7 (3): 378–404.

Dellepiane-Avellaneda, Sebastian. 2015. "The Political Power of Economic Ideas: The Case of 'Expansionary Fiscal Contractions.'" *British Journal of Politics & International Relations* 17 (3): 391–418.

DeLong, J. Bradford. 1997. "America's Peacetime Inflation: The 1970s." In *Reducing Inflation: Motivation and Strategy*, edited by Christina D. Romer and David H. Romer, 247–276. Chicago: University of Chicago Press.

Deutsche Welle. 2021. "Top German Court Rejects Challenge to ECB Bond-Buying Scheme." *DW.com*, May 18, 2021. https://www.dw.com/en/top-german-court-rejects-challenge-to-ecb-bond-buying-scheme/a-57566117.

Deyris, Jérôme. 2023. "Too Green to Be True? Forging a Climate Consensus at the European Central Bank." *New Political Economy* (January): 1–18.

Diessner, Sebastian, and Giulio Lisi. 2020. "Masters of the 'Masters of the Universe'? Monetary, Fiscal and Financial Dominance in the Eurozone." *Socio-Economic Review* 18 (2): 315–335.

Dietsch, Peter, François Claveau, and Clément Fontan. 2018. *Do Central Banks Serve the People?* New York: John Wiley & Sons.

Djankov, Simeon. 2014. *Inside the Euro Crisis: An Eyewitness Account.* Washington, DC: Peterson Institute for International Economics.

Domanski, Dietrich, Michela Scatigna, and Anna Zabai. 2016. "Wealth Inequality and Monetary Policy." *BIS Quarterly Review* (March): 45–64.

Dossche, Maarten, Jiří Slačálek, and Guido Wolswijk. 2021. "Monetary Policy and Inequality." *ECB Economic Bulletin* 2:84–103.

Dotti, Giulia M., and Beatrice Magistro. 2016. "Increasingly Unequal? The Economic Crisis, Social Inequalities and Trust in the European Parliament in 20 European Countries." *European Journal of Political Research* 55 (2): 246–264.

Draghi, Mario. 2012. Speech at the Global Investment Conference, London, July 26, 2012. http://www.ecb.europa.eu/press/key/date/2012/html/sp120726.en.html.

Drechsler, Itamar, Thomas Drechsel, David Marques-Ibanez, and Philipp Schnabl. 2016. "Who Borrows from the Lender of Last Resort?" *Journal of Finance* 71 (5): 1933–1974.

Ehrmann, Michael, Sarah Holton, Danielle Kedan, and Gillian Phelan. 2021. "Monetary Policy Communication: Perspectives from Former Policy Makers at the ECB." ECB Working Paper Series 2627, December 2021.

Ehrmann, Michael, Michel Soudan, and Livio Stracca. 2013. "Explaining European Union Citizens' Trust in the European Central Bank in Normal and Crisis Times." *Scandinavian Journal of Economics* 115 (3): 781–807.

Eich, Stefan. 2022. *The Currency of Politics: The Political Theory of Money from Aristotle to Keynes.* Princeton, NJ: Princeton University Press.

Eichengreen, Barry. 1992. *Golden Fetters: The Gold Standard and the Great Depression, 1919–1939.* Oxford: Oxford University Press.

Eichengreen, Barry. 2015. *Hall of Mirrors: The Great Depression, the Great Recession, and the Uses—and Misuses—of History.* New York: Oxford University Press.

El-Erian, Mohamed. 2016. *The Only Game in Town: Central Banks, Instability, and Avoiding the Next Collapse.* New York: Random House.

European Central Bank. 2011a. *Monthly Bulletin* (September).

European Central Bank. 2011b. "Statement by the President of the ECB," August 7 2011. https://www.ecb.europa.eu/press/pr/date/2011/html/pr110807.en.html.

European Central Bank. 2012. "Comparing the Recent Financial Crisis in the United States and the Euro Area with the Experience of Japan in the 1990s." *Monthly Bulletin* (May): 95–112.

European Central Bank. 2014. "Decisions Taken by the Governing Council of the ECB (in Addition to Decisions Setting Interest Rates)," October 2014. https://www.ecb.europa.eu/press/govcdec/otherdec/2014/html/gc141017.en.html.

European Central Bank. 2021a. "Detailed Roadmap of Climate Change–Related Actions." https://www.ecb.europa.eu/press/pr/date/2021/html/ecb.pr210708_1_annex~f84ab35968.en.pdf.

European Central Bank. 2021b. "ECB Listens—Midterm Review Summary Report." https://www.ecb.europa.eu/home/search/review/html/ecb.strategyreview001.en.html.

European Central Bank. 2021c. "ECB Listens—Summary Report of the ECB Listens Portal Responses." https://www.ecb.europa.eu/home/search/review/html/ecb.strategyreview002.en.html.

European Central Bank. 2021d. "ECB Presents Action Plan to Include Climate Change Considerations in Its Monetary Policy Strategy," press release, July 8, 2021.

European Central Bank. 2021e. "The ECB's Monetary Policy Strategy Statement." https://www.ecb.europa.eu/home/search/review/html/ecb.strategyreview_monpol_strategy_statement.en.html.

European Central Bank. 2021f. "Our Response to Coronavirus (COVID-19)." https://www.ecb.europa.eu/home/search/coronavirus/html/index.en.html.

Farrell, Henry, and John Quiggin. 2017. "Consensus, Dissensus, and Economic Ideas: Economic Crisis and the Rise and Fall of Keynesianism." *International Studies Quarterly* 61 (2): 269–283.

Federal Reserve. 2009a. "Transcript of the Meeting of the Federal Open Market Committee," January 27–28, 2009. https://www.federalreserve.gov/monetarypolicy/files/FOMC20090128meeting.pdf.

Federal Reserve. 2009b. "Transcript of the Meeting of the Federal Open Market Committee," March 17–18, 2009. https://www.federalreserve.gov/monetarypolicy/files/FOMC20090318meeting.pdf.

Federal Reserve. 2010. "Transcript of Meeting of the Federal Open Market Committee," November 2–3, 2010. https://www.federalreserve.gov/monetarypolicy/files/FOMC20101103meeting.pdf.

Federal Reserve. 2013. "Transcript of Chairman Ben Bernanke's Press Conference," December 18, 2013. https://www.federalreserve.gov/mediacenter/files/fomcpresconf20131218.pdf.

Federal Reserve. 2020. "Federal Open Market Committee Announces Approval of Updates to Its Statement on Longer-Run Goals and Monetary Policy Strategy." Press release, August 27, 2020. https://www.federalreserve.gov/newsevents/pressreleases/monetary20200827a.htm.

Federal Reserve. 2022 "Federal Reserve Board—Fed Listens." Board of Governors of the Federal Reserve System. https://www.federalreserve.gov/monetarypolicy/review-of-monetary-policy-strategy-tools-and-communications-fed-listens-events.htm.

Ferguson, Thomas, and Robert Johnson. 2009. " Too Big to Bail: The 'Paulson Put,' Presidential Politics, and the Global Financial Meltdown." *International Journal of Political Economy* 38 (2): 5–45.

Fernández-Albertos, José. 2015. "The Politics of Central Bank Independence." *Annual Review of Political Science* 18:217–237.

Ferrara, Federico M., Donato Masciandaro, Manuela Moschella, and Davide Romelli. 2022. "Political Voice on Monetary Policy: Evidence from the Parliamentary Hearings of the European Central Bank." *European Journal of Political Economy* 74 (September): 1–23.

Ferrara, Federico Maria. 2019. "The Battle of Ideas on the Euro Crisis: Evidence from ECB Inter-Meeting Speeches." *Journal of European Public Policy* 27 (10): 1463–1486.

Feyen, Erik, and Inés González del Mazo. 2013. "European Bank Deleveraging and Global Credit Conditions Implications of a Multi-Year Process on Long-Term Finance and Beyond." *World Bank Policy Research Working Paper* 6388.

Feygin, Yakov. 2021. "The Deflationary Bloc." *Phenomenal World*, January 9, 2021. https://www.phenomenalworld.org/analysis/deflation-inflation/.

Financial Times. 2013. "Central Bankers Say They Are Flying Blind," April 17, 2013.

Financial Times. 2018. "Lehman Insider: Why the Bank Could and Should Have Been Saved." September 6, 2018.

Financial Times. 2015a. "Anti-Capitalist Protesters Target ECB in Frankfurt," March 18, 2015.

Financial Times. 2015b. "ECB Adjusts to Life amid the Protests," April 23, 2015.

Fischer, Stanley. 2011. "Central Bank Lessons from the Global Crisis." Dinner lecture at the Bank of Israel conference on "Lessons of the Global Crisis," Jerusalem, March 31, 2011.

Fisher, Paul. 2010. "The Corporate Sector and the Bank of England's Asset Purchases." Speech given at the Association of Corporate Treasurers, London, February 18, 2010.

Foster, Chase, and Jeffry Frieden. 2017. "Crisis of Trust: Socio-Economic Determinants of Europeans' Confidence in Government." *European Union Politics* 18 (4): 511–535.

Fraccaroli, Nicolò, Alessandro Giovannini, and Jean-François Jamet. 2018. "The Evolution of the ECB's Accountability Practices during the Crisis." *ECB Economic Bulletin* 5:47–71.

Frank, Barney. 2011. "Foreword." In *On the Brink: Inside the Race to Stop the Collapse of the Global Financial System*, by Henry M. Paulson, Jr., xxxvix–xlviii. New York: Business Plus.

Friedman, Milton, and Anna J. Schwartz. 1963. *A Monetary History of the United States, 1867–1960*. Princeton, NJ: Princeton University Press.

Gabor, Daniela. 2021. "Revolution without Revolutionaries: Interrogating the Return of Monetary Financing." Center for Open Science Working Paper.

Gabor, Daniela. 2022. "Green Central Banking." In *Making the Great Turnaround Work: Economic Policy for a Green and Just Transition*, 39–45. Berlin: Heinrich Böll Foundation.

Galí, Jordi, and Luca Gambetti. 2019. "Has the US Wage Phillips Curve Flattened? A Semi-Structural Exploration." NBER Working Paper 25476, January 2019.

Gandrud, Christopher. 2012. "The Diffusion of Financial Supervisory Governance Ideas." *Review of International Political Economy* 20 (4): 881–916.

Geithner, Timothy F. 2014. *Stress Test: Reflections on Financial Crises*. New York: Random House.

Gilad, Sharon. 2015. "Political Pressures, Organizational Identity, and Attention to Tasks: Illustration from Pre-Crisis Financial Regulation." *Public Administration* 93 (3): 593–608.

Gilad, Sharon, Moshe Maor, and Pazit Ben-Nun Bloom. 2015. "Organizational Reputation, the Content of Public Allegations, and Regulatory Communication." *Journal of Public Administration Research and Theory* 25 (2): 451–478.

Giles, Chris. 2013. "Central Bankers Say They Are Flying Blind." *Financial Times*, April 17, 2013.

Gocaj, Ledina, and Sophie Meunier. 2013. "Time Will Tell: The EFSF, the ESM, and the Euro Crisis." *Journal of European Integration* 35 (3): 239–253.

Goodfriend, Marvin. 2005. "The Monetary Policy Debate since October 1979: Lessons for Theory and Practice." *Federal Reserve Bank of St. Louis Review* 87 (March/April, part 2): 243–262.

Goodfriend, Marvin. 2007. "How the World Achieved Consensus on Monetary Policy." *Journal of Economic Perspectives* 21 (4): 47–68.

Goodhart, Charles. 2005. "Safeguarding Good Policy Practice. Panel Discussion II." *Federal Reserve Bank of St. Louis Review* 87 (2): 293–306.

Goodhart, Charles. 2010. "The Changing Role of Central Banks." BIS Working Paper 326, November 2010.

Goodhart, Charles, and Rosa Lastra. 2018. "Populism and Central Bank Independence." *Open Economies Review* 29 (1): 49–68.

Goodman, John B. 1991. "The Politics of Central Bank Independence." *Comparative Politics* 23 (3): 329–349.

Gopinath, Gita. 2020. "The Great Lockdown: Worst Economic Downturn since the Great Depression." *IMF Blog*, April 14, 2020. https://blogs.imf.org/2020/04/14/the-great-lockdown-worst-economic-downturn-since-the-great-depression/.

Gourevitch, Peter A. 1986. *Politics in Hard Times: Comparative Responses to International Economic Crises*. Ithaca, NY: Cornell University Press.

Grabel, Ilene. 2000. "The Political Economy of 'Policy Credibility': The New-Classical Macroeconomics and the Remaking of Emerging Economies." *Cambridge Journal of Economics* 24 (1): 1–19.

Grabel, Ilene. 2003. "Ideology, Power, and the Rise of Independent Monetary Institutions." In *Monetary Orders: Ambiguous Economics, Ubiquitous Politics*, edited by Jonathan Kirshner, 25–53. Ithaca, NY: Cornell University Press.

Greenspan, Alan. 2002. "Economic Volatility." Remarks at a symposium sponsored by the Federal Reserve Bank of Kansas City, Jackson Hole, Wyoming, August 30, 2002.

Grilli, Vittorio, Donato Masciandaro, Guido Tabellini, Edmond Malinvaud, and Marco Pagano. 1991. "Political and Monetary Institutions and Public Financial Policies in the Industrial Countries." *Economic Policy* 6 (13): 342–392.

Hall, Peter A. 1986. *Governing the Economy: The Politics of State Intervention in Britain and France.* New York: Oxford University Press.

Hall, Peter A., and Robert J. Franzese, Jr. 1998. "Mixed Signals: Central Bank Independence, Coordinated Wage Bargaining, and European Monetary Union." *International Organization* 52 (3): 505–535.

Hall, Robert E., ed. 1982. *Inflation: Causes and Effects.* Chicago: The University of Chicago Press.

Hall, Rodney Bruce. 2008. *Central Banking as Global Governance: Constructing Financial Credibility.* Cambridge: Cambridge University Press.

Hardie, Ian, and David Howarth, eds. 2013. *Market-Based Banking, Varieties of Financial Capitalism and the Financial Crisis.* Oxford: Oxford University Press.

Harris Interactive. 2009. "Monthly Opinions of Adults from Five European Countries and the United States." Access date August 28, 2022.

Hayo, Bernd. 1998. "Inflation Culture, Central Bank Independence and Price Stability." *European Journal of Political Economy* 14 (2): 241–263.

Hayo, Bernd, and Carsten Hefeker. 2010. "The Complex Relationship between Central Bank Independence and Inflation." In *Challenges in Central Banking: The Current Institutional Environment and Forces Affecting Monetary Policy*, edited by Mark E. Wohar, Martin T. Bohl, and Pierre L. Siklos, 179–217. Cambridge: Cambridge University Press.

Helgadóttir, Oddný. 2016. "The Bocconi Boys Go to Brussels: Italian Economic Ideas, Professional Networks and European Austerity." *Journal of European Public Policy* 23 (3): 392–409.

Helleiner, Eric. 1994. *States and the Reemergence of Global Finance: From Bretton Woods to the 1990s.* Ithaca, NY: Cornell University Press.

Helleiner, Eric. 2011. "Understanding the 2007–2008 Global Financial Crisis: Lessons for Scholars of International Political Economy?" *Annual Review of Political Science* 14:67–87.

Helleiner, Eric. 2014. *The Status Quo Crisis: Global Financial Governance after the 2008 Meltdown.* New York: Oxford University Press.

Henning, Randall C. 2016. "The ECB as a Strategic Actor." In *The Political and Economic Dynamics of the Eurozone Crisis*, edited by James A. Caporaso and Martin Rhodes. Oxford: Oxford University Press: 167–199.

Hernàndez, Enrique, and Hanspeter Kriesi. 2016. "The Electoral Consequences of the Financial and Economic Crisis in Europe." *European Journal of Political Research* 55 (2): 203–224.

Hetzel, Robert L. 2008. *The Monetary Policy of the Federal Reserve. A History.* New York: Cambridge University Press.

Hetzel, Robert L. 2013. "The Monetarist-Keynesian Debate and the Phillips Curve: Lessons from the Great Inflation." *Federal Reserve Bank of Richmond Economic Quarterly* 99 (2): 83–116.

Hinterleitner, Markus, and Fritz Sager. 2017. "Anticipatory and Reactive Forms of Blame Avoidance: Of Foxes and Lions." *European Political Science Review* 9 (4): 587–606.

Hoenig, Thomas M. 2005. "The Greenspan Era: Lessons for the Future." *Proceedings of the Jackson Hole Economic Policy Symposium*. Kansas City: Federal Reserve Bank of Kansas City: vii–viii.

Hood, Christopher. 2011. *The Blame Game: Spin, Bureaucracy, and Self-Preservation in Government*. Princeton, NJ: Princeton University Press.

Hooghe, Liesbet, and Gary Marks. 2009. "A Postfunctionalist Theory of European Integration: From Permissive Consensus to Constraining Dissensus." *British Journal of Political Science* 39 (1): 1–23.

Hooper, Peter, Frederic S. Mishkin, and Amir Sufi. 2020. "Prospects for Inflation in a High Pressure Economy: Is the Phillips Curve Dead or Is It Just Hibernating?" *Research in Economics* 74 (1): 26–62.

Hopkin, Jonathan. 2020. *Anti-System Politics: The Crisis of Market Liberalism in Rich Democracies*. Oxford: Oxford University Press.

Howarth, David, and Peter Loedel. 2003. *The European Central Bank: The New European Leviathan*. London: Macmillan.

Howarth, David, and Lucia Quaglia. 2015. "The Political Economy of the Euro Area's Sovereign Debt Crisis: Introduction to the Special Issue of the Review of International Political Economy." *Review of International Political Economy* 22 (3): 457–484.

Howarth, David, and Lucia Quaglia. 2016. *The Political Economy of European Banking Union*. Oxford: Oxford University Press.

Howarth, David, and Charlotte Rommerskirchen. 2013. "A Panacea for all Times? The German Stability Culture as Strategic Political Resource." *West European Politics* 36 (4): 750–770.

Howarth, David, and Charlotte Rommerskirchen. 2016. "Inflation Aversion in the European Union: Exploring the Myth of a North–South Divide." *Socio-Economic Review* 15 (2): 385–404.

Ioannou, Demosthenes, Jean-François Jamet, and Johannes Kleibl. 2015. "Spillovers and Euroscepticism." ECB Working Paper Series 1815, June 2015.

Ihrig, Jane E., and Scott A. Wolla. 2022. "How Will the Fed Reduce Its Balance Sheet?" *Federal Reserve Bank of St. Louis Open Vault Blog*, May 11, 2022.

IMF. 2003. *Deflation: Determinants, Risks, and Policy Options—Findings of an Interdepartmental Task Force*. Washington DC: International Monetary Fund.

IMF. 2008. *Global Financial Stability Report: Containing Systemic Risks and Restoring Financial Soundness*. Washington, DC: International Monetary Fund.

IMF. 2010. *World Economic Outlook*. Washington, DC: International Monetary Fund.

IMF. 2013. "Unconventional Monetary Policies—Recent Experience and Prospects." *Policy Papers*, April 2013.

IMF. 2018. "The Global Recovery 10 Years after the 2008 Financial Meltdown." In *World Economic Outlook*, October ed., edited by International Monetary Fund, 71–100. Washington DC: International Monetary Fund.

IMF. 2020a. *Regional Economic Outlook for Europe, October*. Washington, DC: International Monetary Fund.

IMF. 2020b. *World Economic Outlook*, April ed. Washington, DC: International Monetary Fund.

Inui, Masayuki, Nao Sudo, and Tomoaki Yamada. 2017. "Effects of Monetary Policy Shocks on Inequality in Japan." BIS Working Papers 64, June 2017.

Irwin, Neil. 2013. *The Alchemists: Three Central Bankers and a World on Fire*. New York: Penguin Books.

Issing, Otmar. 2000. "Why Price Stability?" Paper prepared for the ECB Central Banking Conference, Frankfurt, November 2000.

Issing, Otmar. 2003. "Monetary Policy in Uncharted Territory." Stone Lecture, London, November 3, 2003.

Issing, Otmar. 2004. "The ECB and the Euro—the First Five Years." Mais Lecture delivered at the City University Business School, London, May 12, 2004.

Issing, Otmar. 2017. "Central Banks: Are Their Reputations and Independence under Threat from Overburdening?" *International Finance* 20 (1): 92–99.

Issing, Otmar, Vitor Gaspar, Ignazio Angeloni, and Oreste Tristani. 2001. *Monetary Policy in the Euro Area. Strategy and Decision-Making at the European Central Bank*. Cambridge: Cambridge University Press.

Ito, Takatoshi. 2004. "Inflation Targeting and Japan: Why Has the Bank of Japan Not Adopted Inflation Targeting?" In *The Future of Inflation Targeting*, edited by Christopher Kent and Simon Guttmann, 220–267. Sydney: Reserve Bank of Australia.

Ito, Takatoshi. 2006. "Japanese Monetary Policy: 1998–2005 and Beyond." In *Monetary Policy in Asia: Approaches and Implementation*, edited by Bank for International Settlements, 105–132. Basel: Bank for International Settlements.

Ito, Takatoshi, and Frederic S. Mishkin. 2004. "Two Decades of Japanese Monetary Policy and the Deflation Problem." NBER Working Paper 10878, October 2004.

Iversen, Torben. 1998. "Wage Bargaining, Central Bank Independence, and the Real Effects of Money." *International Organization* 52 (3): 469–504.

Jabko, Nicolas. 2003. "Democracy in the Age of the Euro." *Journal of European Public Policy* 10 (5): 710–739.

Jacobs, David, and Lindsey Myers. 2014. "Union Strength, Neoliberalism, and Inequality: Contingent Political Analyses of U.S. Income Differences since 1950." *American Sociological Review* 79 (4): 752–774.

Jacobs, Lawrence, and Desmond King. 2016. *Fed Power: How Finance Wins*. New York: Oxford University Press.

Jacobs, Lawrence, and Desmond King. 2021. *Fed Power: How Finance Wins*. New York: Oxford University Press.

Jacobs, Meg, and Isabella M. Weber. 2022. "The Way to Fight Inflation without Rising Interest Rates and a Recession." *Washington Post*, August 9, 2022.

James, Harold. 2012. *Making the European Monetary Union: The Role of the Committee of Central Bank Governors and the Origins of the European Central Bank*. Cambridge, MA: Belknap Press of Harvard University Press.

Jeffery, Christopher. 2020. "El-Erian on COVID-19 Policy Risks, 'Zombie' Markets and Central Bank Capture." *CentralBanking.com*, April 14, 2020. https://www.central banking.com/central-banks/financial-stability/7524736/el-erian-on-COVID-19 -policy-risks-zombie-markets-and-central-bank-capture.

Johnson, Juliet, Vincent Arel-Bundock, and Vladislav Portniaguine. 2019. "Adding Rooms onto a House We Love: Central Banking after the Global Financial Crisis." *Public Administration* 97 (3): 546–560.

Johnson, Juliet. 2016. *Priests of Prosperity: The Transnational Central Banking Community and Post-Communist Transformation*. Ithaca, NY: Cornell University Press.

Jones, Erik. 2009. "Output Legitimacy and the Global Financial Crisis: Perceptions Matter." *JCMS: Journal of Common Market Studies* 47 (5): 1085–1105.

Jones, Erik, and Matthias Matthijs. 2019. "Rethinking Central-Bank Independence." *Journal of Democracy* 30 (2): 127–141.

Joyce, Michael, Matthew Tong, and Robert Woods. 2011. "The United Kingdom's Quantitative Easing Policy: Design, Operation and Impact." *Bank of England Quarterly Bulletin* 51 (3): 200–212.

Kahn, George. 2005. "The Greenspan Era: Lessons for the Future—An Introduction to the Bank's 2005 Economic Symposium." *Proceedings of the Jackson Hole Economic Policy Symposium*. Kansas City: Federal Reserve Bank of Kansas City: xxiii–xxxi.

Keefer, Philip, and David Stasavage. 2003. "The Limits of Delegation: Veto Players, Central Bank Independence, and the Credibility of Monetary Policy." *American Political Science Review* 97 (3): 407–423.

Khaler, Miles, and David A. Lake, eds. 2013. *Politics in the New Hard Times: The Great Recession in Comparative Perspective*. Ithaca, NY: Cornell University Press.

King, Mervyn 2000a. "Balancing the Economic See-Saw." Speech delivered to the Plymouth Chamber of Commerce and Industry's 187th Anniversary Banquet, April 14, 2000.

King, Mervyn. 2000b. "Monetary Policy: Theory in Practice." Address by the Deputy Governor, January 7, 2000. https://www.bankofengland.co.uk/-/media/boe/files/speech/2000/monetary-policy-theory-in-practice.pdf?la=en&hash=79C2DFA1 5AF5A73F13F373567F82A5C4FCE17974.

Kirshner, Jonathan. 2000. "The Study of Money." *World Politics* 52 (3): 407–436.

Kirshner, Jonathan. 2001. "The Political Economy of Low Inflation." *Journal of Economic Surveys* 15 (1): 41–70.

Kirshner, Jonathan, ed. 2003. *Monetary Orders: Ambiguous Economics, Ubiquitous Politics*. Ithaca, NY: Cornell University Press.

Kohn, Donald L. 2010. "The Federal Reserve's Policy Actions during the Financial Crisis and Lessons for the Future." Speech delivered at Carleton University, Ottawa, Canada, May 13, 2010.

Krugman, Paul. 1998. "Japan's Trap." Blog post, May 1998. http://web.mit.edu/krugman/www/japtrap.html.

Krugman, Paul. 2014. "Four Observations on Secular Stagnation." In *Secular Stagnation: Facts, Causes and Cures*, edited by Coen Teulings and Richard Baldwin, 61–68. London: Centre for Economic Policy Research.

Kumar, Manmohan S., Taimur Baig, Jorg Decressin, Chris Faulkner-MacDonagh, and Tarhan Feyzioglu. 2003. "Deflation: Determinants, Risks, and Policy Options." *IMF Occasional Papers* 221.

Kuttner, Kenneth N., and Adam S. Posen. 2004. "The Difficulty of Discerning What's Too Tight: Taylor Rules and Japanese Monetary Policy." *North American Journal of Economics and Finance* 15 (1): 53–74.

Kydland, Finn, and Edward Prescott. 1977. "Rules Rather Than Discretion: The Inconsistency of Optimal Plans." *Journal of Political Economy* 85 (3): 473–491.

Lagarde, Christine. 2013. "The Global Calculus of Unconventional Monetary Policies." Speech delivered at the Federal Reserve Bank of Kansas City Economic Symposium, Jackson Hole, Wyoming, August 23, 2013.

Lagarde, Christine. 2014. "The Global Economy in 2014." Speech at the National Press Club, Washington, DC, January 15, 2014.

Lagarde, Christine. 2020. "Introductory Statement," Frankfurt, March 12, 2020.

Lagarde, Christine. 2022. "Introductory Statement at the Plenary Session of the European Parliament," Strasbourg, February 14, 2022.

Lane, Philip R. 2020. "The Monetary Policy Package: An Analytical Framework." *ECB Blog*, March 13, 2020. https://www.ecb.europa.eu/press/blog/date/2020/html/ecb .blog200313~9e783ea567.en.html.

Lane, Philip R. 2022. "The Monetary Policy Strategy of the ECB: The Playbook for Monetary Policy Decisions." Speech delivered at the Hertie School, Berlin, March 2, 2022.

Lavelle, Kathryn C. 2013. *Money and Banks in the American Political System*. Cambridge: Cambridge University Press.

Leeper, Eric M. 2010. "Monetary Science, Fiscal Alchemy." NBER Working Paper 16510, October 2010.

Liaquat, Ahamed. 2009. *Lords of Finance: The Bankers Who Broke the World*. New York: Penguin Press.

Lindsey, David E., Athanasios Orphanides, and Rober H. Rasche. 2005. "The Reform of October 1979: How It Happened and Why." *Federal Reserve Bank of St. Louis Review* 87 (March/April, part 2): 187–236.

Lohmann, Susanne. 1998. "Federalism and Central Bank Independence: The Politics of German Monetary Policy, 1957–92." *World Politics* 50 (3): 401–446.

Lohmann, Susanne. 2003. "Why Do Institutions Matter? An Audience–Cost Theory of Institutional Commitment." *Governance* 16 (1): 95–110.

Lombardi, Domenico, and Manuela Moschella. 2016. "The Government Bond Buying Programmes of the European Central Bank: An Analysis of Their Policy Settings." *Journal of European Public Policy* 23 (6): 851–870.

Lucas, Robert E. 1976. "Econometric Policy Evaluation: A Critique." *Carnegie-Rochester Conference Series on Public Policy* 1:19–46.

Mabbett, Deborah, and Waltraud Schelkle. 2019. "Independent or Lonely? Central Banking in Crisis." *Review of International Political Economy* 26 (3): 436–460.

Mandelkern, Ronen. 2016. "Explaining the Striking Similarity in Macroeconomic Policy Responses to the Great Recession: The Institutional Power of Macroeconomic Governance." *Comparative Political Studies* 49 (2): 219–252.

Maor, Moshe. 2011. "Organizational Reputations and the Observability of Public Warnings in 10 Pharmaceutical Markets." *Governance* 24 (3): 557–582.

Maor, Moshe, Sharon Gilad, and Pazit Ben-Nun Bloom. 2013. "Organizational Reputation, Regulatory Talk, and Strategic Silence." *Journal of Public Administration Research and Theory* 23 (3): 581–608.

Marcussen, Martin. 2006. "The Transnational Governance Network of Central Bankers." In *Transnational Governance: Institutional Dynamics of Regulation*, edited by Marie-Laure Djelic and Kerstin Sahlin-Andersson, 180–240. Cambridge: Cambridge University Press.

Marcussen, Martin. 2009. "Scientization of Central Banking: The Politics of A-Politicization." In *Central Banks in the Age of the Euro*, edited by Kenneth Dyson and Martin Marcussen, 373–390. Oxford: Oxford University Press.

Masciandaro, Donato. 2007. "Divide et Impera: Financial Supervision Unification and Central Bank Fragmentation Effect." *European Journal of Political Economy* 23 (2): 285–315.

Masciandaro, Donato, and Francesco Passarelli. 2018. "Populism and Central Bank Independence." *SUERF Policy Note* 33 (May).

Masciandaro, Donato, and Davide Romelli. 2015. "Ups and Downs of Central Bank Independence from the Great Inflation to the Great Recession: Theory, Institutions and Empirics." *Financial History Review* 22 (3): 259–289.

Massoc, Elsa. 2021. "Having Banks 'Play Along': State-Bank Coordination and State-Guaranteed Credit Programs during the COVID-19 Crisis in France and Germany." *Journal of European Public Policy* 29 (7): 1135–1152.

Matthijs, Matthias, and Mark Blyth, eds. 2015. *The Future of the Euro*. Oxford: Oxford University Press.

Matthijs, Matthias, and Mark Blyth. 2017. "When Is It Rational to Learn the Wrong Lessons? Technocratic Authority, Social Learning, and Euro Fragility." *Perspectives on Politics* 16 (1): 110–126.

Matthijs, Matthias, and Kathleen McNamara. 2015. "The Euro Crisis' Theory Effect: Northern Saints, Southern Sinners, and the Demise of the Eurobond." *Journal of European Integration* 37 (2): 229–245.

Maxfield, Sylvia. 1997. *Gatekeepers of Growth: The International Political Economy of Central Banking in Developing Countries.* Princeton, NJ: Princeton University Press.

McKinsey & Company. 2020. "Total Stimulus for the COVID-19 Crisis Already Triple That for the Entire 2008–09 Recession," June 11, 2020.

McNamara, Kathleen. 2002. "Rational Fictions: Central Bank Independence and the Social Logic of Delegation." *West European Politics* 25 (1): 47–76.

McNamara, Kathleen R. 1998. *The Currency of Ideas: Monetary Politics and the European Union.* Ithaca, NY: Cornell University Press.

McPhilemy, Samuel, and Manuela Moschella. 2019. "Central Banks under Stress: Reputation, Accountability and Regulatory Coherence." *Public Administration* 97 (3): 489–498.

Meltzer, Allan H. 2009. *A History of the Federal Reserve, Volume 2, Book 2, 1970–1986.* Chicago: University of Chicago Press.

Milstein, Eric, and David Wessel. 2021. "What Did the Fed Do in Response to the CO-VID-19 Crisis?" *Brookings Hutchins Center Explains*, December 17, 2021. https://www.brookings.edu/research/fed-response-to-covid19/.

Mishkin, Frederic S. 2007. "Will Monetary Policy Become More of a Science?" Paper prepared for the Deutsche Bundesbank Conference on Monetary Policy over Fifty Years, Frankfurt, September 21, 2007.

Mody, Ashoka. 2018. *Euro Tragedy: A Drama in Nine Acts.* Oxford: Oxford University Press.

Mody, Ashoka, and Milan Nedeljkovic. 2018. "Central Bank Policies and Financial Markets: Lessons from the Euro Crisis." CESifo Working Paper 7400, December 2018.

Moschella, Manuela. 2016. "Negotiating Greece. Layering, Insulation, and the Design of Adjustment Programs in the Eurozone." *Review of International Political Economy* 23 (5): 799–824.

Moschella, Manuela, and Nicola M Diodati. 2020. "Does Politics Drive Conflict in Central Banks' Committees? Lifting the Veil on the European Central Bank Consensus." *European Union Politics* 21 (2): 183–203.

Moschella, Manuela, and Luca Pinto. 2019. "Central Banks' Communication as Reputation Management: How the Fed Talks under Uncertainty." *Public Administration* 97 (3): 513–529.

Moschella, Manuela, Luca Pinto, and Nicola Martocchia Diodati. 2020. "Let's Speak More? How the ECB Responds to Public Contestation." *Journal of European Public Policy* 27 (3): 400–418.

Moschella, Manuela, and Davide Romelli. 2022. "ECB Communication and Its Post-Pandemic Challenges." *Monetary Dialogue Papers*, February 2022.

Mukherjee, Bumba, and David Andrew Singer. 2008. "Monetary Institutions, Partisanship, and Inflation Targeting." *International Organization* 62 (2): 323–358.

Nelson, William R. 2014. "Lessons from Lender of Last Resort Actions during the Crisis: The Federal Reserve Experience " *BIS Papers* 79 (September).

Nocera, Joe. 2009. "Lehman Had to Die so Global Finance Could Live." *New York Times*, September 11, 2009. https://www.nytimes.com/2009/09/12/business/12nocera.html.

OECD. 2020. "Job Retention Schemes during the COVID-19 Lockdown and Beyond," October 12, 2020. https://www.oecd.org/coronavirus/policy-responses/job-retention-schemes-during-the-covid-19-lockdown-and-beyond-0853ba1d/.

Orphanides, Athanasios. 2003. "Monetary Policy in Deflation: The Liquidity Trap in History and Practice." *North American Journal of Economics and Finance* 15 (1): 101–124.

Orphanides, Athanasios. 2013. "Is Monetary Policy Overburdened?" BIS Working Papers 435, December 2013.

Orphanides, Athanasios, and Daniel L. Thornton. 2005. "Editors' Introduction: Reflections on Monetary Policy 25 Years after October 1979." *Federal Reserve Bank of St. Louis Review* 87 (March/April, part 2): 139–143.

Papademos, Lucas. 2007. "The Science of Monetary Policy: Past Advances And Future Challenges." Speech delivered at Deutsche Bundesbank Conference on Monetary Policy over Fifty Years, Frankfurt, September 21, 2007.

Papadia, Francesco, and Tuomas Välimäki. 2018. *Central Banking in Turbulent Times.* Oxford: Oxford University Press.

Park, Gene, Saori N. Katada, Giacomo Chiozza, and Yoshiko Kojo. 2018. *Taming Japan's Deflation: The Debate over Unconventional Monetary Policy.* Ithaca, NY: Cornell University Press.

Paulson, Henry M., Jr. 2009. "Letter to Timothy F. Geithner," March 17, 2008. http://online.wsj.com/public/resources/documents/Treasuryletter0308.pdf?mod=WSJBlog.

Paulson, Henry M., Jr. 2011. *On the Brink: Inside the Race to Stop the Collapse of the Global Financial System.* New York: Business Plus.

Peters, B. Guy. 2018. "The Challenge of Policy Coordination." *Policy Design and Practice* 1 (1): 1–11.

Pew Research Center. 2015. "Americans' Views of Fed Depend on their Politics," December 16, 2015. https://www.pewresearch.org/fact-tank/2015/12/16/americans-views-of-fed-depend-on-their-politics/.

Pew Research Center. 2020. "Public Holds Broadly Favorable Views of Many Federal Agencies." Topline questionnaire, March 24–29, 2020. https://www.pewresearch.org/politics/wp-content/uploads/sites/4/2020/04/PP_2020.04.09_Agencies_TOPLINE.pdf.

Pierson, Paul. 2004. *Politics in Time: History, Institutions, and Social Analysis.* Princeton, NJ: Princeton University Press.

Pisani-Ferry, Jean. 2014. *The Euro Crisis and Its Aftermath.* New York: Oxford University Press.

Polanyi, Karl. 1944. *The Great Transformation: The Political and Economic Origins of Our Time.* Boston: Beacon Press.

Politi, James. 2021. "Powell Moves to Stamp Out Market Fear of Exit from Loose Policy." *Financial Times*, January 14, 2021.

Polyak, Palma. 2022a. "External Enablers of Eurozone Austerity: Exploring the Link between the Ease of Suppressing Domestic Spending and Trading Partners' Demand." *New Political Economy* 7 (5): 754–770.

Polyak, Palma. 2022b. "The Silent Losers of Germany's Export Surpluses: How Current Account Imbalances Are Exacerbated by the Misrepresentation of Their Domestic Costs." *Comparative European Politics*, April 13, 2022. https://dx.doi.org/10.1057/s41295-022-00291-8.

Posen, Adam. S. 1995. "Declarations are Not Enough: Financial Sector Sources of Central Bank Independence." Paper prepared for the Symposium on Central Bank Independence, National Bureau of Economic Research, Tenth Annual Conference on Macroeconomics,, March 10–11, 1995.

Potter, Simon M., and Frank Smets. 2019. "Unconventional Monetary Policy Tools: A Cross-Country Analysis." Committee on the Global Financial System Papers 63, October 2019.

Powell, Jerome H. 2020. "New Economic Challenges and the Fed's Monetary Policy Review." Speech delivered at the Federal Reserve Bank of Kansas City Economic Symposium, Jackson Hole, Wyoming, August 27, 2020.

Powell, Jerome H. 2021a. "Community Development." Speech delivered at the Just Economy Conference sponsored by the National Community Reinvestment Coalition (via webcast), May 3, 2021.

Powell, Jerome H. 2021b. "Getting Back to a Strong Labor Market." Speech delivered at the Economic Club of New York (via webcast), February 10, 2021.

Quaglia, Lucia, and Amy Verdun. 2023. "Explaining the Response of the ECB to the COVID-19 Related Economic Crisis: Inter-Crisis and Intra-Crisis Learning." *Journal of European Public Policy* 30 (4): 635–654.

Quealy, Kevin. 2021. "The Complete List of Trump's Twitter Insults (2015–2021)." *New York Times*, January 19, 2021. https://www.nytimes.com/interactive/2021/01/19/upshot/trump-complete-insult-list.html#the-fed.

Rabouin, Dion. 2021. "Poll Indicates Low Trust, Poor Public Perception of the Fed." *Axios*, April 5, 2011. https://www.axios.com/2021/04/05/federal-reserve-poll-low-trust-poor-public.

Rajan, Raghuram. 2017. "Central Banks' Year of Reckoning." *Project Syndicate*, December 21, 2017. https://www.project-syndicate.org/magazine/central-banks-unvoncentional-monetary-policies-by-raghuram-rajan-2017-12.

Ratner, David, and Jae W. Sim. 2022. "Who Killed the Phillips Curve? A Murder Mystery." Finance and Economics Discussion Paper Series 2022-028, May 2022.

Reisenbichler, A. 2020. "The Politics of Quantitative Easing and Housing Stimulus by the Federal Reserve and European Central Bank, 2008–2018." *West European Politics* 43 (2): 464–484.

Reuters. 2011. "Exclusive: Germans Lead Resistance to ECB Bond Buying," August 5, 2011. https://www.reuters.com/article/us-ecb-bondbuys-idUSTRE7741QJ20110805.

Reuters. 2012. "Avoid Ideology over ECB Bond-Buying—Nowotny," August 31, 2012. https://www.reuters.com/article/uk-ecb-nowotny-idUKBRE87U0A220120831.

Reuters. 2016. "Lawmakers Call on Dutch Government to Oppose ECB Bond Buying," October 5, 2016. https://www.reuters.com/article/netherlands-ecb-bond-buying-idINL5N1CB4FA.

Rogoff, Kenneth. 1985. "The Optimal Degree of Commitment to an Intermediate Target." *Quarterly Journal of Economics* 100 (4): 1169–1190.

Romer, Christina D., and David H. Romer. 2002. "The Evolution of Economic Understanding and Postwar Stabilization Policy " NBER Working Paper 9274, October 2022.

Rostagno, Massimo, Carlo Altavilla, Giacomo Carboni, Wolfgang Lemke, Roberto Motto, Arthur Saint Guilhem, and Jonathan Yiangou. 2019. "A Tale of Two Decades: The ECB's Monetary Policy at 20." ECB Working Paper Series 2346, December 2019.

Roth, Felix, Daniel Gros, and Felicitas Nowak-Lehmann. 2014. "Crisis and Citizens' Trust in the European Central Bank—Panel Data Evidence for the Euro Area, 1999–2012." *Journal of European Integration* 36 (3): 303–320.

Sablik, Tim. 2021. "The Fed's New Framework: With a Revised Strategy, the Fed Responds to Challenges Facing Central Banks Today." *Federal Reserve Banak of Richmond Econ Focus* (First Quarter), https://www.richmondfed.org/publications/research/econ_focus/2021/q1/federal_reserve.

Sacchi, Stefano. 2015. "Conditionality by Other Means: EU Involvement in Italy's Structural Reforms in the Sovereign Debt Crisis." *Comparative European Politics* 13 (1): 77–92.

Saez, Emmanuel, and Gabriel Zucman. 2019. *The Triumph of Injustice: How the Rich Dodge Taxes and How to Make Them Pay.* New York: W. W. Norton.

Sandbu, Martin. 2015. *Europe's Orphan: The Future of the Euro and the Politics of Debt.* Princeton, NJ: Princeton University Press.

Schelkle, Waltraud. 2017. *The Political Economy of Monetary Solidarity: Understanding the Euro Experiment.* Oxford: Oxford University Press.

Scheve, Kenneth, and David Stasavage. 2017. "Wealth Inequality and Democracy." *Annual Review of Political Science* 20 (1): 451–468.

Schmidt, Vivien A. 2016. "Reinterpreting the Rules 'by Stealth' in Times of Crisis: A Discursive Institutionalist Analysis of the European Central Bank and the European Commission." *West European Politics* 39 (5): 1032–1052.

Schmidt, Vivien A. 2020. *Europe's Crisis of Legitimacy. Governing by Rules and Ruling by Numbers in the Eurozone.* Oxford: Oxford University Press.

Schwartz, Herman Mark. 2009. *Subprime Nation: American Power, Global Capital, and the Housing Bubble.* Ithaca, NY: Cornell University Press.

Shin, Hyun Song. 2009. "Reflections on Northern Rock: The Bank Run That Heralded the Global Financial Crisis." *Journal of Economic Perspectives* 23 (1): 101–119.

Siklos, Pierre L. 2002. *The Changing Face of Central Banking. Evolutionary Trends Since World War II.* New York: Cambridge University Press.

Silva, Luiz Awazu Pereira da, Enisse Kharroubi, Emanuel Kohlscheen, Marco Lombardi, and Benoît Mojon. 2022. *Inequality Hysteresis and the Effectiveness of Macroeconomic Stabilisation Policies.* Basel: Bank for International Settlements.

Skocpol, Theda. 1992. *Protecting Soldiers and Mothers: The Political Origins of Social Policy in the United States.* Cambridge: Harvard University Press.

Smith, Colby. 2020. "The Fed's Quest for Higher Inflation Looks Doomed without Congress." *Financial Times*, September 4, 2020.

Sorkin, A.R. 2010. *Too Big to Fail: The Inside Story of How Wall Street and Washington Fought to Save the Financial System—and Themselves.* New York: Penguin Books.

Steelman, Aaron. 2011. "The Federal Reserve's "Dual Mandate": The Evolution of an Idea." *Federal Reserve Bank of Richmond Economic Brief*, December 2011.

Steinmo, Sven, Kathleen Thelen, and Frank Longstreth, eds. 1992. *Structuring Politics: Historical Institutionalism in Comparative Analysis.* Cambridge: Cambridge University Press.

Stempel, Jonathan, and Elinor Comlay. 2008. "Bank of America Takeover to End Independent Merrill." *Reuters*, September 15, 2008. https://www.reuters.com/article/us-merrill-bankofamerica-idUSN1445019920080915.

Stock, James H., and Mark W. Watson. 2002. "Has the Business Cycle Changes and Why?" In *NBER Macroeconomics Annual, Volume 17*, 159–224. Cambridge, MA: National Bureau of Economic Research.

Streeck, Wolfgang, and Kathleen Thelen, eds. 2005. *Beyond Continuity: Institutional Change in Advanced Political Economies.* Oxford: Oxford University Press.

Summers, Larry. 2014. "US Economic Prospects: Secular Stagnation, Hysteresis and the Zero Lower Bound." Speech delivered to the National Association for Business Economics, February 24, 2014.

Summers, Lawrence H., and Anna Stansbury. 2019. "Whither Central Banking?" *Project Syndicate*, August 23, 2019.

Svensson, Lars E. O. 1999a. "Inflation Targeting as a Monetary Policy Rule." *Journal of Monetary Economics* 43 (3): 607–654.

Svensson, Lars E. O. 1999b. "Price-Level Targeting versus Inflation Targeting: A Free Lunch?" *Journal of Money, Credit and Banking* 31 (3): 277–295.

Svensson, Lars E. O. 2003. "Escaping from a Liquidity Trap and Deflation: The Foolproof Way and Others." *Journal of Economic Perspectives* 17 (4): 145–166.

Taylor, John B. 2005. "The International Implications of October 1979: Toward a Long Boom on a Global Scale." *Federal Reserve Bank of St. Louis Review* 87 (March/April, part 2): 269–275.

Temin, Peter. 1989. *Lessons from the Great Depression.* Cambridge, MA: MIT Press.

Temin, Peter. 2010. "The Great Recession and the Great Depression." *Daedalus* 139 (4): 115–124.

Tesche, Tobias. 2018. "Instrumentalizing EMU's Democratic Deficit: The ECB's Unconventional Accountability Measures during the Eurozone Crisis." *Journal of European Integration* 41 (4): 447–463.

Teulings, Coen, and Richard Baldwin. 2014. "Introduction." In *Secular Stagnation: Facts, Causes and Cures.* London: Centre for Economic Policy Research.

The Economist. 2022. "Too Much to Do: Central Banks," April 23, 2022, https://www.economist.com/special-report/2022-04-23.

The Economist. 2011. "Central Bankers to the Rescue?" August 13, 2011. https://www.economist.com/weeklyedition/2011-08-13

Thelen, Kathleen. 2004. *How Institutions Evolve: The Political Economy of Skills in Germany, Britain, the United States, and Japan.* Cambridge: Cambridge University Press.

Thiemann, Matthias. 2023. *Taming the Cycles of Finance? Central Banks and the Macro-Prudential Shift in Financial Regulation.* Cambridge: Cambridge University Press.

Thiemann, Matthias, Carolina Raquel Melches, and Edin Ibrocevic. 2021. "Measuring and Mitigating Systemic Risks: How the Forging of New Alliances between Central Bank and Academic Economists Legitimize the Transnational Macroprudential Agenda." *Review of International Political Economy* 28 (6): 1433–1458.

Thompson, Helen. 2009. "The Political Origins of the Financial Crisis: The Domestic and International Politics of Fannie Mae and Freddie Mac." *The Political Quarterly* 80 (1): 17–24.

Tognato, C. 2012. *Central Bank Independence: Cultural Codes and Symbolic Performance.* New York: Palgrave Macmillan.

Tooze, Adam. 2018. *Crashed: How a Decade of Financial Crises Changed the World.* New York: Viking.

Tooze, Adam. 2021. *Shutdown: How Covid Shook the World's Economy.* Dublin: Allen Lane.

Treeck, Johanna. 2021. "Greenpeace Lands on ECB Tower in Climate Finance Protest." *Politico*, March 10, 2021. https://www.politico.eu/article/greenpeace-protest-european-central-bank-paraglider-climate-finance-carbon/.

Trichet, Jean-Claude. 2010. "The ECB's Response to the Recent Tensions in Financial Markets." Speech delivered at the Thirty-Eighth Economics Conference of the Austrian National Bank, Vienna, May 31, 2010.

Tsingou, Eleni. 2014. "Club Governance and the Making of Global Financial Rules." *Review of International Political Economy* 22 (2): 225–256.

Tucker, Paul. 2009. "The Repertoire of Official Sector Interventions in the Financial System: Last Resort Lending, Market-Making, and Capital." Speech given at the Bank of Japan International Conference, Tokyo, May 28, 2009.

Tucker, Paul. 2018. *Unelected Power: The Quest for Legitimacy in Central Banking and the Regulatory State.* Princeton, NJ: Princeton University Press.

Ueda, Kazuo. 2001. "Japan's Liquidity Trap and Monetary Policy." Speech given at the semiannual meeting of the Japan Society of Monetary Economics, Fukushima, September 29, 2001.

Ugolini, Stefano. 2017. *The Evolution of Central Banking: Theory and History*. London: Palgrave Macmillan.

Van der Veer, Reinout Arthur. 2020. "Audience Heterogeneity, Costly Signaling, and Threat Prioritization: Bureaucratic Reputation-Building in the EU." *Journal of Public Administration Research and Theory* 31 (1): 21–37.

Van 't Klooster, Jens, and Nik de Boer. 2023. "The ECB's New Strategy and the Paradox of the Secondary Mandate." *Journal of Common Market Studies*, 61 (3): 730–746.

Van 't Klooster, Jens, and Clément Fontan. 2019. "The Myth of Market Neutrality: A Comparative Study of the European Central Bank's and the Swiss National Bank's Corporate Security Purchases." *New Political Economy* 25 (6): 865–879.

Verdun, Amy. 1999. "The Role of the Delors Committee in the Creation of EMU: An Epistemic Community?" *Journal of European Public Policy* 6 (2): 308–328.

Verdun, Amy. 2017. "Political Leadership of the European Central Bank." *Journal of European Integration* 39 (2): 207–221.

Viñals, José. 2000. "Monetary Policy Issues in a Low Inflation Environment." Paper prepared for the "Why Price Stability?" ECB Central Banking Conference, Frankfurt, November 2–3, 2000.

Volcker, Paul, and Martin Feldstein. 2013. "An Interview with Paul Volcker." *Journal of Economic Perspectives* 27 (4): 105–120.

Wæraas, Arild, and Moshe Maor. 2015. "Understanding Organizational Reputation in a Public Sector Context." In *Organizational Reputation in the Public Sector*, edited by Arild Wæraas and Moshe Maor. New York: Routledge.

Wall Street Journal. 2010. "Open Letter to Ben Bernanke," November 15, 2010. https://www.wsj.com/articles/BL-REB-12460.

Walter, Stefanie. 2021. "The Backlash against Globalization." *Annual Review of Political Science* 24:421–442.

Wasserfallen, Fabio. 2019. "Global Diffusion, Policy Flexibility, and Inflation Targeting." *International Interactions* 45 (4): 617–637.

Weber, Axel. 2010. "Monetary Policy after the Crisis: A European Perspective." Keynote at the Shadow Open Market Committee Symposium, New York, October 12, 2010.

Weber, Isabella. 2021. "Could Strategic Price Controls Help Fight Inflation?" *The Guardian*, December 29, 2021.

Wessel, David, ed. 2014. *Central Banking after the Great Recession: Lessons Learned, Challenges Ahead*. Washington, DC: The Brookings Institution.

Wessel, David. 2017. "Central Bank Communications Evolving, but Has a Ways to Go." *Wall Street Journal*, November 28, 2017. https://www.wsj.com/articles/wessels-take-central-bank-communications-evolving-but-has-a-ways-to-go-1511868081.

Woodford, Michael. 2012. "Methods of Policy Accommodation at the Interest-Rate Lower Bound." Paper presented at the Federal Reserve Bank of Kansas City Symposium on the Changing Policy Landscape, Jackson Hole, Wyoming, August 31, 2012.

Woodward, Bob. 2000. *Maestro: Greenspan's Fed and the American Boom*. New York: Simon Schuster.

World Bank. 2020. "Transcript: A Conversation with David Malpass and Janet Yellen at an Event Hosted by Bipartisan Policy Center," Washington, DC, February 4, 2020. https://www.worldbank.org/en/news/speech/2020/02/04/transcript-a-conversation-with-david-malpass-and-janet-yellen-at-the-bipartisan-policy-center.

Yellen, Janet L. 2016. "Macroeconomic Research after the Crisis." Speech given at the Elusive "Great" Recovery: Causes and Implications for Future Business Cycle Dynamics, Sixtieth Annual Conference, Federal Reserve Bank, Boston, October 14, 2016.

Index

Page numbers in italics refer to figures and tables.

www.ingramcontent.com/pod-product-compliance
Ingram Content Group UK Ltd.
Pitfield, Milton Keynes, MK11 3LW, UK
UKHW041814020225
454515UK00004B/166/J